Lisa Maxwell

# Not That Kinda Girl

## A STORY OF SECRETS, LONGING AND LAUGHTER

HARPER

HarperCollins*Publishers*
77–85 Fulham Palace Road,
Hammersmith, London W6 8JB

www.harpercollins.co.uk

This paperback edition published in 2012
First published by HarperCollins*Publishers* 2011

1 3 5 7 9 10 8 6 4 2

© Lisa Maxwell 2011

Lisa Maxwell asserts the moral right to be
identified as the author of this work

A catalogue record of this book is
available from the British Library

ISBN 978-0-00-741891-6

Printed and bound in Great Britain by
Clays Ltd, St Ives plc

**MIX**
Paper from
responsible sources
**FSC˙ C007454**

# Not That
# Kinda Girl

*For Paul and Beau*

# Contents

*Lisa Maxwell*

# INTRODUCTION

## Down at the Duke

As I walked towards the Duke of Sutherland in Walworth I could hear Nan's voice belting out one of her favourite songs:

> 'I'd like to be good …
> And I know that I should …
> I'm just not that kind of a girl …'

Just hearing her voice gave me a warm feeling. I'd always loved these words, because they're funny and so familiar to me, from my earliest memories. As I pushed the heavy pub door open she was still at the piano, her left hand vamping a rhythm without moving across the keyboard, her right picking out the tune. She reached the last two lines:

> 'Old Tommy Tucker …
> Everyone knows he's a dirty old … fella!'

The pub erupted in cheers and laughter, even though everyone there had heard the song before. I made my way through the fuggy, crowded bar, inhaling cigarette smoke and beer fumes, to the upholstered bench seat where Nan always sat with Grandad and their friends. She was basking in the applause and free drinks being sent across to their table.

'Oh my Gawd, look who's 'ere! Hide your wallet, Jim,' she said when she spotted me.

'I'm saying no, clear off out of here!' Grandad would always say before I even had time to speak.

They were both laughing, and so were their friends.

I'd launch into my speech: 'Guess what? I've seen these shoes in Grants in the Walworth Road, and they've only got one pair in my size. They were so nice, they said they'd put them by for me …'

As I wriggled myself in between them on the bench seat, I'd look at Nan.

'You'd better speak to your grandad,' she'd say, so I'd turn puppy-dog eyes on him.

'*Please*, Grandad – they're really nice,' I'd tell him.

'I bet they are,' he'd say.

'*Please*, Grandad, I won't ask for anything else ever again!'

Huge guffaws from everyone round the table.

'How much are they?' he'd ask, already putting a hand in his pocket.

'Only £14.99.'

'Here's fifteen nicker – clear off, that's yer lot!'

I would skip out of the pub with the whole group smiling and watching me and, I imagine, thinking, 'Aw, how could you resist her?' Even though I was 16 I was tiny, slim and, because of my stage-school training, confident. I knew Nan and Grandad were proud of their little Lise whenever I went into the pub, they loved me – and I also knew, from an early age, that when Grandad had a few drinks inside him I could get anything out of him.

Nan, Grandad and Mum adored me. I lived with all three of them and I was the centre of their universes. I never went without anything; they spoiled me rotten. As far as Mum was concerned, nobody could ever point a finger at me and say I lacked anything. Except one big thing she was unable to give me: a father.

On my birth certificate there are two stark words, words branded on my soul: 'Father Unknown'.

Today, with more than half of all babies born to unmarried couples according to the Office of National Statistics, the stigma of being illegitimate has pretty much gone. It's a word you never hear now, and a good thing, too: it means illegal, beyond the law. That's a terrible stamp to put on a child. I was born outside the law, and back then in the 1960s only 5 per cent of all babies did not have married parents.

My birth was something friends and family whispered about, hoping I wasn't listening. A child born 'out of wedlock' was something to be ashamed of, the subject of gossip and innuendo: a stain on a family. This was something I was aware of from the very beginning. I always felt the love I was given was tainted with embarrassment and shame, a shame that has coloured my life in so many ways; it has affected my relationships, my work, everything. It's a shadow that stretched long and deep and out of which I have only recently emerged into the sunshine.

*Lisa Maxwell*

Yes, I have always been bright and bubbly, funny, up for a laugh and a party, but the parties, the drinks and the laughter, everything was a way to keep on moving, to make sure I never stood still long enough to look deep inside myself. Finally, in the last few years, I have come off that merry-go-round and found a quiet, happy place in life where I can face up to myself and my story. I've come to terms with my birth; I know who I am. It's been a long and at times difficult journey, but writing this book has also helped me find myself and lay to rest the ghosts that have haunted me.

# CHAPTER 1

## Meet the Family

I was only three years old, too small to see over the balcony outside our second-storey council flat at the Elephant and Castle, but there was a metal grille set into the brickwork that gave me a view of the estate below. While Nan tried to drag me back indoors, I was clinging to the bars, screaming and kicking hysterically. Below, I could see my mum getting into a minicab with a man in the back.

'Your mother's entitled to go out …' Nan was saying as she struggled to contain my hysteria.

'She's with a man, she's with a *man*!' I was yelling.

'Just get in the car, Val. She'll be all right,' Nan shouted to Mum as she finally prised me away and dragged me back inside.

Mum seemed to be in some sort of danger: the thought of her with a strange man was disturbing – I felt she couldn't protect herself. And I hated her for leaving me to be with a man. This is my earliest memory. I can't say exactly how I knew it was wrong; at that age you simply sense it from the way the grown-ups are trying to hide it. Mum didn't say goodbye – she slipped out, secretively – and when I asked where she was, Nan and Grandad had exchanged sideways glances. So I panicked: I wanted her to come back. In some childish, unrealised way I wanted to save her from the terrible things about to happen to her.

Even then, too young to understand it properly, I had taken on board so much of the shame of being born out of wedlock and all the judgement that went with it that I felt my mum should be whiter than white and live like a nun. I had no idea how or why, but I knew a man had been involved in my arrival and this was something to be ashamed of, that it had been wrong. How did I develop such dark thoughts from such an early age, such fully formed moral opinions about her life? It was as though they seeped into me without anyone ever sitting me down and really spelling it all out. I don't remember Nan and Grandad ever saying bad things about her, they were kinder than that, but the disapproval and half-heard gossip about my own mysterious 'Father Unknown' became part of me by osmosis.

I had picked up, probably from the whisperings of the grown-ups, that Mum had ruined her life by going with a man, and so I was terrified whenever I saw her with one. Men spelt trouble: disaster, shame, something dirty. So any attempt she had at a private life was thwarted, partly by the stigma of being an unmarried mother, but also – I'm ashamed to admit – by me, and from an early age I was determined to sabotage any chances she might have.

Mum never talked about it properly to me: the usual way of dealing with things in our family was to try and ignore them. She never said it was OK for her to have a boyfriend and she was entitled to some happiness and a loving relationship. All she ever said was that no one wanted her because of me. Imagine having that on your shoulders all your life. For her part, she felt she had to compensate, to make sure I missed out on nothing because I didn't have a dad. I ruled the roost. From the day I was born I controlled her life. Obviously any baby and small child must be the first priority, but Mum lost herself completely the day I was born.

The Rockingham Estate at the Elephant and Castle was where I grew up, living with Mum, Nan and Grandad at 15 Stephenson House. The estate is a collection of red-brick, four-storey blocks of flats built in the 1950s, with scrubby, worn grass in between. To get to our flat we had to go up two flights of stairs and then walk along the balcony in front. We were round the corner of the building, the last stretch of balcony, so quite private.

It was a comfortable home and a good place to grow up. Nowadays estates like this are rough, with gangs and the associated drugs and violence, but when I was little the only 'gang' was the knot of kids I played with – endless games of 'Penny Up', 'Cannon' or 'Run Outs'. We ebbed and flowed around the area between the flats, hiding and chasing each other all day through the school holidays until our mothers stood out on balconies calling us in for tea, which was what the evening meal was called ('dinner' was served at midday). Next to the estate was the strangely named Jail Park (I think it got its name because it was beside the Inner London Sessions court) and this, too, was a safe playground.

Mum has an old black-and-white photo of the Coronation party held on the estate in 1953. All the mums and teenagers stand in the background while 50 kids sit at a great long table, stuffing themselves with jelly and ice cream. It seems like a different era, an age when neighbours looked out for each other and everyone helped out, but it was only 10 years before I was born and the estate was still a friendly, caring place to grow up. At least, that's how it seemed to me.

Because it was a council estate all the front doors were painted the same colour: red. To this day whenever I move into a new house the first thing I do is change the colour of the front door just because I can. The only bit that scared me was the stairwell: the stairs were made of concrete with sparkly bits in it – for some reason, you only see this in council flats of that age. Yellow tiles ran halfway up the walls. There was no graffiti and it didn't smell like a public urinal but it was dark and grubby and made me nervous. I don't know what I thought would happen but I used to run up those stairs as fast as I could, often shouting, 'Come on, Billy, there's a good Alsatian!' to my protector, an imaginary dog.

Our flat had three bedrooms, a living room, kitchen and bathroom. When I was really small my Uncle Alan lived there too. But let's go back to the very beginning. How did I come to be living with Nan and Grandad and sharing a room with Mum?

Let's start with Nan and Grandad. They were such an important part of my life. A typical working-class couple, they were strong characters. Grandad drove a road sweeper for the council, which was a bit embarrassing because he parked this big yellow-and-black vehicle near our flats – I think he even went down the pub in it. He also did planting for the council in Battersea Park. He liked his work, and we had window boxes at home. Grandad won an award for the best window boxes on the estate – I've a feeling we were perhaps the only people there who had them.

Grandad's shoes were always immaculate and he stored them in a little cabinet with all his kit for cleaning them. In cold weather he wore a flat cap. He had a tiny moustache, a bit like a Hitler moustache, like a bit of black tape stuck under his nose. For years I never had a clue what colour his hair was because it was Brylcreemed down. It was only when he was old that I could tell it was grey underneath. He rolled his own cigarettes with Golden Virginia tobacco, but Nan never smoked. Mum still has his toolbox with the nails and screws sorted and stored in old tobacco tins.

Nan and Grandad met when they were young, childhood sweethearts. He was the only man she'd ever been with. Her family was very poor, but his were a bit better off because his mother was a moneylender. In the old photos I've seen they look quite smart and Nan's family seem really ragged in comparison. Grandad (Jim Maxwell) was a cheeky lad: his nickname was 'Bagwash' because there was a laundry round where he lived called 'Maxwell Bagwash'. He saw this young girl (Rose) eating chips and said, 'Give us a chip, Ginge' – he called her 'Ginge' because there's a bit of ginger colouring in her family, and as Nan grew older and greyer she always had her hair tinted a reddish colour. Alan was born ginger, and there were lots of jokes about how he must be the milkman's, but it's in the family. When they got married Grandad's family felt he could have done better for himself, but he and Nan were together for the rest of their lives.

They both worked hard – Grandad was still working when he died at 76. Nan was always doing jobs and usually more than one: cleaning, working at the bookies. Their social life revolved around the pub. Nan was musical, and it's fair to say she had a showing-off gene (in case you're wondering where I get it from). She taught herself to play the piano by ear, never had a lesson, and would belt out songs like 'Tommy Tucker' and 'Slap a Bit of Treacle on Your Pudding, Mary Ann'. She loved it, and that's why she insisted Mum should look after me at weekends – nothing, not even me whom she idolised, could get in the way of their time down the pub. Nan loved having an audience in the palm of her hand. Everyone in the pub knew each other, knew all about their kids, there was a great sense of community.

I can still sing all her good old London songs. Nan was singing until she was in her eighties and perfected the same throaty wobble in her voice on a big note that Vera Lynn had. In April 2003, when I was the subject of *This Is Your Life*, she had Michael Aspel eating out of her hand and insisted on singing, finally getting her break on national television. As she got older and her voice wasn't so strong, she would hold the mike too close (which gave a fuzzy edge to the sound), but my memories are of her belting the words out.

Nan was of average height (there's nobody else in our family who is small like me) and the only make-up she ever wore was lipstick, which to be perfectly honest was never expertly applied. Let's just say her lipstick thought her lips were bigger than they were. At home she wore a pink nylon overall, the sort of thing only Nans had.

So that's Nan and Grandad, and now it's Mum's turn. Obviously I wasn't around when all this happened, but eventually, years after my childhood, I heard it from her. It was not easy for Mum to tell her story, or to live it either: life on the estate may have been safer and friendlier in those days, but people were also a lot more judgemental and it was tough for a single mother. Her story has been shrouded in shame and half-truths for most of my life. In fact, it's only in the past few years that I've managed to piece it all together.

My mum Val is the second eldest of Nan and Grandad's four children: Shirley was four years older and after Mum came Jim and Alan. As a small child Shirley had TB, and at 18 months she went into hospital and only left when she was six. When she came home she thought Nan and Grandad were a nurse and a doctor; it was ages before she called them 'Mum' and 'Dad' again, and they were overjoyed when she did. This was at a time when families could only visit children in hospital for a couple of hours every day so it must have been very hard on them all. Val always felt Shirley was the favourite, and perhaps she was because of what she'd been through. Anyway, she was the one who could do no wrong and I think in a way both she and Mum fell into their roles: Shirley did everything right, while Val was the rebellious, cheeky one.

All Nan's children attended the Joseph Lancaster school, which I went to later, which felt nice for me because I liked that feeling of continuity, of being part of the family, one of Nan's children. Afterwards, they all attended the same grammar school: Walworth Central. Despite being the only member of her family to pass the 11-Plus, Mum left school at 15 and worked in office jobs. She was doing the wages at Arthur Miller & Co just off the Bermondsey Road (a firm which made donkey jackets) when she became pregnant with me at the age of 22. By then Auntie Shirley was married – she married early, her first serious boyfriend – and Uncle Jim was working in the Channel Islands, so only Mum and Alan were living at home.

Mum was very glamorous-looking – 5'8". I've got a picture of her sitting like a model with her big peroxide-white hair back-combed up and wearing her winklepickers and a tight little cardigan. She looks so powerful, so in control of her life. Yet she didn't handle anything difficult that happened to her in the way you'd imagine the woman in the photo would. It was the early sixties and in some ways women were beginning to take charge of their lives, but the moment they became pregnant it was right back to the fifties, the days when nice girls didn't part their legs until they were married and any girl who got pregnant was 'no better than she ought to be'.

Everyone who knew Mum when she was young says she was extremely attractive, great fun, very into how she looked and having boyfriends. Even now, when I say those things, I feel I have to add, 'but not in a tarty way'. I think I just imbibed the general feeling in the household that my mother was a bad girl who liked boys a bit too much and ended up getting pregnant like girls who sleep around. That was the way of thinking of Nan and Grandad's generation, the judgemental view I grew up with.

Mum used to go out with a friend, Norma, who worked as a receptionist at the same firm. One evening on the way home from work, Mum (who was 20 at the time) bought 'Let's Twist Again' by Chubby Checker. After playing it back at the flat, she wanted to go out and have fun, so she rang Norma – I've a lot to thank Chubby Checker for! They went to a pub in Lambeth Walk and a couple of guys came in, one of them wearing what my mum described as a 'Frank Sinatra' hat.

'He's gorgeous, he reminds me of Paul Newman,' Mum told Norma as soon as she clapped eyes on John Murphy. Luckily, Norma fancied the other one. Mum liked the self-assured look of John – she always went for the cocky ones. After the ritual chatting-up, Mum and Norma agreed to go on to a drinking club in the Strand. Being close to Fleet Street, it was a place mostly used by printers (John worked 'in the print' for a firm of typesetters in Shoe Lane). As Mum was to learn much later, he was married, but his job gave him great cover for their affair because everyone knew printers worked shifts so on the nights he wasn't able to see her he had a perfect excuse.

Mum and Norma were bowled over by these two blokes, but Mum admits they were much keener than the men so they took to hanging around in the drinking club in the hope of seeing them. Sometimes John would ring Mum at work and she'd walk around on Cloud Nine for the rest of the day. She'd really fallen for him. She admits she always knew she was more into the relationship than he was, but that's young love for you. And she's often told me she was bang in love with him. She used to say, 'You always kid yourself that they will get keener, don't you?' John would sometimes come to the flat and go to the pub, so Nan and Grandad met him too, but he never fully played the role of Mum's boyfriend – he always had a mate with him.

It was an erratic affair: Mum could go weeks without seeing him, but she was always desperate for him to call, and whenever he did she would drop everything. She was mad keen and that's why she says she slept with him: desperate to hang on to him, she was trying to take the relationship to another, more committed level. Some nights he would come round to Nan and Grandad's at about 2 a.m. after he'd finished work and Mum would let him in. He'd stay for a few hours and creep out later. Two years into the relationship, however, Mum found she was pregnant and John Murphy was about to become 'Father Unknown'.

I think she didn't believe it could happen to her: she admits she was in denial. When she missed her first period she thought it must be because she had a cold, and the next time it had to be an upset stomach. When she faced up to it she started jumping down whole flights of stairs, drinking neat gin and taking hot baths, but I was determined to make my entrance – Mum says I was a 'clinger'. You couldn't have abortions in those days (they were illegal) and besides, she wouldn't have known where to start.

At first the only person she told was her friend Norma. When she was sure, she told John Murphy, and that's when he dropped the bombshell in her hour of need: 'I can't do anything, I'm married,' he confessed. Mum says it never occurred to her that he might be married. She admits she should have questioned him more and should have known because he wouldn't commit, but she never did: she just wanted him.

Mum was devastated, but told no one else, and because she was tall and slim she managed to conceal her bump for a long time. Eventually, when she was about six months pregnant, she broke down in floods of tears at work and confessed to one of the directors. He asked why she was so upset and she said, 'Because I am not married.'

In that moment of utter despair he gave her the support she so badly needed. 'A baby is a joyous event,' he told her. 'You have to embrace it.' The owner of the company told Mum that they would do anything they could to help, so it's unfair to say everyone was judgemental, but in reality no one could do much to help her.

For Mum, the biggest problem was that she had not told her parents. A daughter 'in trouble' was such a shameful thing and she was terrified of Grandad's reaction. He was old school: he'd sit in his chair and call for Nan to pour him a cup of tea, even if the teapot was in front of him and even though Nan went out to work and probably needed a sit down, too. Some things were women's work.

Somehow, Mum heard about a mother and baby home in Streatham and she got herself booked in there. But she didn't like it when she went to see the people in charge: she sensed their disapproval and they made her feel there was a lot of shame involved in going there – which, of course, in those days there was. This is not the place to go into the conditions of homes for unmarried girls, but I don't think many who went there in the fifties and sixties would describe them as happy, caring places. Mum was at her wit's end and had no idea what else to do: she was supposed to move into the home six weeks before the birth, give the baby (me) up for adoption as soon as it was born and then stay for six weeks afterwards. She packed her bag and even wrote some letters, which she was going to send to Uncle Jim in Jersey for him to post one back to Nan and Grandad each week as if she was working out there.

'I don't think I ever said the word "adopted", even to myself,' she later told me. 'I was in denial about what would happen to my baby. I didn't think about it.' I can hardly imagine how scared and alone she must have felt as she made these elaborate plans. In the end, it was clearly too much: Mum couldn't keep it a secret from Nan any more and confessed she was pregnant. Nan was upset at the news but even more concerned about the idea of Mum going into the home and having to give the baby away. She told her not to go and said they would face Grandad together.

Mum says she would not have gone through with it. She didn't really want to, but she needed someone to say the words 'Don't go', and when they did it was a terrific relief. Mum and Nan had a cry together, unpacked her bag and threw away the letters. Meanwhile, Nan was just as scared of Grandad's reaction as Mum was, so they put off telling him, but at least Nan helped her daughter to face up to the reality of the situation. She insisted she saw a doctor and about six months into her pregnancy Mum attended antenatal classes at Guy's Hospital.

In the end Grandad heard the news in the worst possible way. Word must have got round because one night in the pub great-Uncle Dick (Grandad's brother) asked, 'Has our Val had the baby yet?'

Grandad went ballistic, not just because she was pregnant but because he'd been kept in the dark. He stormed home from the pub. Mum was cowering under the sheets while he shouted and swore and banged on the bedroom door. He called her a slag and worse, then yelled: 'Why didn't nobody tell me? We could have done something. Now it's too late!' It was the worst rage any of them could remember hearing from him, and Mum was sobbing, clutching her pillow over her head to drown out the noise. I think the whole of Stephenson House knew about it that night.

Meanwhile, Nan was trying to soothe him. He'd never laid a finger on her or any of the children, but he was very strict and absolutely furious, so it could have been a whole lot worse. As it was, it was all shouting and swearing. The next day, when things had calmed down a bit, Nan said to Mum: 'We're going up to Johnny Murphy's to sort this out. Can we have his address?'

By this point John had left his wife and was living back home in Streatham. Mum had already visited him there a couple of months earlier, after his wife (also pregnant at the same time) had confronted her. 'Are you Val Maxwell?' she asked. 'I'm not here to cause trouble – Johnny has left me and gone back to his mother's. Will you come there with me? I want to front up to him with this business that you and me are both pregnant.' Mum had heard that John was a real player, but she was so desperate to be with him that she naively went along with it, hoping she might convince him to choose her.

Anyway, after they found out, Nan and Grandad went to see John at his mum's house and he looked very uncomfortable, so they arranged for him to come round to their flat the next day, but when they saw him again all he said was: 'I can't do anything – I'm married. But I'll help out financially.' Mum felt she didn't want his money, but at least it was finally clear to her.

Mum says Grandad was kind to her after that, but I'm not sure she's telling the whole truth. I think he gave her a hard time, because years later, when she was very drunk one Christmas, she started to knock him: she said he may have been a good grandfather to me but he wasn't a good father. I was very upset at the time because my memories of him were good and I felt she was taking that away from me, but I didn't have any idea of what she went through. Grandad felt the shame bitterly and I'm sure he let Mum know on every occasion he could.

I was born three weeks early. Mum was washing and setting Nan's hair (she always did this every Saturday, like clockwork) when the labour began. I was born three minutes after 8 p.m. on Sunday, 24 November 1963, two days after President Kennedy was shot. Mum has often told me she remembers hearing about the assassination just before she went into hospital.

I weighed 5lb 13oz, small but not worryingly so, and had jaundice. Mum stayed in hospital for 10 days, like they did in those days. She admits she had no idea what having a baby entailed – all the sleepless nights, endless washing and feeding – she thought she would just get on with her life. She also hoped that when John Murphy saw me he'd want to be with her, but once again she had her head in the clouds and he never saw his new baby daughter.

Looking back, Mum says she never doubted she did the right thing in keeping me – women who give their babies up for adoption are often tortured souls. But that's not to say it was easy. In those days the damage was also profound for those who went through with keeping an illegitimate baby, and she would not be free of the shame of my birth for many years, if ever. In reality this was just the beginning: the beginning of my life and the beginning of a struggle that would exist between us for the next 40 years.

When we came back home from hospital, Nan was in charge. Mum liked dressing me up, but Nan did most of the other stuff – the bottles and the nappy changing. Apparently Grandad said to Mum at one stage: 'It's about time you did something for your baby – it's yours, not hers.' Mum says she regrets not doing more but at the time she was more than happy to hand me over. Whatever he felt about the way I was conceived, from the moment I arrived home Grandad adored me, though. I won him over straight away and any doubts he might have had before I was born were gone: I was the apple of his eye.

It has made my life very awkward having three parents: Mum, Nan and Grandad. I've always had to be careful – I could never say how much I loved Nan for fear of upsetting Mum. It was a strange upbringing in that way. And now, with hindsight, Mum thinks it was a mistake to stay at home with her parents all her life and she should have found a place for the two of us. But living at home meant she could go back to work after 10 months off on maternity benefit. 'I don't mind looking after her all week, but at the weekends you have to stay in,' Nan told her. She and Grandad liked to go down the pub every Friday, Saturday and Sunday.

For Mum, living at home with her parents meant that she never found out about running a home. She never had to cook because Nan did it all, but she did her share of the washing, putting my terry nappies in the old boiler in the washhouse next door to the flat. Because Nan was always there, Mum didn't have the confidence to break out on her own. She tried to take responsibility for me – 'She's *my* daughter,' I remember her saying to Nan. 'Well, stop fucking having a go at her then!' Nan would say.

Now I can see that Nan was undermining Mum, but as a child I thought she was just taking care of me. Nan was a strong personality and you'd need a hell of a backbone to go against her wishes. Mum never could, and I can see why not: she was formidable. Both had big mouths and big voices, and they'd go at it hammer and tongs – lots of door slamming, lots of swearing. But Nan always had the last word and it was always the women making the noise: Grandad never took part.

He also made it difficult for Mum to be a normal mother to me. She remembers he was always telling her off for nagging me because as far as he was concerned I could do no wrong. Mum couldn't stand up to him because she felt obliged to her parents for letting us live there. Looking back, I can see it was very hard for her.

I do remember Mum was usually there to put me to bed. She'd do the rhyme about the little piggies – 'This little piggy went to market, this little piggy stayed at home …' playing with my toes. And she would hold my hand and recite, 'Round and round the garden, like a teddybear …' Both ended with me being tickled, which I loved.

Having a social life was difficult for Mum, and not just because I was hell bent on stopping her. As she says, in those days a woman with a baby was not a good proposition. She had a couple of chances: at one stage she got engaged to a guy called Johnny who she'd been seeing for about a year (somehow Nan must have persuaded me he was all right). Auntie Shirley even found a flat for Mum, him and me to move into. A mate of Grandad's brought some rings to the pub and Mum chose one. They were discussing wedding dates and she was over the moon: at last she would have the respectability she craved. I was about five at the time and he got on well with me, lying on the floor with me doing puzzles. Finally, Mum's life was taking shape.

When Johnny's mother found out, she told him: 'If you marry that girl, I want nothing more to do with you.' It seemed he cared more for her than he did for Mum because he sent round a letter:

Dear Val, I won't be there tonight. My mum and dad are going down to Cornwall and I'm going with them. I think it's time we called it a day.

Mum left me with Grandad and rushed to where Johnny worked, but he'd already gone and she never saw him again. It was so cruel, and once again she was devastated. Every time she went out with a man she dreaded telling him she had a kid because she knew he wouldn't want to see her again, she says. Although she didn't tell me the story of my father until many years later when I had a family of my own, at the time she told me that no one wanted her because of me.

# CHAPTER 2

## Early Days at the Elephant

From the moment Nan and Grandad accepted me into their home, nothing was too good for me, no hand-me-downs. I had a big Silver Cross pram bought new for me from Morleys of Brixton. It was navy-blue and silver and Mum said she felt so proud of me when I was in it. She chose my name after Lisa Marie (the actress from *Rock Around the Clock*).

From day one, the way I looked was top of her list of priorities. She would do me up like a piece of installation art, all the best clothes, like a 'Tiny Tears' doll in my little white crochet bonnets and capes. She'd bump me down the stairs of Stephenson House and leave me on display for passers-by to admire. It was two floors down and she couldn't see me from the balcony, but in those days no one worried about children being kidnapped. Perhaps there was a much greater sense of community – no one would do it today. Anyway, if anyone did want to snatch me they'd have to get past our old bulldog, Ricky, who was tied to the pram. Call it Elephant and Castle childcare.

Mum loved buying me clothes. When I was older she'd dress me up and take me over to the park, where she'd take pictures of me smelling flowers. She used to clean my patent shoes with milk to make them shine and spend ages on my hair, giving me doorknocker plaits with loops and always with ribbons. I remember when I was old enough for school she'd stand me on the side in the kitchen and make sure I looked immaculate while Noel Edmonds prattled away on Radio One.

As I grew older I identified with her need to create a good impression on the outside. I loved shopping for clothes, picking out my outfits for family dos. Whenever I got new clothes, I would ask Mum to hang them on the back of the bedroom door so I could fall asleep gazing at them. For Mum, dressing me up was a way to validate us both. ''Course we love 'er – look how nice she looks' was the message she was sending out. It rubbed off on me and I've always worried about creating the right visual image, wanting people to like how I look; what started as a love of fashion became a way of controlling people's perceptions of me. If I looked great on the outside, no one would search for the real stuff underneath. The last thing I ever wanted was for people to feel sorry for me – 'Poor little Lise' were not words I ever wanted to hear.

We were a lively family and there were lots of dos to dress up for. Nan and Grandad liked a good time and there were a few parties at number 15, spilling over from big family get-togethers in the pub. They used to put a board over the bath and put all the drinks in the bath. When I was a baby there was a scare because they thought someone had sat on me: it was one of my family's favourite stories – even as a baby I was the butt of Nan's humour. Apparently Alan's friend Mickey lurched about drunkenly and had flopped down almost on top of me. When someone realised they couldn't see me they thought I was squashed underneath him. They all thought it was hilarious.

Nan only ever expected one thing from me: if she was having a good time, I had to join in. 'You've gorra have a laugh, int'yer?' was her motto. She didn't do misery. If anyone tried to burst her bubble, she'd say: 'Fuck 'em if they can't take a joke!' And she'd encourage me to get up and dance in the middle of the boozed-up adults. 'Gorn, babe,' she'd say, and as the spirit of Chubby Checker entered my body I'd dance and shout.

'Is it a *bird*?'

Boozed-up adults: '*No!*'

'Is it a plane?'

'*No!*'

'Is it a twister?'

'*Yeah!*' and the whole of number 15 would be up on their feet, twisting the night away, with Little Lise right at the heart of it.

'Aw, in't she lovely?' people would say. I knew I was everyone's favourite.

As Nan's granddaughter it was no surprise that I was a born entertainer, and she and Mum encouraged me. She enrolled me for dancing classes when I was about three and a half at the Renee Hayes Dancing School in a church hall just off the Walworth Road. I had a little red leotard and white tap shoes, through which my mum threaded red ribbons.

I was walking there one day with Mum when I was attacked by a dog off the lead: it was only little, like a Yorkshire terrier or something, but it bit my leg and locked its jaws onto me. Mum tried to kick it off, then picked me up and tried to swing it off. Eventually, when it was off me, I was taken to hospital for a tetanus jab which made me scream and put me off injections, so that put paid to my dancing for a while. I refused to go again but I still danced around at home. I remember once climbing on top of the sideboard, which had a drinks cabinet in it. This cabinet was made of shiny, fake walnut wood – I know it was plastic because we didn't have any real wood in the house. Suddenly it fell over on top of me and there was smashed glass all around. I was badly cut and Mum had to rush me to hospital again; luckily this time I didn't need an injection.

I wasn't just spoilt with clothes, I was given every toy I ever wanted: if I wanted a walking, talking doll the same size as me, I got one. When I asked for a Swingy Doll, with beautiful white nylon hair she could swing to and fro, it was the same. And when I wanted a whole suite of Sindy bedroom furniture, it was there. I don't remember being denied anything.

I must have been a cute kid when I was at nursery school because the teacher chose me as her bridesmaid when she got married. Mum was so proud: she and Nan took me down to Brighton for the wedding, and she was thrilled when people kept telling her what a pretty child I was. I was the centre of attention, just as I was throughout my childhood.

In some ways, I think Mum loved me too much. I was nearly suffocated by her love and fascination for me. I was top priority. I know that often happens to only children, but even as a child

I found the responsibility of being put on a pedestal almost too great: it didn't allow me to fail.

Nan and Grandad adored me in a more straightforward way, but even that caused problems. Their other kids had children, too, and Mum remembers a bit of resentment. Nothing was ever said openly to me about my father, but I heard things. At family gatherings people would say: 'She's a chip off the old block. She looks just like her dad.' And 'She favours her father, not her mother.'

From an early age there was clearly a short gene in my mix but Mum always tried to pass it off by saying it was to do with an infection after I was born. I'm the only one with a little button nose, too. When Mum introduced me for the first time people would often say, probably just out of politeness, I looked like her. She'd reply, 'No, she's not like me, but she's the spitting image of her father.' This was in my hearing, but not to me.

All I knew about him was his name – John Murphy – and I didn't like it. It made me think I was half-Irish and I didn't want to be a different nationality from everyone else in my family. The kids on the Rockingham Estate made fun of Irish people. Sometimes Mum would say, 'You could have been a Murphy,' and I hated it because I liked being a Maxwell.

I never asked direct questions about my father; somehow I knew not to; but she'd sometimes say things, like he looked like Paul Newman and that he looked fantastic and wore a Frank Sinatra hat. From these snippets I built up my own image: for me, Paul Newman was the definition of a good-looking man and I've always loved the music of Frank Sinatra. Maybe that's just coincidence or perhaps some deep-rooted influence from those days but don't imagine I spent hours thinking about my

'Father Unknown' – I didn't. I did a really good job of putting him out of my mind. Somehow it seemed an insult to Mum to harp after a father figure when I could see she was doing everything she could to make sure I didn't feel abandoned.

Grandad was like a real dad to me although he wasn't cuddly and warm and he didn't seem to be part of my world as much as Nan. But he did the fatherly things: he took the stabilisers off my bike, taught me to ride it, and he made a game for me – a bit like jacks only with wooden cubes. Like lots of men of his generation, he always wore suits (usually brown) and stripy shirts. He got them on Club Row market, next to Petticoat Lane, and whenever he needed a new one he'd take me with him on a Sunday morning. To a child this was a magical place, full of colourful stalls and great characters. My favourite stall was the one where they sold puppies, and Grandad would take me there and let me play with them – we loved our trips together. Afterwards we'd go and see his brother (Uncle Dick) and his son Richard (Little Dick) and I'd get a cup of tea and biscuits, then he'd drop me home before going down the pub.

It was Grandad who reluctantly put up the money when Mum saw an advert for child models (I was seven or eight at the time). She took me along and the people running the 'agency' said we would need to buy a portfolio. This was a scam because they never found me any work, but the photos were great and Mum used them later on when she got me into the Italia Conti.

It was Grandad who brought home one of my closest childhood friends: Pierre the poodle. He was a French poodle, hence the name, who had belonged to Grandad's sister Sarah (famous in the family because she once lived next door to Cliff Richard) but she could no longer keep him. I was thrilled to adopt him and apparently when I was very young I said that when I grew up I was going to marry him. I have to say, the name was a bit of an embarrassment – shouting 'Pierre' off the balcony really wasn't acceptable on the Rockingham Estate – so Uncle Alan quickly renamed him Pete the Poodle.

Grandad was the boss in the house: if the news was on the telly and we were talking, he only had to say 'Shush' and we'd all go quiet. After two or three drinks he was more sociable and he'd have a soppy grin on his face. That's when he would say 'yes' to buying any toys or clothes I wanted and, boy, did I know it.

Mum and me shared our room until I was about 10: I think this contributed to the impression I had from early on that Nan and Grandad were in the role of parents. Mum never grew out of being their child because she always lived with them and it's only recently she's had a double bed, not till after Nan died in 2009.

Running through those years was my ongoing fear of Mum having a life outside our family: I dreaded her going on dates, I felt she was going to do all the things that had given her a 'reputation' in the first place – shocking, horrible things associated with my birth. I remember with horror once walking in when I was about eight and finding Mum in Nan and Grandad's bed with a man: it was terrible. I called her a 'slut' and other things, words I must have picked up from what other people said about her. As far as I was concerned, she wasn't supposed to have a boyfriend or male company. The man had a beard and no one in our family had a beard. To me, he looked debauched, but then any man in a compromising position with Mum would seem that way. Much later, when I was about 14, she had another boyfriend (Bernie). I wasn't going to cut her any slack and used to sit between them on the sofa. As Mum says, she had dates, not relationships.

I've got a picture from a holiday we went on to Portugal when I was a kid and Mum's sitting on the back of a fisherman's motorbike. I hated seeing that picture: he's swarthy, and to me he looks like a highly sexual person. It was terrible for me because I think Mum was having a holiday romance with him and I hated that, I hated anything to suggest she was a normal, sexual being.

Uncle Alan played his part in my upbringing, too. He is only 12 years older than me (Nan's youngest child) and in many ways I grew up thinking of him as a big brother: he used to look after me after school while Mum was working. He'd take me to Nan, who would be at the Elephant and Castle Shopping Centre playing bingo, trying to win food vouchers for our tea. She was no good with money and so she had to come up with creative ways to feed us all, usually involving bingo, the pawn shop or the tally man (the man who collected instalments on money she'd borrowed). Looking back, I can see she probably had a real gambling problem: money always went down the betting shop or the bingo hall and a lot of the time I was with her when she visited there. Grandad never gave her money because he knew what she did with it. She always loved horse racing and followed certain jockeys, working out the odds. At one time she worked in a betting shop and if a punter came in with a bet she knew was hopeless she'd pocket the cash and not put the bet on. Thank God it never came down on her. Later in life she'd watch the racing on telly, screaming and shouting at her horse.

I remember hiding with Nan when the tally man came round (I don't know how she knew it was him). Suddenly there'd be a knock at the door and she knew not to answer as if she could smell him. So we'd hide and I'd have to be really quiet, like a game. If we were in the passage when he came, we'd have to get down really low because he could peer through the letterbox. When he'd gone, she'd laugh about it and get on with the rest of her day. If he caught her out and she had to open the door, it would only be a crack, a few inches. I'd be hanging round her legs, trying to see him, but she'd always push me back. I could never put a face to the tally man but the thought of him scared me: he was like a bogeyman.

I don't think Mum or Grandad knew about the tally man or the clothing club Nan paid into; maybe it was only Uncle Alan and me who were in on it. Alan got a leather jacket from the tally man money, which he has never forgotten. Nan told us to keep it a secret.

She was always trying to get money out of Grandad, but he knew better. Whatever excuse she used, he knew it would go down the betting shop or the bingo; they rowed about it a lot. When they were cleaning offices together in the City they would take me with them. I'd sit there making false nails for myself out of Sellotape (a skill used later in life) while they cleaned. She'd be having a go at him about money. Sometimes she'd forge notes from one of the other cleaners (a man), asking to borrow a tenner until next week, and Grandad would hand it over, not realising it was going into her purse. If she had money, I'd be taken to the betting shop and had to hang around outside waiting for her, even after the age of 11 when I was in my posh Italia Conti uniform.

Feeding us all was very hand to mouth: she'd count out the money, sometimes coppers, and go shopping every day. We all ate at different times: the only time we tried to have a meal together was Sunday lunchtime but because Nan and Grandad had been in the pub for hours it was often burnt. We had a drop-leaf table under the window that would only be pulled out on Sundays or at Christmas. Normal meals after I came in from school were egg and chips or ham, egg and chips if there was more money, a bit of brawn some days. I loved fish paste and used to eat it with a spoon from the jar. Nan would sometimes make shepherd's pie and I loved her rice pudding with a skin on top, made in a bowl that looked about 100 years old. We all loved it when Nan brought pie and mash home: there was a real ritual to ripping the paper off, carving a cross and pouring in the bright green liquor from a polystyrene cup, then smothering it in vinegar and pepper. It was a real treat, bought from Arments in Westmoreland Road, off the Walworth Road. I think we only had pie and mash if Nan won a bit on the horses.

I loved the Joseph Lancaster School. When I started there at five, the head teacher remembered Alan and said he hoped I would do better: 'Alan came in through the front door and out through the back and was home before your nan.' But I was a good girl: my school reports are all great except every teacher said I was very chatty (nothing much has changed). We didn't have to wear a uniform and, as you've gathered, I was always fashionably dressed. Mum used to buy me clothes in Carnaby Street, *the* trendy place in those days, from a shop called Kids in Gear. I loved my patent leather hot pants with yellow leather braces on them. In another shop (Buttons & Bows) she bought silk ribbons, buttons and bits and pieces to sew onto my clothes to jazz them up. The shopkeeper made a dress for me, crocheted in white with red satin ribbon woven through and a matching beret. It was for the wedding of one of Mum's friends (they weren't having bridesmaids but they wanted me in the pictures) so I was star of the show, my favourite place.

I wore the dress to school as well: there was never any of that saving your best for weekends in our family, I was always done up like the dog's dinner. It was part of our thing. Look at us Maxwells: we're not failures, we've got all the latest gear and everything we've got is on our backs. A lot of working-class people are like that. Nan had a ring on every finger, she'd bung it all on: it was about telling the world we didn't need charity. There's a pattern emerging when I look back at my life.

I was Miss Popular at school: bright, funny and loved by everybody except those I took the mickey out of. Putting the focus on someone else's shortcomings meant no one got round to asking me the dreaded question: 'Why haven't you got a dad?' Without thinking about it, I was always trying to recruit friends: believers in Lisa Maxwell, people who would think, isn't she great? I'm glad Lisa is on the planet! One of the reasons why I liked being well dressed was that I thought it would make people like me more if I looked as if I came from a well-off family who could afford to buy nice things. Even as a kid I was acting out the philosophy that took me through a lot of my life and stopped me ever having to face up to myself: keep busy, stay at the centre of things, have a laugh. Whatever you do, don't stand still long enough to be alone with yourself or to let other people ask too many questions. If I was funny and popular, who would care if I didn't have a father?

Maybe the other kids did notice but they didn't say anything to my face. Maybe the others clocked my background, but I was protected from name-calling and nasty comments because all the scary kids liked me, which meant no one else gave me any trouble. I was tiny, but I had this really tall friend called Delphine. Her sister Jackie could beat anyone up, including the boys. My loose tongue and ability to mimic people meant I was always taking the mickey, but I managed to duck out of trouble: if anyone threatened to meet me after school, I'd walk out with Delphine and the troublemakers would melt away.

Mum never admitted she was a single parent, deserted before her baby was born. At the offices where she worked she always said she was divorced or separated, and for years she told me my father had 'died in the war'. I was too young to ask '*What* war?' because it didn't make any sense (there was no war when I was born, unless you count Vietnam) and what was an American GI doing hanging around South London with Mum? But it was something women always said, an excuse the previous genera-tion had been able to use, so that's what I told the kids at school. When I look back, I'm amazed, but they accepted it just as I did.

I found out my dad wasn't dead from Nan, but not in a proper sit-down-and-we'll-have-a-talk kind of way. We were in the pub when I was seven or eight and I said something about him being dead (I think a kid at school had asked me). 'Oh, your dad ain't dead, don't be silly,' said Nan casually, then turned to the barman: 'Scotch and American and a martini, please, Jim. Oh, and can you tell the pianist to play "When Your Old Wedding Ring Was New" …'

It was just slipped in: it wasn't explained, just a quick refer-ence before ordering the next drink. I don't remember being shocked or the news having a massive impact, so I think deep down I probably already knew but didn't understand. Although I carried on pretending, the story changed: instead of saying Dad was dead, now I said he left when I was very young. It was a world away from being illegitimate because at least I had a father when I was born. If I had a dad, even for a day or two after my birth, it legitimised me being on the planet.

Secrets and lies and shame have had a profound effect on me. There was a big chunk of my life that I didn't know about – 'Father Unknown' – but I also knew from early on that I mustn't ask questions. Again, I don't know how I knew this, but subliminally someone must have made me feel it was not a good idea: we don't talk about things that hurt. It was a defence mechanism, I guess, filtered down to Mum from Nan and Grandad's generation, who believed you put up and shut up.

As I grew up, I became adept at not dealing with things: I simply put my head in the sand. From a young age children pick up when something causes pain, and I didn't want to put my mum through that agony. The bits of information I was given about myself were just snippets or downright lies; you become numb to the good stuff, the bad stuff, everything … Somehow you know some of it's not true but you also understand the reason why they're not telling you the truth is because it's too hard for them so you never try to unravel things. Not that I went through childhood having deep thoughts about all of this; I was enjoying myself too much.

I was a bit of a star at school: the singing teacher (Miss Stokes) really encouraged me, telling me I was a natural. She gave me the role of Mrs B in our little production about Peter Rabbit when I was about six and I remember hearing my voice singing through a microphone, a song about Mrs Rabbit going through the wood with her shopping basket – I loved it. It was a massive moment in my life, hearing my voice amplified and performing to an audience.

I was clever at school but that didn't matter in my family, they weren't interested in academic things. For some reason, I had a reading age of 16 at 11 years old. We all took a test to see who should be on the school team for the Panda Club Quiz, an event started by the Met Police, and I was chosen. The four smartest kids took part in this quiz with all the other schools in London and we won, which made us celebrities at school for a while – it was a really big deal, everyone was very pleased. We had to answer questions about the history of the police, which is funny because many years later I would join the Force myself in *The Bill* – I guess my research started early.

Breaks and lunchtimes were spent playing and our favourite games were French Skipping, with girls jumping through a large loop of knicker elastic, and Two Ball Up the Wall – I always had two tennis balls with me and was a whizz at throwing them against the wall and reciting rhymes like 'Holy Mary, mother of God/Send me down a couple of bob'. Blasphemous, but we never thought about the meaning. We weren't a religious family, the Maxwells, although I was sent to Sunday school at the Abdullam Mission from about seven years old. I took a shine to a dog living next door to the room where Sunday school was held. I'd knock at the door and ask if I could take Teddy for a walk. A lady in an overall, just like Nan wore, would hand him over on an old chain lead with a worn leather handle.

'Here you are, love,' she'd say.

'When do I have to bring him back?'

'When you've had enough.'

Off I'd skip with Teddy, who wasn't exactly pretty. He was part-Doberman and part-Whippet, and probably lots of other things in there as well: skinny, brown and black with a strange little stump where his tail should have been. I loved walking round the estate with him, pretending he was mine.

One day Teddy made a run for it, with me desperately trying to keep hold of him, which was difficult because the leather handle had snapped and I was grasping the end of the metal chain. Then the metal hook, which held the chain to the leather, pierced the skin between thumb and forefinger: the more Teddy ran, the more it bit into my hand. The pain was excruciating and I was screaming in agony. Somehow I managed to yank the hook out and ran home, yelling my head off.

'All right, babes, calm down,' said Mum. 'Let's have a look.'

I got on top of my breath slightly and became calmer, desperately hoping Mum wouldn't take me to hospital – I dreaded having an injection.

'We've got to go, babes. You might have lockjaw.'

'What the hell is that?' I wailed. 'Am I going to get a stiff head and never speak again?'

'No, you just need a little tetanus. Let's just get you up the 'ospidal.'

By this time I was hysterical. 'Do I have to have a needle?'

'No, darling, they don't give you needles now – they give you sweets nowadays.'

So we went to Guy's Hospital, but I soon realised I'd been tricked when two nurses held me down and a giant in a white coat came towards me with a needle like a pneumatic drill. I screamed, kicked and wriggled and tried to punch, but in the midst of this maelstrom the needle went in without me noticing it.

'There, there, it's all over – calm down,' I was surprised to hear the doctor in the white coat say. And then, 'Now, I hear you wanted sweets?' and he waggled a bag of Jelly Tots at me. So I got the sweets but it was not the way Mum said it would be. Lying was her first line of defence under pressure and I don't blame her because all she was worried about was getting me to hospital. I would have preferred to know what was coming, though!

In my later years at primary school I used to bunk off a bit. We'd go round to the flat of a black lad called Jimmy Paul, who had the 'Telegram Sam' record by T-Rex, which we would play endlessly. Jimmy scared a lot of kids – he was a good fighter with a bit of attitude, but I was his mate and so was Wendy Donovan. I really liked her clothes and she lent me her Starsky and Hutch chunky-knit cardie. When we went on our one and only school trip, a week in Norfolk, she lent me her edge-to-edge cardigan for the whole time. A really thin knit that joined in the middle, no buttons or fasteners, worn with a thin knitted belt, it was beige and came down to just cover my bum: I wore it with plat-form shoes.

I don't think I knew the word 'chic' then, but that's exactly what I would have used. To me, that cardigan looked like it cost a fortune. I remember that I extended the loan period, keeping it for the whole trip, and it was out of shape by the end. That trip was the first time I ever fancied a boy – Gary Weston. I showed off by dancing in front of him, wiggling my derrière. It was the start of another pattern in life: I've always used dancing to attract blokes I fancy.

In those days there was a great deal of freedom for children. As soon as I was big enough, Nan and Mum would let me loose to play with the other kids on the estate. They'd call from the balcony when they wanted me and often it would be after dark and I'd still be running around. We used to run everywhere, hiding from each other; we'd even play on a rubbish dump. Although we never got in big trouble, we could be naughty. I remember we played Knock Down Ginger (knocking on the door and running away) on the door of a little round Irish man, who looked like a leprechaun ('Thick Mick') – the political correctness police would be after us today. But we never did any harm and he was lovely to us.

There was a sandpit in Jail Park, where we played endlessly. I once got a mouthful of bird pooh, which gave the other kids a good laugh. Even then, I was talking the whole time and I must have looked up with my mouth still motoring. Another time I was wearing a gold ring with a tiny diamond in it. (What was Mum thinking of, sending a six-year-old out to play like that? Typical of us Maxwells, all part of making me look high-end.) Anyway, I swapped it for a bag of Maltesers. Mum had to go round to the girl's house to retrieve it.

My babysitter Sandra lived on the ground floor of Stephenson House: I used to play with her brother Raymond, who was a couple of years older than me, and his cousin Rachel. Raymond was mad about Elvis and we'd all be doing Hound Dog impressions on the bit of lawn at the back of his flat. I was keen on David Cassidy and Sandra took me to see him when I was about seven or eight at the Wembley Empire. Because I was only little and sitting on her shoulders we were allowed right through to the front, and he sang 'The Puppy Song' for me and gave me a rose. I was so in love – I remember crying and kissing the television whenever he was on. When he came back to London the next time I was so upset he was kept on a launch on the Thames to stop the fans stampeding him. He was the first person I ever saw wearing Yeti boots, and he was the coolest thing on the planet.

I rode around the estate on my bike, a red second-hand Raleigh that my mum bought from her friend Shirley Delannoy, whose name I loved because it sounded exotic and foreign. Shirley was a travel agent with bleached blonde hair. She was married to a man from Belgium so by the standards of my childhood she *was* exotic. It was sometimes a volatile union – they lived on the sixteenth floor of a Bermondsey tower block and she would joke that one day she would deliberately leave open the balcony door when he was out drinking in the hope that he might fall over in his drunken state.

I got another kind of education from Uncle Jim and Auntie Wendy. Jim had done well for himself, running a successful haulage company, and they had a big house with a swimming pool. He was always supportive of Mum and me and I used to spend part of my summer holidays with his family. I'd be put on a Green Line bus in London and they'd pick me up at the other end. It was there that I learnt to eat posh.

I remember four-course dinners at their house, everyone round the table. And I learnt how to eat in a restaurant – they took me for my first-ever trip to a Chinese. When I used to pretend I had a father to kids who thought my parents were divorced, all the information I gave about my imaginary dad was based on Jim.

When I was 10, Jim and Wendy took me to Devon for a holiday. I was with my cousin Samantha and there was this lovely-looking French boy playing near us. He looked like a mini Sacha Distel, with a navy blue jumper. Young as I was, my taste in boys was already refined – I've always liked the preppy French look (for a girl from a council flat, I have a taste for 'a bit of posh' in terms of looks). So Samantha and I kept smiling at this boy and eventually we got talking to him. I was a bit surprised by his high voice.

'Lauren,' he said, when I asked his name.

'*Laurence*?' I asked, puzzled.

'No, *Lauren* – I am a girl …'

I was gutted but we still became pen pals and I think when I was writing to her I secretly imagined she was a boy.

When I was about 12, I was at Uncle Jim's house, sitting in the front of the Jag that Auntie Wendy had parked in the drive. Their Alsatian was in the car with me and I was trying to get the Stylistics' eight-track cassette out of their cassette player. Somehow I knocked the car, an automatic, into reverse and we started to roll backwards down the hill. I was a tiny kid so if anyone had seen this it would have looked really odd. The dog started howling – he knew this wasn't right. We were heading towards the swimming pool but luckily I managed to grab the brake and pull it on. We stopped within a couple of feet of the pool. Thank God we haven't hit anything, I thought, as I climbed out.

'I'm sure I left the car under the kitchen window,' said Auntie Wendy.

'No, it's always been by the pool, Auntie Wendy,' I told her, all innocent.

The dog didn't snitch but he looked a bit worried around me for a while.

We always had holidays and most years we went abroad: Spain, Italy and Portugal. Grandad paid for it all, putting money away every week. Usually it was Nan, Grandad, Mum and me, but sometimes Nan and Grandad's friends Lil and Bill Holt came as well. They were always called Lil'Olt-and-Bill'Olt, like one word. Their daughter had a son – Gary – born in the hospital at the same time as me, so Lil was one of the first to see me after I came into the world. They were always part of our lives.

We went to Pontinental in Torremolinos a few years running – that's Pontins, but abroad. It was two huge tower blocks, one next to the other. I loved it because they had a disco and a talent competition. It was always a big old booze-up and I was very spoiled. There were day trips to Morocco but the only one of us who would go was Grandad – the others just wanted to bake our tans. In one of my favourite pictures, he is sitting on a camel in Morocco. Years later, my friend Caroline Sargeant who lived in the block of flats opposite ours, Telford House, told me she thought we were a posh family because we always went abroad.

There was one time, however, when I really didn't want to go to Spain. It was my last year at Joseph Lancaster and the singing teacher who I loved was putting on a production of *The Wizard of Oz*. Who do you think landed the part of Dorothy? I auditioned with a pretend American accent, which I'd been perfecting for years. For some reason I thought it was really cool and I would go round the Elephant and Castle asking grown-ups the time in this funny voice. I thought they would all be wondering why a little American girl was there, but probably they just thought I was a silly kid pretending. Anyway, I remember auditioning, saying 'Where am I? This isn't Kansas. Oh, Toto, *Toto* …' – I loved Judy Garland and the part seemed made for me – I really felt this was my moment. Then I couldn't do it because the show clashed with our trip to Pontinental. At this point I got in a real strop and told Mum I didn't want to go, that I would stay with one of my friends to do the show. But I had to go and I cried at the idea of some other girl being Dorothy. I knew they'd give the part to a girl called Titia, who was very blonde and pretty. When I got back, I dreaded school because everyone would be talking about the show and how good she was.

It was no wonder I was the natural choice for Dorothy: from the age of eight I'd been going to stage school every Saturday. When I left Joseph Lancaster I attended full time, but that's a story worth a whole chapter of its own.

# CHAPTER 3

## Italia Conti Girls

My stage career happened almost by chance. I was lucky because among the other kids on the Rockingham Estate were the three Sargeant girls: Caroline, Lynn and Elaine. Caroline, who was about four years older than me, spoke differently to the rest of us, a bit like a BBC announcer, and Mum was very impressed. She and Nan spoke fluent Rockingham, but Mum reckoned if I ended up talking like the rest of my family then I wouldn't get anywhere in life; if I had a posh accent it would give me a start in life.

'Why does she talk like that, Liz?' she asked Caroline's mum, who was also a single mum. She went on to explain about Italia Conti.

'My Lisa would like some of that! How do you get her in?' asked Mum.

It seemed a charitable trust had helped out because 11-year-old Caroline had talent. The trust found a sponsor, a photographer called Alan Olley, who helped pay for her to attend the fee-paying stage school. It was the first time Mum or any of us had ever heard of Italia Conti. For years my mum called it 'Italian Conti' and most people round our way thought I was learning Italian. I was eight then, too young to go full time. Mum rang the school to ask about elocution lessons, but they said they weren't doing them any more. They told her they were giving speech and drama lessons on Saturday mornings and this was just as good for teaching me to speak properly. So I was enrolled, and every Saturday morning she would take me to the school in Clapham. Her ambition, as she told me often enough, was for me to marry Prince Andrew so she needed to make sure I could talk proper and was prepared to make sacrifices.

I used to love going round to Caroline's flat because she had The Monkees' album and we'd mime to 'Daydream Believer' and 'Last Train to Clarksville' and put on our own plays. Because she was at Italia Conti full time, she had scripts of real plays: we especially enjoyed putting on *Billy Liar* because every other word was 'bloody' so we could swear away in her bedroom all day and say, 'It's *all right*, it's in the script!'

Her sisters and me would play at auditioning for the lead roles, but because Caroline was the eldest and went to stage school she always won. We'd be Charlie's Angels and she was always Farrah. Once we'd established the game, I'd play it with other kids – I remember doing it with my cousins out at Uncle Jim's house in Buckinghamshire. That was great because then it was my game so I could be Farrah and, believe me, I *was* Farrah like my life depended on it. I've always had thin hair, so it did wonders for my confidence pretending I had this big mane to flick. We'd run around the house hiding behind rubber plants, then leap out and shout 'Freeze!' with our fingers shaped like a gun.

From the word go, I loved Italia Conti. We learnt to enunciate properly and memorised speeches from Shakespeare, taking exams run by the London Academy of Speech and Drama. Soon the other girls were staying on for dancing lessons after drama and I joined those classes, too: doing tap, ballet and modern dance.

I made friends straight away: Laura James was one of my best friends, Karen Halliday was another and Amanda Mealing, who went on to a big role in *Holby City*. We four were working-class kids, so I didn't feel out of place. Laura and Karen knew each other as they were both from Stockwell and Amanda came from Lambeth. We all spoke pure South London, but within weeks I was talking like Princess Lisa of Rockingham with this perfect cut-glass accent.

Soon it was time to move on from primary school and all I wanted was to attend Italia Conti full time. Of course it cost money: Mr and Mrs Sheward, who ran the school, told Mum that the Inner London Education Authority normally gave four scholarships but they'd cut it down to two that year and so we had to audition. There were about 20 of us, all there with our mums, who were probably even more nervous than us. I auditioned with a modern piece, a ballet piece, a speech and a song: I didn't have a serious acting piece so I did a poem called 'Worms', which was short and silly. Looking back, I didn't do myself justice but I wasn't at all nervous – I never had a problem walking into a room and showing off. I had three 'parents' putting me on a pedestal, who thought I was the bees' knees, so my self-esteem was pretty high.

We had to wait for two weeks for the results (Mum says they were two of the longest weeks of her life). When Mr Sheward rang it was not good news: I'd come third. My friends Laura and Karen got the scholarships. I was offered a place but the fees were well beyond our means. At a meeting with Mr Sheward, he told Mum, 'She's one of the most talented kids we've come across and we have to find a way to get her into this school.' He had a book called *The Directory of Grant Making Trusts* and gave her lots of numbers to ring to see if they could offer any help. They were mostly single-parent charities but because we lived with Nan and Grandad we didn't really qualify. Nobody could help – I guess they had far more pressing problems than a kid who had a decent home but needed the money to go to stage school. I remember thinking, why does everything come down to the fact that I haven't got a dad? Why doesn't Mum just get the money, couldn't someone leave it her in an inheritance or something?

It wasn't looking good but Mum was determined not to give up. She was the receptionist at Gaskett, Metcalfe & Walton, a firm of solicitors, and approached her boss, Michael Harris. Mum volunteered to work lunch hours and longer hours so that she could save the money (she had already surrendered an insurance policy to help but was worried about further payments). Michael could see there was no way she would save enough by the time I had to start and so he came to an arrangement with her: the firm advanced my fees and they stopped £25 a week from Mum's wages to pay them back. I'm so grateful to him for help when we needed it, and later on he became a trusted friend and handled several legal matters for me.

His firm also helped Mum get more money from my dad, John Murphy, although at the time this wasn't properly explained to me. I remember, when I was about 12, being taken to a court near Tower Bridge in my school uniform. The whole experience didn't gel – I think I'd have rather done without the money. I didn't like the role of poor kid outside court with a begging bowl: they needed to recast the part for another child, I thought, not one who went to stage school, had a posh accent and believed she would one day be a big success. I stood outside the court building with a strange sick feeling in the bottom of my tummy because I believed I must have done something wrong. Courts were for criminals, weren't they?

One of the clients at the firm where Mum worked was Bruce Forsyth's first wife, and when she heard about me going to Italia Conti she gave us her daughter Debbie's old cape. Some of my uniform came from Dickens & Jones, the official school supplier, which to me was a really high-end shop up West and I know it cost an arm and a leg. Mum got a lot of it from a second-hand shop in Battersea, though. The cape was dark blue with a collar like Mary Poppins's cape, a bit like the ones nurses wear; there were silver buttons each side with chains going across. Underneath we wore a royal-blue blazer and then a blue jumper and grey skirt. Later on, little kilts. In winter, I had a blue velour hat and a straw boater for summer.

But the uniform was only the start: I had to have a bag containing *The Complete Works of Shakespeare*, which I never used because we'd have the parts printed out on paper. I also needed loads of ballet shoes, tights, a leotard and all the other accessories a dancer has to have. Imagine me walking from Stephenson House to the Elephant and Castle tube station done up like something out of *Bedknobs and Broomsticks*. I was so proud because it was obvious I was going to a fee-paying school.

Grandad thought Mum was mad to be paying out all that cash. 'You're wasting your bloody money! Why don't you send her to Pitmans?' he used to say. Learning shorthand would be more useful, he thought. Meanwhile, Mum fought her corner.

'No, it's what she wants to do,' she insisted.

'Are you sure it's not what *you* want her to do?' he said.

And it's true: I was living out Mum's dream for her, but it was also *my* dream, my lifeline, my chance to be someone different. Mum saw that, too: she felt that I wouldn't end up like some of the other girls round there, marrying a gangster or a petty criminal or even becoming a single mum like her. Although I didn't realise it at the time, we were making a point to my absent father: trying to prove he'd made a big mistake when he turned his back on us.

In those days the Italia Conti building was so imposing. Years later, when I was doing *The Bill*, I used to drive past it, and it doesn't look anything special now – I guess that's normal when you look back on things from an adult perspective. Back then I was very impressed by the vast entrance hall. On the first day, Mum and the other mothers came with us and there was a real excited buzz about the place.

I don't ever remember not fitting in: if they'd all been talking with Geordie accents I'd have adopted one, too. As a kid I was a complete chameleon. It was a useful skill in my working life but one that came, I believe, from my upbringing: I always had to put whatever trauma we were going through behind me. Don't think about it too much, just get on with it, was the family philosophy.

Looking back, going to stage school should have been daunting, but it wasn't at all, and this is a testament to the self-esteem

Mum had given me. As a child, you could throw me in at the deep end in any situation and I'd swim. Besides, what was there to be scared of? Laura, Amanda and Karen were going, too. That doesn't mean I wasn't impressed: we first years shared a dressing room with the older girls and I remember being bowled over by Leslie Ash, who was a fifth former. I was mesmerised by her beauty and sophistication; she was the most stunning girl I had ever seen. She wore drainpipe jeans tucked into her boots, had feather-cut hair and always seemed to be carrying a large portfolio, probably full of gorgeous 10" by 8" headshots. We all wanted to be Leslie Ash.

The whole place was magical. In the loos were slim white paper bags with a picture of a crinoline lady on the front. We four thought they were there for our ballet pumps (one shoe fitted perfectly in each bag) and we lined them up in the dressing room. I'm sure the older girls must have been in fits of laughter. We were also convinced there was a ghost in one of the classrooms (we called him 'Ghost Boy Blue') and left notes out for him. They always disappeared, which meant he was real. Years later, when Karen and I were revisiting the school, we discovered the teachers had been nipping in to take them – they thought it was very funny.

Italia Conti was run by the Shewards, whose four children had all been taught there and now helped out: I got to know the youngest, Graham, really well. They are a brilliant family, dedicated to the school and the kids who go there. I think I was the smallest in our year, but from the beginning it worked out well for me. Even before I started full time in the summer holidays we got a call from the Conti Agency (when you attended the school you were automatically placed on the books). The BBC were casting a TV show (*Ballet Shoes*, based on the book by Noel Streatfeild) and they were looking for girls under 4'6" to play extras. We had to be aged 11 or over to be allowed to work, yet most girls that age were too tall. I was nearly 12, but only 4' 2½".

'Oh, bless her!' said the girl from the agency when Mum told her how tall I was, and we could hear them laughing in the background. She then had to check with the casting director that I wasn't *too* small, and luckily I wasn't. I was thrilled to be working and being paid about £50 before I'd even started at stage school. But it wasn't all happy memories, and this was also my first experience of something that would haunt me throughout my time as a child actor.

In order to work, all child actors had to go to the Inner London Education Authority and jump through hoops put in place to ensure we weren't being exploited. We were weighed and measured, then had to prove our schoolwork was up to date and a third of our earnings was being saved. For me, the worst part was that I had to produce my birth certificate every time, and whenever I pulled it out there it was in big bold letters: 'Father Unknown'.

Why couldn't Mum just make up a name? Why does everyone have to know? I would think to myself. We lie about everything else in our family, so couldn't she have told 'just a little fib'? The school would ring up to say I had a job, adding casually, 'Make sure Lisa brings in her birth certificate.' Of course it was no big deal to them, but my heart would sink. If only one person could have put it in perspective. I wish someone had said, 'Your mum had a really shit time because everyone judged her but actually they got it wrong, it doesn't matter – she and your Nan and

Grandad should stop worrying about what other people might say and accept the situation.' But no one did, and it was years before I could tell myself the same thing. As it was, I couldn't be in the same room when they looked at the birth certificate, I couldn't bear seeing someone else's eyes reading 'Father Unknown' – it made me feel physically sick. The worst thing was people feeling sorry for me. I can't stand pity.

For most of the filming of *Ballet Shoes* I was at the barre doing exercises. I was never the best at ballet and the teacher in the film would come up behind us and whack my backside, which was always sticking out. When the programme was finally broadcast on television it was hard to spot 'class member number three, second from the left' with my hair scraped back and the same clothes as everyone else. Then again, had I stood out I wouldn't have been doing my job properly. We didn't have video in those days to pause and freeze frame, but Mum, Nan and Grandad all went along with it, claiming they knew me. Although I was only an extra, it was still exciting to be in front of the cameras, and the experience gave those of us taking part a bit of prestige when we arrived at the beginning of term. My friend Laura was in it with me and we felt like the chosen ones.

And the parts kept coming in. Next, I was in a TV sitcom called *The Many Wives of Patrick* with Patrick Cargill, who was very upper class. With my Italia Conti vowels, I could also play posh. Around this time I also did a pilot for *The Gender Gap* with Judy Parfitt and Francis Matthews, and again I was supposed to be from the top drawer. I think they got a surprise when I muffed a line and suddenly said 'Oh fuck it!' Not just the sound of a 12-year-old swearing, but a real Cockney accent when I was acting so terribly, *terribly* proper. Just after that I landed another part in a kids' series: *A Place Like Home*. It was great, not just because I loved acting: it meant that I could secure my full Equity membership (in those days it was tough to get into the actors' union and impossible to secure work unless you happened to be in it).

*A Place Like Home* was about growing up in a foster home (Pauline Quirke from *Birds of a Feather* played one of the other kids). I had a lead role: a sweet little kid with my hair in plaits, always planting things in the garden. However, I caused real problems by catching chicken pox in the middle of filming and they had to rewrite the scripts around my absence. Years later, when I worked with Pauline again, she told me she was cursing me at the time because she had to learn a lot of my lines as well as her own. She even had to play a game of Monopoly on-camera, playing my part, too! When I went back, the make-up girls worked hard to paint out the last three spots on my face.

Having these jobs so early on was a huge boost to my confidence because everyone there wanted to work. The school were very kind to Mum and me: they knew how much of a struggle it was for us financially and so they put me up for any job going. I was very happy at school, although I know some of the other pupils weren't – you've got to remember every kid who goes there is the best in their local dancing school, and then they get to Conti's, where they meet 15 or so other versions of themselves, some more talented and more confident. This can have two effects: either it boosts your confidence and sends you on your way, reaching for dazzling showbiz heights, or it can do the exact opposite and make you realise you're not so talented or as special as you thought.

For me, it opened up a wonderful escape. Italia Conti was completely classless, with working-class pupils like me and other kids from well-set-up, middle-class backgrounds, who lived in the suburbs in houses with gardens. Most of them had brothers and sisters, and to me this meant they were not accidents – their parents had wanted to have them and that's why they had more kids afterwards. I always felt being an only child was part of the shame of my birth, and for years I was under the impression only children were unplanned and unwanted.

Although the friends I knew when I first started were other working-class girls, soon I was mixing with others from privileged backgrounds and they spoke nicely (without pretending) and lived in big houses. I was always self-conscious about where I lived, and if anyone gave me a lift I'd be dropped off round the corner in Bath Terrace (which sure didn't sound like a council estate). Later, I found that the well-to-do kids didn't have an issue with where I was from. I had a South African friend called Renee who used to stay and her family were fine about it, even though they were wealthy. I was forever borrowing her clothes (she was the first girl in school to wear trousers) and I kept a pair of her grey flannels for months. To me, her Mason & Pearson hairbrush seemed like the height of posh and I swore I'd have one of my own as soon as I could afford it.

Today I'm embarrassed by the young Lisa who was ashamed of the Rockingham Estate because I'm a very down-to-earth person, the complete opposite of a snob: at the time I was so self-conscious about being out of wedlock it made me feel bad about my whole background. What I loved was being able to blag my way through to convince everyone I had the right to be there. Deep down, I felt like a pretender. Then again, a lot of actors admit they are always afraid someone will come up to them and say, 'You're not actually very good at acting, are you?' They always think they're going to get found out. That's how I've felt all my life, but not about my acting – about me: 'I know who you are, you're that little kid who hasn't got a dad, who comes from a council estate at Elephant and Castle,' they'll tell me. Confident in my acting, I was also comfortable with walking into a room and talking to anyone. I wasn't scared of anything … except the truth coming out.

I used to lie about the most stupid things. There was a school fête and Mum's friend Margaret made some lovely cakes but I pretended Mum had made them – I wanted the teacher in charge to think I came from the sort of family where the mother bakes cakes. The teacher was really pleased and said, 'I must thank Mrs Maxwell' (Mum was always 'Mrs' Maxwell at school). And to my deep shame I even denied knowing my mum when I first started at Conti. She took me to the tube station every day and waited until I was on the train: I always wanted her to go because on the platform would be lots of other kids in the same uniform as me, all looking like we belonged to some secret society. It was a bit like Harry Potter and his friends waiting for the train to Hogwarts.

'What's going to happen between now and the train arriving?'

'You never know, there are some funny people about,' she'd say, and all the while I'd be thinking, one of them is you …

Perhaps she was right to be concerned: we were almost all girls and we looked like everyone's idea of typical schoolgirls, which attracted a fair few dodgy types. We were all very blasé at the time and I can't remember any of it being a real threat, but looking back I guess she had a point. But I was very self-conscious about Mum being there and shouting 'Love you, Babes!' when everyone could hear.

I can remember so clearly one of my first days at the school: I got into the carriage and became aware, as the train started moving slowly off, that she was running alongside it. The tube went a bit faster and when I glanced out the window she was still there. But now she was shouting: 'Help, my coat – it's stuck in the door … Open the bloody doors!' The guard noticed and so the train quickly stopped and her coat was released, but I'm deeply ashamed because when one of the Conti kids who'd seen it asked 'Who was that woman?' I shrugged and said, 'No idea.' With that, I turned my back on Mum. All she was trying to do was protect me, but I was embarrassed and ashamed – I hate the fact that I was like that.

Later on, everyone would get to know my mum and they'd all be shouting, 'Bye, Lisa's mum!' when she did her big 'Bye, Babes, I love you!' routine (she took me to the tube every day until I was 16). On the train it was a wonderful little bubble. Because we were stage-school kids we were naturally noisy, and we'd sing songs and recite bits from plays – I felt extremely special and happy as soon as I entered that bubble.

The arrival of Bonnie Langford in our class at school a year later was a big event. We'd been told she was coming and couldn't wait. She'd been a big star on Broadway in *Gypsy* (Noël Coward reputedly said about the show: 'They should cut the second act and the child's throat') and we'd seen her in the film *Bugsy Malone*, but I don't think any of us anticipated what a consummate pro she was. Twelve-year-old Bonnie arrived at school every day as if she was going into rehearsals: her hair was fabulous, bright red and teased into a million ringlets, every single one immaculate and held back by a headband that matched her school uniform. Everything about her was 'finished' – that's the only word I can think of. We were all learning, works in progress, but she was already the complete deal: the perfect package.

Her pencil case had her name on it and all her pencils had her name in gold letters along the side. Over her leotard and tights she'd wear a black T-shirt with her name in diamante and a big star with lights shooting out of it. She was good at everything, could put her leg up by her ears without wobbling and she was also clever, getting straight As for all subjects. Bonnie was a few months younger than me and already famous; I couldn't believe we were in the same class. We wanted to criticise her to make ourselves feel better because she was such a high achiever, but we just couldn't because she was brilliant at everything, also lovely to everybody else. She had black eyelashes that she told me were dyed – it was the first time I'd heard of anyone doing this.

Laura James was my best mate at this time: so pretty and super talented, I was always proud she chose me. If anyone should have been the next Liza Minnelli or Barbra Streisand, it had to be Laura (she's now happily married to Jonathan Ross's younger brother Adam, with two lovely girls). A right pair, we bonded over our sense of humour. We were a bit mean to Bonnie: she sat in front of us in class and we used to dip her ringlets in the inkwells. I've never owned up to this before and when I meet Bonnie – we are good friends – she may go off me, now she knows!

Laura and me would slip into Frank Spencer impersonations and keep it up all day (the older girls used to get us to do it; I think they thought we were a pair of freaks). She lived just three or four stops up the Northern line from me in Stockwell and I loved going to her house. It was my idea of what the perfect family should be: a mum, a dad and an older brother. I hardly ever invited her to mine, but I think she worked out that it was because I was ashamed of our flats. She was always very sensitive and never asked why.

We used to spend hours together at the Elephant and Castle Shopping Centre, pulling faces in the photo booth and buying Snoopy and Holly Hobbit pencil cases and rulers. At least, Laura was buying hers and I was demonstrating how good I was at nicking them. I got away with quite a few and shared the spoils with her – luckily, I was never caught. We'd also buy our favourite magazines: *Bunty*, *Jackie*, *My Guy* and *Photo-Love*. At 16 I made it onto the cover of *Photo-Love*, in my eyes one of my greatest achievements.

It was while Laura, Karen and I were mooching around in the school holidays that we were flashed at in the street. A man walked towards us with a coat over his arm, and when he moved it, 'Run, he's got his *willy* out!' Laura shouted. We weren't scared – we just thought it was funny. Laura and Karen started running but I was laughing so hysterically that when I tried to run I wet myself so I had to stop and cross my legs. We went to Laura's house and then her mum and Karen's mum took us to the police station to report it. Being 12-year-old stage-school girls, we loved the drama – I think we thought we were in an episode of *Dixon of Dock Green*. 'Oh my God, you should have *seen* it! It was right down here …' we babbled, gesturing down towards our knees.

The policeman asked the mothers if we knew what 'erect' and 'flaccid' meant. When they said no, he asked us whether it was pointing North or South. Finally Laura drew it for him by pointing towards the South. I've always said it was Karen who wet herself, but this book is about the truth: it was me who had to walk around in a pair of wet jeans and I've only recently apologised to her.

Meanwhile, back in the school dressing room we would play performing games: our favourite was *Grease* after Mum took a group of us to see it at the Elephant Odeon. We took it in turns to be John Travolta and Olivia Newton-John. Bonnie didn't always join in our games but she loved playing *Grease* and if she was Danny she would leap off the table like the Russian gymnast Olga Korbut, singing, 'It's *electrifying*!'

Danielle Foreman was also a good friend at Conti's, although like Bonnie she started a bit later than the rest of us. She's the sister of the actor Jamie Foreman and their dad was Freddie Foreman, a well-known gangster (Jamie used to babysit me when Mum was going out – Danielle would come over and he'd be left in charge of us at our flat). The family lived in Dulwich and their dad wasn't around some of the time because he was in prison but I can remember the thrill of him turning up at school to pick Danielle up in his sky-blue Rolls-Royce Corniche. Freddie was part of the whole gangster scene going on in London: he knew the Krays and the Richardsons and he was involved in a couple of murders as well as some big heists. I didn't know any of this at the time but I think I was savvy enough to know he didn't get his Rolls working down the market.

# Not That Kinda Girl

When 50p was nicked from Bonnie Langford's moneybag, the finger of suspicion was unfairly pointed at Danielle and me for some reason: it wasn't us. About six of us had been in the dressing room at the time and we were interrogated by Mrs Sheward. Afterwards Danielle and me were kept behind, probably because we refused to allow them to search our bags. It wasn't because we had anything to hide; we were just being difficult.

A girl in our year had already started her periods and she seemed to be excused almost everything. She was always missing things because of her period – blimey, when you start your periods you become practically disabled, I remember thinking. So when they wanted to search our bags we told them: 'You can't search our bags! We may have personal things in there, like Pantie Pads.' It was an invasion of our privacy, we said. We didn't even know the right name for sanitary protection – we just thought it sounded good.

Being taken to Mrs Sheward's office was a bit frightening. There were two offices: one for the agency, where everyone was chatty and the walls were covered in pictures of us all; and then her own, which was formal and contained a big desk with an embossed leather top. Mrs Sheward was a small woman, with lots of hair piled up on top of her head, like wedding hair – Marje Simpson could have been modelled on her. I always thought she got up at about 4 a.m. every day just to get the hair right. If you were called into her office, it was serious (I only went there twice). Anyway, she interviewed us separately, trying to get us to grass each other up, but we refused to do so.

I'm certain Danielle didn't take the money. And I didn't take it either, but it meant we were late leaving the school that day and Danielle's dad was meeting us in the Rolls.

'Don't you ever let me catch you thieving, you little toe-rags! I'll burn your fucking fingers off if I catch you at that game,' he yelled at us. Looking back, it was funny coming from a man involved in all sorts of crime, but I can see he was just as determined his kids would have a completely different life. We never heard any more about the 50p at school.

At the weekend he'd sometimes pick me up in the Rolls (which I loved) to take Danielle and me out. I liked the neighbours in Stephenson House to see me, and Mum loved it, too. One Saturday we went on one such trip. We drove up the Old Kent Road with the roof down on the Rolls, even though it wasn't that warm, but I didn't care about being cold – I loved sitting in the back of the car with everyone looking at me.

Then he said: 'We're going up West now'. So we went to Ronnie Knight's drinking club, which was called J. Arthurs. Because Danielle was Freddie's daughter everyone made a big fuss of her: the barmen and all the staff treated her with real reverence. When they asked Danielle what she would like to drink, she said: 'I'll have a Harvey Wallbanger.' So I said I'd like one of those, too, even though I had no idea what it was.

'Why are you talking funny?' asked Mum after Freddie had dropped me back home, and my speech was slurred (she knew I might be drunk but because I wasn't ill she didn't say anything). I told her I'd had Harvey Wallbangers. I think she thought they were some kind of hamburger.

'Oh he's *lovely*, that Freddie!' she said.

For some reason Mum always thought Freddie was a saint. I used to rollerskate round the Elephant and Castle and about 8 p.m. one night I was skating in front of the Charlie Chaplin when he came past.

'What you doing here, you little so-and-so?' he asked. 'Bet your mother's worried out of her life about you. Go on, clear out of it! Clear off home and get some sweets.'

He gave me a £50 note – the highest note I'd ever seen. I gave it to Mum, who said: 'God love him, he's like the Pope – a *god*! He picks 'er up in a Corniche, buys 'er Harvey Wallbangers and sends her home in case something dodgy happens …'

My friend Danielle was beautiful, with lovely dark hair: she wore mascara and bright red lipstick, and to me she looked just like Snow White. Her mum had an antique stall on the Bermondsey Market and she gave me a keeper (friendship) ring. She was very into horoscopes, mediums and reading the future. I was once in Danielle's room when I watched a lamp fly off the windowsill without anyone touching it. Oh God, her mum's going to think I broke it! How was I going to tell her it just came off on its own? All she said was: 'Don't worry, darling – it's only Danielle's poltergeist.'

Danielle and me used to spend all our time together talking about boys – we even practised kissing just to know what it felt like. When I was 14 I really fancied this boy called Lee who used to sell newspapers at the Elephant and Castle. He looked cheeky and funny, like a squashed version of Mike Reid, and would call out the newspapers in a singsong voice, which I found very attractive. Danielle passed a note to him saying I fancied him and he arranged to take me out on a date. I remember he turned up in a little beige suede bomber and wore gold chains. We did have a kiss, my second ever, and I seem to remember it lived up to expectations. Funnily enough, I have clearer memories of kissing Danielle – what does *that* mean? But I didn't see him again: I remember thinking myself a bit above him, which sounds snobbish, I know. I'd been brought up to believe only Prince Andrew was good enough for me.

Danielle pursued acting for a while, but family life took her in another direction. Her brother Jamie, however, in my opinion became one of the best actors of his generation.

Another of my really good friends was Suzy Fenwick, whose cousin Perry plays Billy Mitchell in *EastEnders*. When we were kids, Perry was appearing at the Shaftesbury Theatre in a production of *Peter Pan* as one of the Lost Boys. Suzy and I used to hang around with them. She fancied one of Perry's mates, a lad called Nick Berry. We were mucking about at my flat one day when we found his phone number. Suzy rang and asked, 'Is that Nick Berry?' When he said yes, she replied: 'I went through the phone book and I only found one berry, so I picked it!' Suzie had to put the phone down – she couldn't speak, we were laughing so much: it was really silly teenage girl stuff.

Back home, life wasn't all rosy, though. When I was a teenager, Mum and I used to fight a lot in the way that I think sisters sometimes fight; Grandad would have to tell us to calm down. Both of us knew (and still know) which buttons to press. Our fights would be about trivial things but underlying them would be pent-up feelings about each other.

Mum never did things by half. I remember she was on tranquillisers and decided to come off them abruptly after hearing on Esther Rantzen's *That's Life* that you shouldn't take them for more than three weeks or so. By then she'd been on them for six years. She just threw the whole lot down the toilet and went cold turkey, but you're supposed to come off them gradually. I remember having to hold her in the night when she was freaking out – I was about 12 or 13 at the time. She was shivering, sweating and rocking her body backwards and forwards. Even after that first terrible night I'd still hear her whimpering and moaning, but she did it: when Mum decides on something, she is very single-minded.

She gave up cigarettes in the same way. When I was 18 she went to see a doctor about a cough, and when she came back she said: 'He told me I've got very thin airways.' She used to smoke 40 Consulate menthols a day but gave up there and then at the age of 40. I wish I could have had the same self-discipline: it took me several attempts to quit.

Whatever was happening at home, I still had my escape route: the train that took me to my beloved school every day, where I could sing, dance and be with my friends all day long. For me, schooldays really were among the happiest of my life.

It wasn't always wonderful, though.

# CHAPTER 4

## *My Secret Shame*

I'd been nursing a secret for a whole week after I was summoned once again to the principal's office. On this occasion Mrs Sheward stressed it was nothing to worry about but the staff had noticed I'd put on a bit of weight and they didn't want it to get any worse. She told me to be careful with what I ate and said they would keep an eye on me. By then I was 13.

Afterwards I was so upset and embarrassed and I couldn't understand it. I knew another girl who had been put on a diet but she was really fat – how could I have let myself get that big without noticing? When I looked in the mirror I didn't see fat, but if they thought I *was* fat then I must be so. I kept the conversation to myself, but then it got worse, far worse: I was about to be outed as a fattie.

'Lisa, will you come here, please. I just need to check how you're doing with your weight.'

Having been called to the front of the class, I had to stand on some scales next to the teacher's desk. I was mortified, more embarrassed than I'd ever been in my whole life. Now all my friends and classmates knew: I was officially fat. And that terrible feeling, as I walked from my desk to the front of the classroom, has never left me: with one massive blow it seemed to destroy the image I had of myself. No matter how many times my friends told me that I was nothing like the other girl on a diet, the damage was done. I think I was a little bit chubby. My body had started to change and fill out; I remember lying down next to one girl in jazz class doing floor exercises and just coveting her hipbones, thinking how cool it was to have your bones sticking out like that. For dancers, all the moves look better when you have thin arms and legs. In ballet classes the boys had to lift us, and this was another reason why we were more aware of what we weighed: some boys didn't half make a meal out of it, groaning and carrying on as if they had to lift a ton of coal.

At stage school you're in front of a mirror every day in a skimpy leotard and tights. How we looked was a big thing: we were performing children and the school made it clear from the word go that casting directors could come round at any time, picking kids for jobs or to appear in advertisements, so you always think they will choose the most beautiful and you buy into the idea that thin is beautiful. I was worried because I thought if I was chubby then when I was doing all that dancing and exercising I'd be massive by the time I left school.

I still didn't tell Mum I'd been put on a diet. Years later, when I gave interviews about being told to lose weight so young, I described my mother going up the school to object, but this was just one of my fantasies. I never gave her chance to protest – it was my problem to deal with. Also, I never really talked to my friends about it and I didn't cry: I just took it on the chin, absorbed it and kept any hurt buried inside me in the same way that I always dealt with difficult feelings.

Somehow, I lost the extra pounds. I'd skip school lunch, which wasn't difficult. Mrs Stooks, who served in the canteen, always had a fag in her mouth so we'd all be focused on whether that tower of ash was about to drop into our Spag Bol. Often it did, which put us off eating there. Instead I'd head straight for the chocolate machine in the hallway. I'd get a Bar Six and a hot chocolate, then dip the Bar Six into the drink and suck the chocolate off until all that was left was the crispy bit; often that was all I had.

I think I must have developed some kind of body dysmorphia: I no longer trusted what I saw in the mirror because in my mind I was fat, end of, but that's not what the mirror said and so what I was seeing must have been wrong. Body-conscious ever since, I can't help but feel thin is more beautiful, although as I get older I know it can also be ageing. However, this view is deeply ingrained and although I would not become one of the anorexic ones at school I can easily see how it happened to others because it's a very fine line.

One of my Italia Conti classmates was the brilliantly talented Lena Zavaroni, who died of anorexia just weeks before her thirty-third birthday, having battled the condition all her adult life. I was deeply sad when I heard the news of her death but, like everyone else who knew her, not surprised. I'd heard she got married and I hoped she had her life back in shape, but eating disorders are not always easy to defeat.

Just three weeks older than me, Lena had already won the *Opportunity Knocks* talent show and was a big star when she joined our class, but she wasn't like Bonnie, who could handle her fame. Lena was very quiet (I remember her hardly ever speaking) and she always seemed to be on her own. No end of pupils were eager to be her friend because she had the two things we all craved, success and fame, but she was withdrawn and seemed to prefer her own company. Lena had an amazing voice (she was a good old-fashioned belter) but she was not cut out to be so far from her Scottish home and she didn't fit in at a London stage school. She was very thin, with a head that looked far too big for her body, and massive hair.

I'm not blaming the school for Lena's anorexia – there were plenty of other reasons in her sad life – but it's easy to see how any girl might slip into an eating disorder. Somehow I managed to avoid it, although the demons still moved in and would come back to haunt me years later. It was drilled into us that how we looked and presented ourselves was very important. My friend Caroline was told she should always have a full face of make-up because you never knew when you might bump into a casting director. She was mortified one day when she finally met one and didn't have her face on: she wanted to hide, but the woman commented on how pretty she was without make-up.

Despite the emphasis on looks, we did have one girl in my class who stuck out like a sore thumb. She had very irregular teeth: someone once described them as looking like 'a row of bombed houses'. No one could work out why she was at stage school, but I thought I knew. 'She's probably here because they need people to work in horror movies,' I explained, and I meant it sincerely, genuinely thinking this was a nice thing to say. Kids can be so cruel, but she played up to it, pulling faces to frighten us. I don't think she stayed in the industry and I'm sure she grew up looking great because you can't always tell what girls will look like at that age.

At Italia Conti there were boys, too, although they were far outnumbered. We locked one boy (Paul Gadd) into a dark-room with five or six of us and made him kiss us in turn. He rushed around in the dark, air-kissing everyone, but when it was my turn he tripped and fell onto me, so we did touch faces. Does that count as my first kiss? When he got to Danielle Foreman he lingered a bit too long for my liking, and that's when they started going out together. By the way, I should explain Paul's dad was the glam rock star Gary Glitter, which might explain why he was quite a troubled boy with a penchant for letting off fire extinguishers in ballet classes. I can remember Mr Sheward stomping through a tap class, yelling, 'Either that boy goes or I do!' Really, Paul was just mischievous and we all liked him.

Gary Glitter turned up and bought everything at one school fund-raising auction, which he then donated back to the school. Everyone thought, what a lovely generous man. We had absolutely no idea, and I feel sad for Paul now.

It must have been harder for the boys there. One, Peter, had a really fabulous soprano voice and he was a great dancer. Our singing teacher gave him hell one day when he was doing a solo because he started out as a soprano and ended up as a tenor – his voice was breaking. 'Get out of here and work in Woolworths!' he screamed, his standard threat to any of us who seemed to be not putting in enough effort.

I really want to apologise to a boy called Philip, also in our class: I'm ashamed to admit we bullied him horribly. It wasn't done maliciously, we just thought it was funny, but that's the thing about bullying – you don't think how it feels to be on the receiving end. Philip was attractive (and straight) with thick curly hair, but girls of 12 or 13 don't know how to behave around boys and just the fact he had an extra toilet part made him the focus of our attention. We'd sing 'More Than a Woman' from *Saturday Night Fever* with the words: 'Philip's a woman, Philip's a woman to me …' When it came to the 'shuddup bah' chorus we'd go 'bah' right in his face, then do jazz hands and dance around him. We were evil girls. In the end, his mum came up the school to complain about us and we were called in by the head of the academic side. We felt really bad, especially as Philip was moved to another class. It was such a female-dominated environment and all I ever wanted was to make people laugh, but how cruel it was.

We were given pep talks to prepare us for a life in show business. One really savage piece of advice was this: 'You may think certain girls are your best friends, but they're not really. If you are up for a part, and it's down to the last two and it's between you and your best friend, would you want your friend to get it?' It was a way of preparing us for a tough business: more than once the staff told us only the tough would survive. I remember thinking, no, I wouldn't like it if my best friend got a job I was after, but then I felt really guilty for even thinking it. Our school celebrated competitiveness, and it makes me laugh when I hear about schools nowadays where they don't even have sports days because it's not fair on the losers. We were bred to be competitive. But I don't want to make the Italia Conti sound bad – I think girls in ordinary schools get just as many hang-ups, different ones sometimes. Conti's was a fabulous place, a really good establishment for me to grow up in, and I can't imagine enjoying another school anywhere near as much.

At first, being so small seemed a disadvantage. Often I was not selected for dancing jobs because they usually wanted all the dancers in a troupe to be roughly the same height. For acting, it turned out to be a plus, especially as I could play children until I was in my early twenties. And I loved acting the best – I like changing into someone else. Mum had set about changing me and I was happy to carry on with it; not just on stage or in front of the cameras, I was acting every day as if my life depended on it, and I was good at it.

Laura and I were two of the girls recruited by Dougie Squires (a top choreographer of the day) to be in The Mini Generation, a dance troupe. Back then, the New Generation were very big and we'd come on stage after them, a group of kids performing the same sort of dances. We'd dance to 'Crazy Horses' by The Osmonds, all bouncing around as if we'd been plugged into the mains, and we'd do another routine with umbrellas to a Shirley Temple song. We appeared at corporate events and were on TV a couple of times.

Laura, who was so talented, went on to dance with Hot Gossip when she was 16. She was touring the country doing raunchy dances and her mum was still sending her copies of *Bunty*! I remember she came back to school and seemed to have grown up – she had become sexy and glamorous. She could have been a megastar. Bonnie agrees with me that Laura was the most talented girl in our class, but she's opted for marriage and a family instead. Who can blame her?

When it was announced in 1977 that a new production of *Annie* was being put on at the Victoria Palace Theatre in London with Stratford Johns and Sheila Hancock in the leads, there was a mass audition for the orphans. Literally hundreds of us kids turned up at the Theatre Royal Drury Lane and queued down the street with our mums. It felt like every stage-school kid in the country was there. One by one we had to sing 'Happy Birthday' – quite a tricky song because there's a real leap to get to the top note. It was a deliberate choice: they didn't want typical performing children with their pieces all prepared, they wanted natural-sounding kids.

We were whittled down to smaller and smaller groups and then called back for the moment when they line you up and announce who has got the parts. I was to play one of the orphans, but on the first day of rehearsals I was ill and when I travelled up the next day one of the other girls told me that I hadn't got a part after all. I was 'alternative orphan', which meant I had to cover performances when one of the others was away: as children we were only permitted by law to do a certain number of shows each week. I knew then what they meant when they told us at Conti's that you really don't have friends. Perhaps I was being over-sensitive (I'd have found out as soon as I got there that I was an alternative), but I still felt the girls who landed named parts were ever so slightly gloating.

Actually, being an alternative was harder: I did three shows a week, but had to learn different parts. After a few months I was given the role of July, one of the orphans. The lead, playing Annie, was an American girl (Andrea McCardle, who had taken the part on Broadway). When she had to go back to the States we were all in tears, begging to be pen pals. I was sticking my fingers in my eyes to make tears come – I wanted to be part of the big, over-emotional farewells going on, but even though I liked Andrea I wasn't that attached to her.

*Annie* was a happy time. I remember our chaperones taking us to the first McDonald's to open in London for Big Macs. The kids who didn't live in the city stayed in this big flat in Kensington and we all went there for parties. There was a massive sunken bath and wallpaper with shiny silver bamboo trees on it: for a long time this was my definition of posh.

Mum and the other mothers would pick us up after the show wrapped at ten o'clock at night. She would travel on the 21 bus, often with her hair in rollers to set before work the next day. We even had a Royal Command Performance in 1978. The Queen came along the row and stopped at me, asking how old I was. Even though I could imitate Received Pronunciation perfectly well, I really couldn't understand her strangulated vowels: to me it sounded like she was speaking Dutch or something. Every time she asked the question, I said 'Pardon?' It was getting embarrassing, and in the end the girl next to me said, 'She's just saying how old are you.' 'Four'een,' I replied, managing to drop the 't' out of the middle of the word.

The American directors were generous to all us kids in the show, giving us presents and jewellery, usually with a cartoon of Sandy the dog on it (I've kept everything to give to my daughter Beau). Sheila Hancock used to meditate before she went onstage, which I later heard her say in an interview was to help calm stage fright although she never gave any hint of nerves. She bought us all a little silver disc with 'Annie' on it.

I kept the bust binder that I was issued with during *Annie* – it was to flatten our boobs so we looked like young children. I'd wear mine all the time at school because I thought it made me look thinner.

I was in the first run for six months when I was 14 and went back into the show again at 16, playing the lead role of Annie with a different cast. Onstage, we would go into school at odd times and we were put into a classroom to catch up on our academic work because by law we had to do three hours study a day. I'd be with Laura and we'd just natter, though. There was a tutor on set for the children who couldn't get back to their schools, but we always said we were going back. I never paid much attention to schoolwork, something I deeply regret now because there are great gaps in my education, but the performing side was so much more fun.

Yorkshire Television did a documentary about the girls at the school. Of course they were interested in Bonnie and Lena but they also followed Rudi Davies, who was the daughter of the author Beryl Bainbridge. They filmed our classes, culminating in the end-of-term production. I was in the film, though not in a central role.

Rudi went on to appear in *Grange Hill*, the TV series about school kids. I was chosen to be in the series but, unlike her, I didn't have a big role and was only in three episodes. That's where I first met Todd Carty (Tucker Jenkins), who has been a mate ever since. Filming for the part came up while Mum, Nan and Grandad were away in Spain, so I had to stay with a professional chaperone. She took the job of chaperoning very seriously and would even stand outside the loo when we were in there. Whenever Mum rang from Spain she'd stand next to me, which made it hard to say how much I was missing her without sounding as if I was complaining. I remember her rather suddenly waking me up one day by dribbling cold water onto me when I wanted to keep my head on the pillow.

When we were 17, Yorkshire Television came back to see what had happened to us all (they got us together in the pub next door to Conti's). I was one of the ones still working, so I figured more prominently in this programme.

In 1978 there was a big event for my family: the council transferred us to a house. We'd been on the list for ages and may have told one of our 'little fibs' about Nan and Grandad struggling with the stairs at the flats. Anyway, it worked because we were given a three-bedroom near the Walworth Road. We almost got a maisonette in a typical seventies development – all white panels and windows, clean and new looking. I was disappointed when we didn't get it, but the house was better in the long run.

We were all really excited about the move: our new terraced house had a front garden and an alleyway at the back where we'd hear courting couples getting up to no good at night. The road was a cul-de-sac and the walls so thin we could hear the neighbours. Grandad kept the garden immaculate, but because it was at the front we couldn't sunbathe out there: even sitting outside we felt like chimps at the zoo.

Nan and Grandad went on holiday soon after we moved in, so Mum and I redecorated throughout with Laura Ashley-style wallpaper and furnishings, proper curtains, swags and Austrian blinds, all in pale mint green and peach with bows on everything and borders everywhere. We even found a chandelier in a junk shop. It was all very girly and poor Grandad must have thought he'd come home to a tart's boudoir. In fact, there were so many Austrian and festoon blinds that the turning at the junction into our cul-de-sac was soon dubbed 'crossing the Austrian border'.

Although I was happy about the move, I didn't care too much about where we lived – I knew that I wouldn't be living at home forever and this was just a stepping-stone. When I was 15, I used to hang around at Sylvia Young's house. Frances Ruffelle, her daughter, went to Conti's and was a friend of mine. There was a piano at their flat and I'd sing show songs with some of the others who hung out there, including Nick Berry and Suzy Fenwick.

At 16 I left school: I could have stayed on for the student course and more performing arts classes but as far as I was concerned I had my Equity card (unusual at that age) and was convinced the work would flow in. I was very confident and naively thought I knew everything there was to know, a real showbiz veteran … oh, dear! But I was still closely connected to Conti's through the agency – it was not unusual for them to sign up the most promising students for three years. Quite rightly, they felt, as they had given us our training, they should reap some benefits, and it was a compliment to be one of the ones they wanted.

Because I don't come from a showbiz family there was no one to turn to for advice or support at this time. I never asked Mum, Nan or Grandad because they didn't understand what I was doing, although they tried to help and advise me as much as they could. Grandad still thought I could be better off with shorthand and typing; I'd been bitten by the showbiz bug and nothing else would do, though.

Like lots of pretty young girls, I had a shot at becoming a pop star. At 16 I even landed a recording contract. I thought it would all be easy – I'd be a pop star and lead a glamorous life, just by wanting it to happen. Steve Elson, the producer who signed me, said he had a great song and all he needed was a great singer. He gave the impression I'd been chosen out of thousands – well, I was impressed at the time. The song title was 'He's So Nice I Can Hardly Stand It' and that was more or less the lyrics for the first and second verse *and* the chorus. Typically late-seventies pop, it sank without trace once recorded. Although I'd been signed up for five years, my pop career was over in five weeks.

I wasn't out of Conti's for more than a couple of months before I landed my first proper theatre job touring with the Cambridge Theatre Company in a Feydeau farce: *Hotel Paradiso*. After auditioning, I got the part of a 14-year-old girl and appeared with Graeme Garden (*The Goodies*), Sue Hodge (*'Allo 'Allo!*) and Michele Dotrice (*Some Mothers Do 'Ave 'Em*). I was 17, but small enough to play a child, although I had to wear a bust binder again.

It was my first time away from home and although I'd been independent in many ways, taking control of my own career, I'd never received any domestic training. Washing and ironing had never been my department. So Mum took me to Boots and bought me a load of paper knickers (horrible things, the material looked like J Cloths) and they gave me a rash. I quickly learnt a good theatre lesson: make friends with the wardrobe mistress and she'll pop your undies in the washing machine while she's doing the costumes.

For me, the most memorable part of that tour was Brighton, where I snogged a Scottish lad. After the play finished for the night, we'd go on to a club. Sue Hodge (who was as tiny as me) used to bounce up and down, almost levitating, when she danced and we'd have a great time strutting our stuff. This lad looked French – another flashback to Sacha Distel. He had dark hair, a neckerchief and a navy jacket and jeans, very preppy. I knew he'd clocked me, so I danced and wiggled my bottom in front of him to 'Funky Town' – my usual tactic. Sue told me he looked too intense, but that made him all the more attractive to me.

When I spoke to him I discovered he had a strong Glaswegian accent – he might as well have been talking French for all I could understand. We walked along the beach and had a kiss, a cuddle and a little fiddle. We didn't do anything much: I'm very prudish and sex was definitely off-limits. Sex has always been a difficult area for me because I associate it with something shameful and dirty, something I had been led to believe all my life. It has taken me a long time to get over those feelings, but at least I've never rushed into the arms (or beds) of unsuitable men.

Anyway, Scots guy and me sat under the arches on the beach most of the night, talking and having a good old rummage around at each other. I got back to my digs (in a pub) in the early hours. He'd arranged to see me the next afternoon, so when all the rest of the cast were going out I stayed behind. He didn't show up and the pub was empty because in those days they closed on Sunday afternoons. Devastated, I stared out the window at the empty street. I was really hurt, but not because I liked him – it was my pride. I'd never experienced much rejection in life apart from the big one from my father and so I think I felt the hurt really badly.

I must have been experiencing a tiny bit of what my mum went through, I suppose. Even then, I knew not everyone would want to fall at my feet but I made up my mind that I would never let go and make myself vulnerable to hurt. And I never did, not until many years later.

It was an eight-week-long tour and I'm sure Mum must have missed me, even though we talked on the phone a lot – I was still the centre of her life. Together with Nan and Grandad, she came to see the play in Brighton. They had a nightmare journey because the weather was really bad, with heavy snow. I'd left tickets for them at the box office and I remember almost right up to the curtain going up they hadn't collected them, but they made it in the nick of time. I don't think a Feydeau farce was really their cup of tea, and Nan fell asleep. Luckily, I couldn't see that from the stage – I only knew because Mum told me afterwards. When Nan was asleep, her head would fall back and her false teeth would slip so that she looked like Red Rum. Anyway, I expect she needed a doze after their journey.

'Did you enjoy it, Nan?' I said to her afterwards.

'It was all right,' she muttered.

'It's OK, Nan – Mum's told me you were asleep.'

'Didn't it go on! You were very good, but I ain't got a clue what it was all about …'

Soon after the tour ended, the agency rang and asked me to go to Elstree Studios to do a voice test for a French art-house movie, *Nana*. It was being dubbed into English by Louis Elman, famous in the industry as the master of voiceovers. He told me to read a passage and it looked all right on the page but when I saw the footage of a young French girl with heaving breasts I found it hard to keep a straight face – it's weird being in a booth on your own, panting away to a sex scene. It seemed an odd way to make a living. Also, I kept thinking perhaps I wasn't really dubbing a film, but 20 men were getting off on listening to me.

I didn't get the job, but Louis told me that I had a very interesting voice, and soon afterwards, I was called back for the Jim Henson movie, *The Dark Crystal* (1982). Jim and Frank Oz, creators of *The Muppets*, had come up with the idea and I voiced the part of Kira, the female lead gelfling (a creature dreamed up by Jim). Altogether, we had to dub it all the way through three times: the first time they felt we were too English, then too American, and finally we did it in a mid-Atlantic DJ accent.

At this point I learnt an invaluable skill – how to lip sync – and I was taught by the great Jim Henson himself. A black bar comes across the screen, giving you the cue to speak and letting you know when to finish.

'Relax, Lisa – just have fun, play around with it,' Jim told me.

Between them, they decided Kira needed to have a special language when she was talking to the dog (Fizzgig).

'What would Kira say?' Jim asked me.

Having been to Spain with Nan and Grandad for years, I was pretty adept at a pretend Spanish accent and could jabber away in a made-up form of Spanish. They loved it, and so Kira's special language was born in Pontinental, Torremolinos.

Doing the film didn't feel like anything special, though – it was a job, and it involved going to Elstree three times a week. I didn't have any premonition it was so special, but even today *The Dark Crystal* has a huge cult following. When the actor Alan Cumming appeared on *Loose Women* in 2009, the one question he wanted to ask was whether I really was the voice of Kira. He then called his musical director (a man who has worked on massive Broadway productions) over to meet me.

'Oh my *God*! Are you *really* the voice of Kira? This has made my day!' he told me.

Later, when I was on *The Bill*, Honeysuckle Weeks (Julie Nowak) came up and said: 'Someone just told me you are the voice of Kira in *The Dark Crystal*. Tell me it's true!' She told me it's one of her top five films and she even brought in her DVD for me to sign.

In recent years there has been some talk of a remake and people ask if I'm going to be in it. I've heard nothing and I don't think I'd get the gig now, having been an 80-ciggies-a-day girl at one stage in my life, but I'm proud to have been part of such a breakthrough movie.

# CHAPTER 5

## First Love

So I went to stage school and now I earned a living in show business, all my friends were kids who shared my ambitions, and yet the man who was my first lover was nothing to do with all this. I very nearly threw my talent and whole future away on a relationship that could have destroyed me, had I stayed in it.

After all these years I still know why I did it: the young man I fell for was extremely good-looking, with a strong hint of danger that only added to the attraction. He seemed very grown-up and sophisticated, a bad boy with a cockiness that came from knowing that every woman he met fell for him. Just the fact that he fancied me was a heady compliment and I was flattered and easily bowled over at the time.

I first saw him when I was about 14 because he used to come round our area to visit a mate of his. He was only 17 or 18, but with his broad shoulders and handsome face he looked like a man, not a boy. His long hair (light brown with sun streaks) was cut rather foppishly into a wedge – I've always had a thing about

Hugh Grant hair and he walked with a swagger. He and his mate went out wearing long overcoats; they'd jump in a car, drive off and I'd watch until they were out of sight.

Whenever he was in the area I used to spy, clocking him and wondering about him. I never thought he would notice me – after all, I was still a kid and he seemed really cool and much older than he actually was. But a couple of years later he did notice me: I was walking under some railway arches with Mum in my cap and boater school uniform when a white sports car pulled up alongside us and the window went down.

'If she grows up to look like you, I'll marry her,' he told Mum, before pulling away.

Of course this was the perfect chat-up line and Mum was completely flattered by the good-looking young man who had just paid her the ultimate compliment. Meanwhile, I was excited because he fancied me. The more I think about it, it was an extremely clever line: he was a complete charmer.

A few months later, when I had left school, he spotted me again and asked me out on a date this time. Although I didn't know anything about his life or where he was from, I thought he was stunning, so I was more than happy to say 'yes'. His clothes were immaculate – always cashmere, pure wool, fantastic soft leather and none of the cheap man-made fabrics worn by everyone on the Rockingham Estate.

He took me to a club where there was a glass floor with fish swimming around underneath. I thought this the height of sophistication. Afterwards, we went back to his flat, had a little kiss and cuddle and he touched my bum. 'What you doing? Don't take liberties, I'm not that sort of girl!' I told him, and I meant it. Still a virgin, I wanted him to know I was a good girl but I gave off this air of stage-school confidence – we'd all been taught how to carry ourselves, how to 'work it', and this gave a misleading impression. I don't think he'd ever encountered much resistance and so I intrigued him. He wanted to own me, he wanted me to be his little princess and I was so flattered that I was happy to go along with it.

After that first date I pursued him. I took our family dog for a walk all the way from Elephant and Castle to his flat. It was a bloody long walk and Pete the poodle hardly ever got taken out; I don't think he knew what had hit him, and I had to drag him part of the way. I knocked on the door of his flat, trying to make it look as if I was casually passing, and he answered in a dressing gown. He seemed startled to see me and pulled the door behind him so that he could talk to me outside.

'I just wondered if I left my make-up bag here?' I said, using the excuse I'd dreamed up on the way there. 'I left it here or in the back of the cab.'

'I'll have a look and call you,' he told me. 'I need to talk to you, to explain. There's someone here … I'll call you.'

Inch by inch, he shut the door in my face. I'd heard he'd been living with a girl, but assumed it must be over, and so I was devastated. After that I didn't hear from him for some time, and at first I was heartbroken. The next time I heard from him was a few months later in a phone call to tell me he'd been arrested. My heart leapt at the sound of his voice. Instead of alarm bells going off, I really believed him when he told me: 'I've been nicked, but I've been framed. I didn't do it – I've been set up. I'm only allowed one phone call and I knew I had to speak to you.'

He wanted to talk to *me* – how fantastic! I didn't think about the fact he was under arrest, in prison: I was just thrilled to hear from him. He asked me to visit him and said he would send me a VO (Visiting Order) so that I could arrange to see him.

I told Mum straight away. It's not the usual sort of thing you tell your mum, but I had no qualms: I knew she would understand why I found him so attractive, and she liked him, too. I didn't want to go to the prison on my own so she came with me. Like me, she wanted to give him the benefit of the doubt and if he said he'd been stitched up we were happy to believe him. She still thought of him as a gorgeous young man who had paid her a compliment.

On our way to the prison we went on a little shopping spree. We bought him 200 cigs, a Party Seven and a pizza.

'Poor sod, he's in prison – he's going to need cheering up,' we told each other.

How naïve is that? All dressed up, I was wearing a little ra-ra skirt with my legs on show. I never felt overtly sexy – I always thought my look was more 'little girl' because of my height – but I knew I had good legs and was eager to show them. Back then, I spent half my free time on sunbeds so I was very tanned: my legs were brown, not Spammy. And even though my skirts were short, I was always on the tasteful side of suggestive, I thought.

A friend's mum opened a place full of sunbeds in the garage of a pub and that's where I used to go. All these women were in there, lifting names off credit cards with brake fluid and flogging hooky gear. What with that and Freddie Foreman, I wasn't exactly innocent. Things were happening all around me, but it never felt as if I was part of that world – somehow I felt superior. My family were straight, and perhaps naively I believed in the good in people, as did Mum. She and I had no idea about visiting a prisoner, though.

'What's all that?' asked the officer at the first security check when we arrived with all our shopping.

'We thought, as he's going to be here for a while, he'd need cheering up. He may be hungry and we don't want him to run out of fags,' I explained.

At this, he roared with laughter. 'You're not allowed to take it in,' he said, taking it off us. 'What do you want me to do with it all?'

'Can you give it to him?' I asked.

'Yeah, yeah, right! We'll *give* it to him …' He was still laughing.


'Don't worry, you've got a pizza and some fags and beer that we've given to a nice man who was at that window when we came in and he said he'll give them to you,' I told my guy after we'd been through all the security checks.

But he just stared. 'You're having a fucking laugh, aren't you? I can kiss goodbye to that then!' he said.

'Why? We gave it to him to give to you. Where is it?'

'He's probably eaten the pizza by now and he's smoking the fags.'

'*No*, he was a nice man – he wouldn't do that,' I insisted.

'Lisa, he's a *screw*. He is not a nice man, he's a *screw*,' he told me.

'Oh, I didn't realise he was a *screw* …' I had no idea what a screw was, but I did my best to pretend.

'Whatever they say about you, I know it's not true: I'm going to stand by you,' I told him (I think they were lines I'd heard in a film).

It turned out he'd been arrested in town, 'doing the bottle'. I came to know this was rhyming slang ('bottle and glass' equals 'ass') and it means nicking wallets out of back pockets or bags of tourists. I believed him when he said he was set up, but alarm bells really should have gone off when he was sent down for six months and served four of them. While he was in prison I lived from VO to VO: while waiting for them, I hardly left my bedroom, playing Stevie Wonder's *Hotter Than July* album over and over, knowing he was listening to it, too. The lyrics of 'Rocket Love' – 'All I do is think about you' – summed it all up. The other album I played was Phil Collins's *Face Value*, especially the tracks 'In the Air Tonight' and 'If Leaving Me Is Easy', one of the most haunting songs I've ever heard. Those two albums were the soundtrack to my life when he was in jail.

I wrote long love letters and virtually stopped living until the postman brought me a letter or a VO. My letters were complete works of fiction: I tried to make it sound as if I was a really interesting and exciting person, so I made up stories about where I'd been and what I was doing. In truth I was mooching on my bed all day long – I wasn't working at this time, which is quite normal in my job. I remember saying I'd been to The Bombay Bicycle Club as if it was a nightclub when it's just an Indian restaurant. His letters to me were all lovey-dovey, swearing he would never let me down.

At the time a DJ called Robbie Vincent on Radio London did dedications to people in prison, and so I wrote in. I never got my request on air but it made me feel closer to my boyfriend just writing, 'Can you send a dedication to my loved one in prison?' Looking back, the enforced separation heightened my infatuation for him: it gave us both a long time to think so we were red-hot for each other by the time he got out. I don't know what happened to his other girlfriend, but I had a clear field.

His family threw a party at a pub when he was released. There were a few other criminals there, but I was so green, I didn't really understand any of it: there was a lot of talk about 'oysters', but I've only heard it said in a Cockney accent and I now wonder if they meant 'hoisters'. The talk all evening was about jobs people had done. It worried me, but I was thrilled to see him again and his family were nice to me. I wanted him to go straight because I couldn't bear the idea of him going back to prison again. 'I don't care if you do any job, become a postman or something. You don't have to impress me with a sexy job, I love you for you,' I pleaded with him. 'He'll go straight if he loves you,' Mum always said. I think I almost persuaded him because for a time he stopped going out thieving: we were very much in love and I'd spend all my time at his flat. But he didn't get a job; he wasn't trained for any other kind of work. Besides, being a bit of a Flash Harry, it would have been hard to work for someone else. He liked being his own boss and because he had a bit of attitude and was a dominant character he wasn't cut out for a normal job. I sensed his friends treated him with respect and a bit of fear: he was my big man and I was his little princess. Looking back, I can see he was a bit of a father figure for me. He took care of me, and that was powerfully attractive.

It was coming up to Christmas 1981 and he had no money at all because he was still trying to go straight. We were round at a mate's one day for a cup of tea when one of the others there said to him: 'I'll tell you what to get your mum and dad for Christmas. I've been up Jaeger in the West End and just as you go in there are some cashmere sweaters on the left, beautiful. The security is rubbish, you can easily get a couple.' I remember thinking, this is a whole way of life, a whole world, and I can't compete with it.

Meanwhile, Mum could see that despite his brief effort at going straight for me (which lasted for five or six months) my boyfriend had not changed, and she was worried about me. 'This has to stop, Lisa,' she told me. 'He's a thief and you're going to end up like one of those women round here, bringing up kids on your own because your old man's inside. Life will be a misery, with him in and out of prison. I can't stand by and let this happen – I didn't work all my lunch hours to put you through Italia Conti for this.'

One of Mum's favourite expressions was 'I didn't work my lunch hours …' When she said it I would think, I didn't *ask* you to work your lunch hours. I always felt she was holding me to ransom, wanting payback, so I didn't respond very positively – in fact, this was the best way to push me straight into the arms of my unsuitable man. Which is exactly what happened one day after a big row about him, when she gave me an ultimatum: 'If you're going to carry on seeing that bastard, get out of this house! I never want to see you or him again.'

With hindsight, Mum realises it was stupid pushing me like that and I know she regrets saying it. At 17 I just wasn't equipped to deal with a man like him or the world I was going into. Nan and Grandad didn't approve either, and they supported Mum. Remember, I was the apple of all their eyes and they hated seeing me throw myself away. They all thought I was going to be somebody, yet I was doing just what any girl from the Rockingham Estate might do.

The Rockingham Estate coronation party.

Nan and Grandad on the balcony of the Stephenson House flat.

Nan (back left), Grandad (centre right, with cigar in mouth) and Aunt Shirley (centre left) in the local pub.

Nan, down the pub, mid song.

Mum in the early sixties.

With Nan on the balcony, aged three.

As a bridesmaid for my nursery teacher's wedding.

CERTIFIED COPY OF AN ENTRY OF BIRTH

GIVEN AT THE GENERAL REGISTER OFFICE

Application Number

| REGISTRATION DISTRICT | | Southwark | |
|---|---|---|---|
| 1964 BIRTH in the Sub-district of **North Southwark** | | in the | **Metropolitan Borough of Southwark** |

| Columns: | 1 | 2 | 3 | 4 | 5 | 6 | 7 | 8 | 9 | 10 |
|---|---|---|---|---|---|---|---|---|---|---|
| No. | When and where born | Name, if any | Sex | Name and surname of father | Name, surname and maiden surname of mother | Occupation of father | Signature, description and residence of informant | When registered | Signature of registrar | Name entered after registration |
| 383 | Twentyfourth November 1963 Guy's Hospital London Bridge | Lisa Jane | Girl | Father unknown | Valerie Sheila MAXWELL a Wages Clerk of 15 Stephenson House Rockingham Street Southwark | — | V.S. Maxwell Mother 15 Stephenson House Rockingham Street S.E.1. | Thirteenth January 1964 | Cp. Lefer Registrar | |

CERTIFIED to be a true copy of an entry in the certified copy of a Register of Births in the District above mentioned.

Given at the GENERAL REGISTER OFFICE, under the Seal of the said Office, the   **24th**   day of   **February**   **2011**

My birth certificate.

Messing around on the Rockingham Estate with Caroline Sargeant, the girl who had elocution lessons at Italia Conti.

My first ever promo shot. Love the carpet!

Showing off my *Annie* sweatshirt. Not sure why I'm carrying a toy tea set and wearing a straw hat.

Not sure about using photographic equipment as props.

My sultry look. Or am I just mid-blink?

My first proper theatre job, *Hotel Paradiso*.
(I'm the one in the spotty dress on the far right.)

Kira from *The Dark Crystal*. I recorded
the voice for Kira not long after I left
Italia Conti.

In my early twenties. You can see
I was a bit partial to the sunbed!

One of Benny Hill's angels.

Filming *The Lisa Maxwell Show* with Wayne Sleep.

With Jeremy Legg on the set of *No Limits*.

With Kelly Temple, filming *The Biz*.

Filming the *Splash* Christmas special in Disneyland, LA.

With Nino Ferretto, co-presenter for *Splash*.

Nan and Les Dennis.

Getting into the part!

Playing Julie Andrews in a sketch of *The Sound of Music*.

On location with *The Russ Abbott Show*.

On the yellow brick road with Toto and the Tin Man.

At a Christmas karaoke party with Simon and Yasmin Le Bon and Nick Rhodes.

Having a boozy dinner in Hong Kong with my agent Mike Hughes.

Me and Dolph.

Check out the hair! Always been a bit of a poser!

Heading Stateside!

At a pool party in LA. As you can see, by this point my weight was well below healthy.

With my great mate Ron Siegel.

In LA with Darren and my good friends John and Bob.

I was truly in love with him in the way a teenager falls in love. It may not be a mature love, but it's still powerful. I'd been looking at this guy and dreaming about him since I was 14. As I've said, he was very good-looking with an amazing smile, a twinkle in his eye and a beautiful head of hair. He was a great dancer, and when he was in prison I used to dance like him in my bedroom, just to try and remember him. To me, he was so cool. He introduced me to soul music: Lou Rawls, Jean Khan, Roy Ayres and of course Stevie Wonder. To this day, my taste in music is deeply influenced by him.

He seemed to know so much more than me. He was in control of his life; being with him made me feel nothing could hurt me. I also knew other women fancied him – I'd hear them talking about him in the loo at clubs, not realising I was with him. Being on his arm meant other girls envied me, and that was a potent feeling.

When Mum pushed me, the only option was to walk out and live with my boyfriend, something he was very happy about. His flat seemed very upmarket – the curtains with bobbles on the edges had been made to order – and to me, the height of stylish living. It all went with my notion that I belonged in an affluent kind of world. I didn't think about where the money might be coming from, I just shut it out in the same way I'd been brought up to block anything I really didn't want to face up to: so long as it was there and it worked, don't question it. I knew he was back in crime but I didn't allow myself to think it through.

His cronies would come round the flat in the morning and they'd talk about where they were going 'on the bottle'. While he was out, I would spend ages making myself look lovely. It was an empty existence: I just wanted to be his girlfriend, nothing else, and I completely lost my way. Work had become so unimportant that whenever I went for an audition I'd turn up a couple of hours late. God knows how I ever got any jobs.

He'd come and watch me. I'd see him sitting on his own at a table, thinking, that's my bird. It was like that Barry Manilow song, 'Copacabana'. He knew someone with a black cab and he arranged for me to be taken there every night and picked up if he wasn't able to drive me home himself. When he was around we'd go on to nightclubs afterwards. They always seemed to have loads of money, it was never a problem, and I was blissfully happy because I was living with the man of my dreams.

There was no phone at the flat and no mobiles back then, so there was no way for Mum to keep in touch, even if she had wanted to. I think they were all devastated at me going. My Auntie Linda, who was married to Uncle Alan, sent me a card behind Mum's back: 'If you need anything or anyone, I'm here.' She was worried about me being so cut off, and I'm grateful to her.

Linda is a calm, thoughtful person who married into my loud, argumentative family and she has always provided an oasis of calm. I've got other aunts and uncles I adore just as much, but we're all quite similar, with big mouths and lots to say for ourselves. She offers something different.

There was a phone box close to the flat and I used to arrange for people to ring me there at agreed times. If I wanted to speak to my boyfriend before I moved in, I would ring the phone box and someone always answered, just some passer-by (it seems people can't ignore a ringing phone). I never knew who I'd get on the other end, but I had a good line for them:

'There's someone who lives in the block opposite you and it's an emergency, I need to get in touch with them. There's something the matter with his phone. I'm desperate! Can you run over and fetch him for me?' And they always did: I think my acting training came in handy. So when I was living there I'd arrange for the agency to ring me or I'd call them from there – I never had any money, not even for phone calls, so I much preferred people to ring me. I did some more work while I was in the relationship, but resented anything that interfered with my time with him.

I was very isolated from my own life, in a bubble with my bloke. Practically the only person who visited me at his flat was my old friend Renee from school, who came with her dad and took me out for an expensive lunch. Who knows what they thought of me living with this thief, or the other vagabonds (his mates) who were hanging around the flat. And God knows what they might have thought, had they seen me the day before helping make counterfeit money in the living room.

My boyfriend and three or four of his friends had turned up with a guillotine, a printing machine and loads of massive sheets of white paper. He told me to stay in the kitchen. One of them actually said the words: 'This is man's business.'

To me, that sounded really exciting. In those days I loved that kind of sexist stereotypical nonsense, and when I look back I think I was a completely different person to the one I am today. I was happy enough to play the princess, just making tea for the boys and whisking about in my tiny ra-ra skirt. I'd mince in, all giggly, with whisky and lemonade.

'What are you doing?' I asked after I'd plonked the drinks down on the table.

'We're making £20 notes, lots of them,' my boyfriend explained.

Some of the others looked angry he'd told me but didn't dare say anything against him – they were all wary of him. He'd never turned his temper on me and I'd never seen him violent, but I'd heard him put people down and I could see others walked on eggshells around him. There was a pile of new notes on the table and I said: 'They're really good, but they look too new! What you should do is …' I screwed one up into a ball and made it look old. They all agreed it looked better, and so after that I stayed in the room screwing them up.

I kept one of the notes and the next day went across the road to the mini-mart and bought a mint Aero. I remember the buzz of getting more than £19 back in change, in real money. That was the only time I did it, though. If I needed cash he gave it to me, and he was generous. We only ever mixed with other criminals – I suppose that's a bit like actors hanging out together. He and his mates all dressed well and they loved having a trophy bird in tow (I was foolish enough to see it as a compliment). I was also introduced to expensive restaurants, nightclubs and designer clothes … things I didn't know about. It was all very seductive and in some ways educational. I'm not proud of this time and I don't condone it, but the experience taught me a lot.

Mum didn't desert me at this point. She would come round to the flat and bang on the door. I'd tell him I didn't want to see her and he'd open the door and pass the message on. She called him all sorts of names.

'You *bastard*, you've taken away my daughter and you're not good enough for her! You've ruined her life …' That's the sort of thing she'd yell with a few more swear words thrown into the mix. At the time I hated her for creating a scene and not understanding how much I loved him. Looking back, she could see I was under his spell and she just wanted to release me.

One night she turned up with Grandad, who was in his sixties then. I heard his voice outside the door and I was really scared that my boyfriend would hit him – from what I'd heard, I knew he was a good fighter and I knew he had that physical confidence which meant he could hold his own. Even though Grandad was so much older, it was still a male confronting a male.

'Go and get her. She's coming home with me now!' shouted Grandad.

'She doesn't want to,' my boyfriend said

'Then I'll have to come in there to get her!'

'You can't do that, Jim. She doesn't want to go with you.'

Then Grandad lost it: 'You fucking *bastard*, taking that poor baby away from us! I'm going to drag her out.'

Cowering out of sight but peering round the kitchen door, I saw Grandad roll up his sleeves, just as they did in old films when they were about to have a fight.

'Come on then,' he said, squaring up.

'Don't provoke him, Grandad! He'll kill you if you fight him,' I was praying inside. I was extremely touched he was so fearless, taking on a violent young man on my behalf. Sobbing my heart out in the kitchen, all the while I was thinking, what am I doing? What have I done to everyone? Yet I couldn't go: I was still completely in thrall to this man. I'm really ashamed of myself now – it would kill me if my own daughter did anything similar to me.

\* \* \*

We used to go to a pub near where Mum, Nan and Grandad lived. I could easily of nipped home, but at first I didn't call round. Mum never stopped trying to make contact with me, though, and gradually I missed her so much that I started popping in. We were a family who had dramatic rows and they didn't mean half as much as they might in other households – we always excused our outbursts by saying 'it was said in anger' or 'it was said in drink' and then it would all blow over. Sometimes my boyfriend would come with me, and for my sake everyone tried to be polite, but it was a truce: they didn't like him and he certainly didn't like Mum.

Mum's huge generosity towards me continued. For my eighteenth birthday she bought me a red Renault (she gave me driving lessons when I was 17). It was parked outside her house with a big pink bow and the words 'Happy Birthday' written on it. I loved that car – it gave me some independence. Even though it was second-hand, buying it had cost Mum a great deal of her hard-earned salary. Almost inevitably, my boyfriend ended up using it.

I was still very much in love. My family could see I was impressed by his ridiculous material wealth, all ill gotten, and that it had gone beyond him being a bad boyfriend and a bad influence on me – they could tell he was dangerous, but I was totally blinded.

I knew he had a temper and when we'd been out I'd seen him square up to blokes in pubs three or four times. The other guy always backed down, and at first I was impressed: 'He can really handle himself, he's such a man.' Slowly, it became uglier: I saw grown men pussyfoot around him, running errands, treating me like I was something to be revered just because I was his property. I remember thinking, why are they so scared of him? What has he done? I became more and more uncomfortable, but at the same time I liked the idea that everyone else was scared of this man but I could control such an imposing character. In the beginning I felt protected and cherished.

He was extremely possessive, which at first I found flattering: he was pleased if his mates all thought I was a bit of a catch. However, he began to get paranoid, and if one of them looked at me he'd say: 'Don't you fucking go looking at her arse!' I thought it meant he loved me, but after a bit there was always tension and confrontation when we went out. It got to the point where I spent all evening looking at the tablecloth because if I flicked my eyes up to someone else he'd clock it. 'What you looking at him for? D'you fancy him?' And so the interrogation would begin. In the end I daren't look at anyone, not even a waiter and certainly not any of his male friends. Really, it was tragic: they were his mates but he felt they would try and take me away. And it wasn't love for me that drove him on: it was the need to possess me.

The signs were there early on: I remember one New Year's Eve party at a family friend's house when a drunken reveller touched my bum while I was dancing, my boyfriend went ballistic, and after one of my aunties told him to calm down because he was ruining the party he called her a c**t. At this stage I still adored him and I certainly wasn't interested in anyone else, but telling him wasn't enough – I had to prove it by sitting by his side in public, eyes downcast, not speaking the whole time.

His feelings for me became more and more possessive, centred on owning and controlling rather than loving me. In the end even I could see our relationship was dangerous. I have blocked out a lot of the memories because I don't like the person I was then (I'm ashamed of that Lisa), but to survive I had to blank it out, to come through it and put myself back together again.

One night we went to a club with a couple of his friends. Another guy and a girl joined us there. I didn't know them, but I was very intimidated by the girl: she was older than me, very sexy and glamorous, wearing tight leather trousers. She seemed extremely beautiful and sophisticated to me. My boyfriend seemed to think so, too – there was a real connection between them straight away. I was a savvy little kid in some ways and I defi-nitely picked up on something between him and this girl, which made me feel uncomfortable. Somehow I suspected they knew each other far more than just nightclub acquaintances.

We drank a lot that night. In those days there were drugs around and there were times when I suspected my bloke took cocaine. I know nothing about drugs and I'm very naïve about that whole culture, so I don't know whether he used cocaine or something else. Sometimes he seemed even edgier than normal, though.

At the end of a long night we went to a bar. While we were there, a guy came across. He thrust a piece of paper and a pen in front of me and asked me to sign it for him.

'What do you mean?' I said.

'Go on – I know who you are. You're Susan George.'

Wow, I thought. I was extremely flattered because Susan George was a highly successful and very beautiful actress. For a joke I signed it with her name. I was aware that my boyfriend was looking at the guy, as much as to say, 'How dare you speak to my bird?' Perhaps because I'd had a lot to drink or maybe I was fed up with him chatting up the other girl, I enjoyed the attention and was a bit flirty. I could tell my boyfriend was pissed off, but for once I didn't care. 'Bye, Susan!' the man shouted as we left. 'Bye,' I replied, flicking my hair *à la* Susan George, and we climbed into a black cab. Just as we were about to set off, my boyfriend said: 'I've forgotten something.'

He got out and ran back to the club. I could tell by the way he ran, with a sort of hopping, skipping step, trouble was coming. The guy who had been flirting with me was outside and the next thing I saw was that he was on the floor with my boyfriend kicking the life out of him. Kicking, kicking, kicking, in a frenzied way – I'd never seen anything like it. Back in the cab, his friend was screaming: 'Don't look, don't look!' Then he told the driver, 'We're going to have to get out of here fast, mate.'

My boyfriend ran back, jumped in and we drove off. The last thing I saw was the guy on the pavement was not moving.

'At least he wasn't all over me, like you were over that girl,' I foolishly said.

'You fucking *what*?' he roared, turning his attention to me.

As I turned towards him, all I saw was a fist crashing into the window of the taxi. I slid to the floor of the cab, trying to take cover, as he continued to punch the glass, completely smashing through the window. It was terrifying. His mate and his girl-friend were shouting: 'No, *no*!' His friend grabbed him and managed to hold onto him. I was still on the floor, sobbing uncontrollably, while his mate's girlfriend was doing her best to console me. If the cab driver wasn't there, I think he would have turned on me as well. I thought he was going to kill me.

I didn't go home with my boyfriend: I was dropped off at a friend's place. But I didn't sleep. The next day I was in a state and worried about how I could go back to his flat. I decided if I left it until he'd had a good night's sleep it might be calm – I remember thinking how critical it was that I went in at the right moment. At 11 a.m., I let myself in: he was still in bed, so I made myself a cup of tea and sat down. He walked through from the bedroom and I had a good feeling, as if it was going to be peaceful again, but then he strolled across, picked up my tea and hurled it over me before threatening me again. Somehow I managed to escape from the flat and ran out into the street. I can't remember where I went all day – I may have rung Mum and told her we'd had an argument, but I still didn't leave him. Instead I went back later that day: I knew if I didn't, he would come after me, and by now I was too scared to leave.

I'd gone from not wanting to leave him because I loved him although everybody else could read the writing on the wall, to being too terrified and so I went back and placated him. I was just treading on eggshells the whole time, though. It was an incident with a sunlamp, two weeks later, that made me realise I had to get away from him: he had his own sunlamp and I asked if I could borrow it.

'How does it work?' I said.

'Just turn the dial right round, put your face under it and the timer will switch it off,' he told me, but he didn't come to help me set it up – he wasn't interested.

'Have I been under it long enough?' I shouted after I'd been underneath for a while and the timer hadn't gone off.

'Yeah, *yeah*! You can come out now,' he told me.

Because the timer was still running I thought it would be OK, and at first it was. Within an hour my face was bright red, properly burnt as if I was on fire, and I looked awful. Then the skin began to tighten as if it was shrinking and my eyes were closing up: the pain was terrible. He seemed indifferent and didn't offer to take me to hospital, even though I knew I must need treatment. At this point I was panicking, thinking I might be going blind or even be scarred for life. I put on dark glasses and went to the local hospital on my own, where they told me I had third-degree burns and gave me some ointment that made my face very shiny.

After I left the hospital I went to the firm of solicitors where Mum worked. I must have looked like something out of a horror film because when she saw me she burst into tears.

'Oh my God! What has he done to you?' she gasped.

'It wasn't him, it was a sunlamp,' I muttered.

Even then I was defending him, and it must have broken Mum's heart to see me so ground down.

'You've got to get out of this – you've *got* to leave him! Come home,' she pleaded.

'I can't – he'll come after me. I've got to go back,' I said.

So I did go back, but something inside had hardened and now I made my plan to escape. When he went out one morning I said goodbye as normal but then I packed my things and went to Mum's office. In one way this wasn't a smart move because he would know where to look for me, but in another I felt safe surrounded by other people, including the men who worked there. Besides, I didn't want Mum to have to face him on her own because it was the first place he would look for me.

\* \* \*

'That's brilliant,' said Mum after I announced that I'd left him. 'I'm not scared of him – he's not going to hurt you because he's not going to get near you!' She hid me in one of the empty offices. Soon enough, I heard him come storming into the reception.

'Where the *fuck* is she?'

'She's not here.'

'I fucking know she is! She's here somewhere.'

I was terrified because I could hear him opening and slamming doors but the men in the building all came out and threatened him with the police if he didn't leave.

Mum must have realised what I'd been dealing with when she saw him in full flow. I completely understand battered wives who keep going back to abusive husbands: he had such a hold over me. Men like this are damaged, but they're also very clever and you don't realise they're slowly taking you apart, chipping away so that in the end all that's left is this person who doesn't have her own voice. When you really believe you are nobody, how can you survive on your own? You're better off with the devil you know.

Thank God, I managed to get away, and thank God, Mum was there when I needed her. My family was thrilled when I moved back home. One of the main things to help me get away was knowing how disappointed Mum was about my choice of man: he didn't like her and the feeling was mutual. Ultimately, I couldn't be with anyone who didn't like and accept her, but there was no big welcome home because Mum, Nan and Grandad all thought it would be a matter of days before I went back. They knew he had a hold over me and they were right: I wasn't over him yet. He'd come round and bang on the door, trying to get me back. I'd lie there in my old bedroom, safe and secure, and feel excited that he was out there. Usually he came round at the end of the evening when the pubs closed and he'd throw stones at my bedroom window. I'd lean out the window to talk to him, thrilled he still wanted me.

I think my thirst for drama had crept in – I loved playing the part of the young girl separated from the love of her life. Also, I was flattered he loved me more than anyone else. Yet something, and I don't really know what, held me back and kept me from returning to him. Gradually I managed to put the relationship behind me, to realise all the drama I needed could come from my profession, and the fall-out of life with this man was too high a price to pay for my love for him. Slowly, I turned the focus back to my career.

# CHAPTER 6

## Moving On

Emotionally and physically drained, I needed rebuilding and I had to learn to trust again. Let's face it, I'd been programmed from birth to be wary of relationships (men let you down, leave you pregnant, cause you shame) and now my first big, proper affair had turned into hell. But the luck that got me away held, for I met the perfect antidote, a guy who was everything a boyfriend should be: kind, loyal, gentle and good fun to be with.

After moving back to Mum's, I was scared to go out but I couldn't hibernate forever. She and Nan encouraged me to pick up my life and get out there again. I admit there were moments of weakness when I used to drive past the flat where my ex-boyfriend lived, hoping to get a glimpse of him. Thank God I didn't, or I'd have been back with him again: I was so weak, still under his spell.

I started going out with Sylvia O'Donnell, another Conti girl. She was a little older than me and had been in *Striker*, a hit kids' series about football. Her parents ran a pub in Stockwell and we hung out together, going to Stringfellows most nights. She would come to the house and we'd spend all evening getting ready then go out about 11.30 p.m. Mum, Nan and Granddad thought we were odd because we went out as they were going to bed but they were happy to see me back to my old self and never complained. The ritual of getting ready was almost as enjoyable as the night itself. I was still sunbedding, and by this time Mum was renting a sunbed at home (she had it so long that in the end the rental company let her keep it!). Sylvia and me would lie on it for two hours: while one of us was on it, the other would be doing her make-up. We had the brands of the Sunbed Queens: two little white marks at the top of our bums, the pressure points where weight went onto it.

We'd spend ages deciding what to wear. I remember one outfit I had: a little pink and white gingham 1950s-style swim-suit with a tight ruched bodice and a halterneck attached to gathered shorts. I wore it with silver boots.

It was around this time that I first started smoking, and what a mistake it was. Most kids have their first drag really young, but I was 19. Mum brought back 200 Harrods fags duty-free from Spain and I took the green-and-gold packets out with us as a prop to show off. 'You're always carrying fags, but you don't smoke,' friends would say. In the end I started lighting up, and inevitably I was hooked.

I'd first been to Stringfellows with Graham Sheward, the son of the couple who ran Conti's. He used to take a group of us there. Graham was a good mate: we never fancied each other but were always pleased to see each other and hang out. After that I'd been with a couple of other mates, but now I became a regular.

I even went to dinner with Peter Stringfellow a couple of times. He took me to Morton's, a private members' club in Berkeley Square. I don't know how to admit this but in those days I thought he was really attractive (it was before he had the ponytail-thing going on). 'Hello, lovely lady,' he always said in his breathy, Northern accent. His whole demeanour was gentle and I couldn't get my head round him running such a big empire with nothing more than a whisper.

I remember one night we were having a little snog but I couldn't enjoy it because I was so worried about my toenails. Remember I told you how as a kid I used to make my own false fingernails out of Sellotape when I was with Nan and Granddad while they cleaned offices? Well, I used to have a terrible habit of picking my toenails. Being a dancer, I can get my feet right up under my chin and I'd pick away. To make them look even and longer in open-toed shoes, I perfected the art of sticking on Sellotape and then painted the nail and Sellotape extension bright red with varnish. I was doing stick-on nail extensions before anyone else – I wish I'd patented it!

Just as Peter was making a pass at me I realised I'd caught my foot on the base of the table and my Sellotape nails had flicked up and were in danger of coming off! It wasn't exactly the image I was aiming for and I didn't want him to notice: he was used to immaculate girls with everything perfect.

I suppose he must have been a bit kinky because he loved to hear me say the really rude word – you know, the one that begins with 'C' and ends in 'T'. He said it with a flattened Northern vowel whereas I used a polished, rounded one. He kept asking me to say it and I remember thinking, if I keep on saying it perhaps he won't notice the feet (I can count on one hand the number of times I've said that word in my entire life and all of them were that night!).

I was probably one of loads of dolly-birds he took around in those days. We'd meet at the club, go out to dinner and then back to the club again. He always wanted to take me home but I said 'no' because I was quite savvy and didn't want to be on my own in the back of the car with him: I liked him, but I didn't want to take the relationship to another level.

Sylvia looked out for me: 'Make sure he brings you back to the club,' she'd say whenever I went off with Peter. She then asked a friend of hers (Darren Tuohy) to take me home. He always waited sweetly for me to come back. Peter wasn't the only guy I'd go out to dinner with, but I always insisted on going back to the club, where Darren would take me home.

Darren had worked in the film industry, but by the time I met him he was an estate agent and property developer, working for his father's company. It was the eighties' boom. Happy to act as my confidant, friend and driver for a while, Darren never pushed himself at me. He pursued me in a respectful, quiet way, which wasn't something I was used to: most men saw a bubbly stage-school girl and they came on strong.

One day a red rose with no message was delivered to my house. 'Guess what? I think so-and-so has sent me a red rose …' I told him excitedly over the phone. I assumed it was from a gorgeous fella we knew at Stringfellows (it never occured to me that Darren was the only one I'd entrusted with my address). I was so thrilled and excited because this guy was very good-looking, and Darren, bless him, didn't say a word.

He and I would chat about most things. I mentioned in passing that I liked Skips, those smelly prawn cocktail flavour crisps, and a couple of days later a huge catering-size box arrived. This time it had to be him. Velour or towelling tracksuits were really fashionable then and I loved the ones made by Umbro. Darren must have noticed because 10 yellow towelling ones arrived – he'd noticed yellow was one of my favourite colours. By this time his best friend had told me that Darren seriously liked me.

I liked him, too, but it wasn't in the same way as my criminal ex, who for a time I'd been desperate to be around and whose danger was exciting. But I was smart enough to know that I was lucky to walk away and my next choice had to be someone different, so I allowed Darren, who at 20 was a year older than me, to become my boyfriend. If that sounds patronising, it isn't meant to be: it was his choice to wait and allow me time so I guess he was a very good judge of where I was at then. He never took advantage, never tried to take the relationship to a different level until I was ready. Slowly I realised that I should be with Darren – if he went away, there would be a huge hole in my life.

Mum was overjoyed: Darren was a nice boy with a good job and he clearly worshipped me and only had my best interests at heart. After all the heartbreak I'd put them through, I could almost hear the sighs of relief when my family got to know Darren. Grandad used to tease him about spoiling me: 'Just say no,' he would tell him.

I'm ashamed to say I was still not completely over my old boyfriend. He kept turning up outside my house, trying to get back with me, and I was flattered. A few months into the relationship with Darren he found me with my ex – he must have suspected something because he turned up at the flat. I left immediately and we went back to Mum's. I felt so disgusted with myself and I've never seen Darren so upset: normally he was so easy-going. Lisa, you are such a nasty piece of work, I thought to myself. My survival instincts kicked in and because I'm a people-pleaser I told Darren what he wanted to hear: that I was only there to sort some things out and my ex didn't mean anything to me. I think I believed I could juggle them both but when I saw the effect this had on Darren I realised how selfish I was being.

Mum was very supportive at this time. She knew my last relationship was a disaster area but she understood why I found my ex exciting. She also really liked Darren and could see he was so much better for me, although I don't think she ever saw him as my long-term future.

Darren lived in Winchmore Hill with his mum Yvonne and her second husband, Bill. He was close to his father, John, and worked with him. I spent a lot of time there, every opportunity I had. It was a lovely house and a very middle-class lifestyle, but Darren had no issues with my background. I told him my usual lie: Mum and Dad had split up when I was very young and I didn't have any contact with my father. It still sounded a whole lot better than admitting they'd never been together at all and technically my father was 'Unknown'. In all the time we were together I never told Darren the true story.

He was very encouraging about my work, and because he'd been in the industry himself (he'd been a focus puller – one of the crew who adjusts the focus on the camera before working with his dad) he understood the pressures. Soon after we started going out I did a tour in *Babes in Arms*, a show based on a Judy

Garland/Mickey Rooney musical, in which I played Terry, a dumb blonde 1940s starlet. Su Pollard (*Hi-de-Hi!*) and Matthew Kelly also appeared. It was the first time I had ever played comedy, and after I got an exit round (the round of applause after your character leaves the stage) I felt like a comedy god and was on a high. I spent the rest of the tour trying to work out why some lines got that reaction while others didn't.

We had a great tour. I became really good mates with Su and Matthew, one of the best people you could ever meet. He and I were both playing 16-year-olds – not too much of a stretch for me because I'm tiny and I was only 20 at the time, but Matthew was tall and 33. My blonde nymphet had some of the best lines in the show and a fantastic song: 'I Wish I Were in Love Again'.

I ended up having an affair with this ginger actor. He really wasn't my type at all, but when you're on tour things happen. There was a thrill to all the cloak-and-dagger stuff – clandestine meetings, people gossiping about us. I guess at some level I missed the adrenalin.

I still feel terrible about Darren, who didn't deserve such bad behaviour, but I thought I'd really fallen in love. When we got home I told Darren I needed a break in our relationship. I just used that old cliché 'I'm not ready, I need space' – which of course means 'I need space to see someone else'.

What must I have been thinking when I took my latest boyfriend down to the pub to meet Nan and Grandad? I really should have known better than to walk in with a tall, strawberry-blond and ever so slightly fey boyfriend.

'Oh Gawd, Jim! Fucking hell, look what she's walked in with!' was Nan's greeting. And then when he spoke she added: 'He's only got a fucking stutter as well, Jim.' Of course my escort heard all this but he was strong enough to rise above it. I've made him sound extremely unprepossessing, which is unfair: he was a real ladies' man and never had any problem finding glamorous girlfriends.

As the saying goes, 'What goes on tour, stays on tour,' and we were living proof. When we got back to London we tried to make a go of it but the relationship wasn't the same and I ended it. I also wanted to concentrate on my career. Ambition had kicked back in with full force, I was going full throttle and determined not to be derailed by a man again. Work never let me down, I could always count on it and I didn't want to mess things up because of my private life.

Once the affair was over I went back to Darren hoping he knew nothing about it (I don't think he did). A week later my ginger actor was with someone else. It wasn't exactly a long mourning period.

At this stage of my life Darren was the most supportive, uncomplicated and reliable man I had ever been around. I could aim for the sky but I knew he would be there to catch me if I fell. I loved him, but I don't think I ever loved him enough, and looking back I can see he deserved better. He was part of my grand plan to get back on track. I don't think I ever fancied him in the way he fancied me, but I was happy because at that time I didn't want to be distracted by falling madly in love or to change my life plans around a man.

Besides, Darren made it very difficult for me *not* to be with him. He made my life easier, he took care of everything: he was indispensable. If ever I fancied another man (and I did from time to time), I was savvy enough to know it was for the wrong reasons, usually just the ego trip. I always wanted to be loved and it's not hard to get men to fancy you. It doesn't take much to trigger lust, but I was never interested in a purely physical attraction: I always knew what I wanted was love, and Darren gave me that. He was also interested in my career and was the first person close to me that I could talk to about scripts and offers of parts. He was clever, had a natural creative flair and I could introduce him to all my friends. Everyone liked him – he fitted into my showbiz life perfectly; we were a good couple. If you were having a dinner party, you wanted Lisa and Darren because we were like the cabaret. Witty and amusing, we always sang for our supper. Friends thought we were the perfect couple and our relationship was held up as a role model.

When everyone tells you what a fantastic couple you are, after a while you start to believe it yourself and fall into the roles. The truth was there was nothing wrong with Darren and me. If I could put a finger on anything and say it wasn't working, I would have ended it, but how could I do that when I was with the perfect man in the 'perfect' relationship, when all my friends were envious of me and my family was delighted?

I never asked any questions about Darren's business, but I knew he was doing well: property was soaring in the eighties and he always seemed to have loads of money. We sank our earnings into the same pot and as long as I had enough for clothes and anything else I needed I was happy. All of that was Darren's side, and as far as I knew he was very good at it.

After the *Babes in Arms*' tour I made a few TV dramas, including a couple of episodes in a TV sci-fi serial, *The Tripods*. It was a teatime children's programme and I made friends with Liz

Morton, who later married Peter Davison. I was also one of the 'Hill's Angels' for two episodes. Auditioning was bizarre: 10 of us had to do a full-blown dance routine in the living room of Benny Hill's Kensington flat while he sat in an armchair watching us do our hitch kicks. We were taught the routine by a choreographer at Conti's and had to perform in a room no bigger than the average living room. I'm not sure what he was looking for or how he chose the girls he wanted – if there was a chance of a job at the end of it, we'd turn up anywhere.

Around this time I auditioned for a lead in *Castaway* starring Oliver Reed. I got down to the last four and was invited to the office of Richard Johnson, the actor executive producing the film. He asked me how I would feel about eating limpets, but I think my face betrayed me. I didn't have a problem about getting naked with Oliver Reed (or at least, I didn't *think* this would be a problem), but I wasn't prepared for limpets. Usually, I say 'yes' to anything at auditions (I was once asked if I could ride a horse and said 'yes', even though I'd never been on one – I think I was following Nan's philosophy of 'have now, pay later', only in my case it was 'say yes now, learn later' and luckily I didn't get the part). But limpets did for me.

Amanda Donohoe, who got the part, obviously didn't mind limpets or perhaps she was just a better actress than me when zapped with the question. I'm glad I didn't get the job: in retrospect I think I would have found the nudity very difficult.

It's funny that I was auditioning for a stark-naked part when I hadn't even had a screen kiss, but that came next. I was given a part in a sitcom called *Life Without George* with Simon Cadell and he was the first man to kiss me onscreen. Older than me, he was an intellectual and a sensitive kind man and I think he could see I was nervous. On the day we met for the first time, we had to film the kiss. He was great and took time out to talk to me. Since then this is something I've always tried to do with newcomers on a set. It costs nothing and it puts them at ease.

My first big break in television presenting came when the Conti agency rang with an audition for a new magazine show, *No Limits*, produced by Jonathan King. At that time he was huge: he'd had hits in the charts, he'd run Decca Records, he had a big TV series (*Entertainment USA*) and 'Bizarre', a popular column in the *Sun*. He'd put a few paragraphs in his column, saying he was looking for 'the next living sex symbol and superstar' to present his new show, and 3,000 hopefuls wrote in. Like all these things, the producers of the show were not prepared to rely on unknown, untrained presenters and so they cast around the agencies for young talent. Several ex-Conti kids were asked to meet Jonathan at the school and he short-listed some of us to go up to the BBC Manchester Oxford Road Studios for the auditions.

Hundreds of kids were there and we were each thrust in front of a mike for less than a minute to say why we wanted to be the new presenter. Somewhere there's an embarrassing clip of me doing the audition: still the sunbed queen, my skin is the colour of mahogany and I'm wearing a bright orange floral off-the-shoulder top with yellow leggings and salmon pink Converse-type boots. Trust me, those colours were very in at the time.

I put on a posh accent, but also slipped in a slight lisp (very 'OK, yah' eighties). So I rabbited on about wanting to open a poodle parlour called Fifi's to dye poodles pink – not quite Miss World wanting to feed the world, and nothing to do with why I should front the show. Astonishingly, I got through the first round. In the second, we all had to dance to a song I'd never heard before. I was giving it everything, really showing off my moves with my eyes closed as if I'm in the zone, singing 'Badara, badara', which I thought must be the chorus. It turned out to be 'body rock' so I guess I wasn't too far away.

They were looking for two presenters, a boy and a girl, and in the end it came down to me and newcomer Jeremy Legg, a computer consultant from Aylesbury, and another couple. We had to interview a Prince Charles lookalike. The way I interviewed him, with my posh voice and ridiculous Cliff Richard lisp, you'd think I was a member of the Royal Family. Years later, on *Richard & Judy*, they showed a clip of my audition and I was mortified. 'We all had to sound posh in those days, if we were on television,' said Judy. Bless her!

Anyway, Jeremy and I got the gig, which was very exciting. A good-looking blond boy, extremely down-to-earth with spiky highlighted hair, he looked like a pop star. Although a novice, he was still very keen and handled the whole thing well, although he was a little bit star-struck. There was a big launch party for us on a boat in the Thames.

All the auditions had been filmed and the first show of the series was about how they whittled us down to two presenters. After that we travelled to a different town each week, where we'd give out facts about the place and be filmed with iconic landmarks such as the fake cows in Milton Keynes. All this was done with a soundtrack of new US pop music.

It was a great new format with the latest music and state-of-the-art technology. Wherever we went, Jeremy and I had to do stunts, too. In Bournemouth we had to go out on 'wet bikes' (similar to jet skis, but more like motorbikes). While Jeremy got the hang of it quickly, I was hopeless. I got on and fell off, then got on again and fell off again. Meanwhile he was whizzing round, doing figure-of-eights and making it look easy and sexy. Once I managed to stay on I was so excited, revving up and not looking where I was going. Millions of miles of sea were all around but I managed to head straight for a sea wall, the only small wall on Bournemouth beach. I was heading towards it at high speed and just managed to jump off before the bike ploughed into it – when they showed the clip on TV with the music 'She's a Maniac' played over it, a big wave eclipsed the moment I jumped. You couldn't tell whether I hit the wall or not – it looked really dangerous.

The camera then panned to a shot of my head bobbing up out of the water and clearing my nose of snotty seawater with a huge flick. Six million viewers witnessed that! Just thinking about it now makes my bottom go tight. Once you're in telly, you can kiss goodbye to dignity: if they've got a camera on you, they will use it.

The other dangerous stunt was a parachute jump to which I happily agreed. After all, didn't *Blue Peter* presenters do one a week? We did ours on Salisbury Plain and the first thing the instructor (a wonderful man with the nickname Apples) said to me was: 'Right, we're going to do AFF. Are you OK with that?' 'Yeah, I love AFF!' I told him.

I hadn't a clue what it was. Turns out to be Accelerated Free Fall and the accelerated bit was that we only had a day and a half's training. We were shown how to fall, bringing our knees up and rolling from one side to the other. In freefall you have to open your own parachute, and to prevent you from becoming a jelly head when you leave the plane you keep your brain engaged by counting 6,000, 5,000, 4,000 down to 3,000, when you check the canopy.

As usual, Jeremy went first and did it perfectly. Then it was my turn but I was too small and light (they were worried I might never come down on my own when the parachute opened) so I had to have extra weight attached. We were up in the plane when Apples shouted: 'Ready to sky dive?' I was supposed to shout back: 'Yeah, you bet, come on, let's *go!*' and jump out the plane. Instead I said, 'What, now?'

'Yeah, now – *go!*'

So I jumped with two instructors either side, but not touching me. As we went out, we had to arch our backs into a frog position so our bodyweight was central and we didn't spin off. I did it fine and the guys gave me the thumbs-up, then I did the same thing back. There was a tremendous sensation of noise and air gushing into my mouth but although we were falling at 150 m.p.h: there was no sense of movement. I looked down and saw a cloud beneath me. I'm going to go through that, I thought. Automatically I curled up, thinking it would hurt – after all, I'd no idea what clouds feel like. Immediately I started to spin off. The guys had to grab my ankles, pulling me back, and stuck their tongues out at me (sign language for me to arch again). I did so and once they'd got me stabilised they floated off again. Then I saw them giving me the signal to pull my toggle and open the canopy.

Suddenly it's quiet and you feel as if you're no longer falling: it was a wonderfully peaceful sensation. I'm grateful that in those days we weren't miked up to do our stunts because I was talking to myself all the way down: I don't think 'Thank fuck, it's opened!' would have gone down well on an early-evening slot! Just as I was starting to relax and trying to steer the parachute in the way they'd taught us, I looked down and experienced something they call 'ground rush' (when the ground starts flying towards you at huge speed), so I brought my knees up to my chest and rolled over in a perfect landing. Just one small snag: I was about half a mile off-target and they had to come chasing after me in a jeep. The worst bit was that the wind caught the canopy and lifted it: because I'm so light it started to drag me round the field with the instructors' vehicle in hot pursuit. 'I can't get up!' I screamed because every time I tried to stagger to my feet the canopy took off again. Luckily I wasn't injured and it felt exhilarating to have completed the fall, but I've been there, done that and got the certificate. When you're 21 you'll do anything: you don't know fear.

'You've got to let me know when you get down – I need to know you're safe. Find a phone and ring me,' Mum told me before we set off that morning. Afterwards I was so pleased with myself that I completely forgot and we had to dash from Salisbury Plain to London for the big Live Aid concert. It was about 8 p.m. before I remembered and then there was no reply at home. I realised they would all be down at the pub and so I rang there. 'I've been worried out of my mind. Thank God you're safe!' she told me.

We did 10 episodes of *No Limits* but the plan was for each series to have new presenters and so at the end we were filmed auditioning our replacements. Jenny Powell, another Conti girl, took over from me.

Jonathan King was always around when we were filming, arriving in his Rolls. He never offered me a lift in it, but I think he offered Jeremy lifts (he was always giving him pep talks, but it never occurred to me that Jonathan might be gay and like the look of Jeremy – I thought he favoured Jeremy because he was a novice and needed more help. I don't think Jeremy had a clue he was gay either). I was flattered that Jonathan didn't think he needed to pay me so much attention. Of course I knew he liked Jeremy more than me, but that was OK – I didn't expect every man to fall at my feet. Jonathan certainly enjoyed his power and he loved everyone hanging onto his every word. At the auditions all the wannabes crowded round him and he preened and played up to this.

Following this, I never saw him again, but fast forward almost 20 years and I got a call from his agent asking if I would be a character witness at his trial when he was accused of sexually assaulting underage boys. Why me? I thought. After all, I hardly knew him.

Before agreeing, I asked my own agent what I should do and he advised that I should think carefully because there's no smoke without fire. 'Would you be able to say, absolutely and categorically, that you believe he didn't do it or that you feel he wasn't capable of doing it?' he asked. The answer had to be 'no'. All I would have been able to say was that I never saw him making advances to anyone, and I didn't know him personally, so I couldn't give a character reference. I'm glad I didn't give evidence because eventually he was convicted and sentenced to seven years in prison. I'm still astonished to be asked – I can only think his agent must have been scraping the barrel, desperate to find someone who would speak up for him.

# CHAPTER 7

## Down to the Wire

After the first series of *No Limits* ended, I enjoyed a small taste of being famous when I was invited to do guest appearances on shows such as *Cheggers Plays Pop*. Then I landed *The Biz*, an ITV magazine show about the music business, particularly about the making of pop promos. It was thrilling to be offered a job without having to audition, and a first for me. The series had a half-hour teatime slot and was aimed at kids and young teenagers, but there was one major problem: a big dispute about whether or not we could show the promos because the bands objected to the fact that they didn't get paid. In the end we were only allowed to broadcast two each week, which meant for the rest of the half-hour my co-presenter Kelly Temple and I had to prattle on about the promos and what they would have looked like, if only the viewers had been able to see them – compelling stuff! Needless to say, the show completely bombed and was dropped after one series.

Everything has its purpose, however, and *The Biz* introduced me to producer Kate Marlowe. When she took over producing *Splash*, she brought me in as one of the presenters. *Splash* went out live at teatime on Fridays in the late eighties and was meant to be ITV's answer to *Blue Peter*, only with more street cred.

I'd taken over from Victoria Studd (who had a cut-glass accent) and Kate said they wanted someone a bit more real, someone the kids could relate to. Which was great because for some time I'd been trying to be more myself – I'd been picked up for dropping the odd aitch on *The Biz*. In those days there was a strong sense of responsibility about children's education and pronunciation. Heaven forbid, I should give them any of my bad habits! This was a time when presenters started talking more naturally and so I gradually abandoned the Penelope Keith impersonation.

*Splash* was made at the Teddington Studios, where there was a bar overlooking the river. The show was live so there would be a real adrenalin rush, and when it was over we'd go and get hammered. Happy days!

In those days I was a real girl-about-town, driving around in my brand new white convertible Golf GTI, with my long blonde hair and tiny skirts. I bought clothes at Emporio Armani, which had recently opened. They made them in extra-small sizes and it was a novelty to be able to get tailored garments that fitted. If you want a definition of yuppies, it was Darren and I: him in property (the buzz thing in the eighties), me in showbiz. When we were out, I even did the yuppie accent with a peculiar sibilant 's' that posh girls have.

We all used to speed in those days, it was normal, and I remember being stopped sailing through Regent's Park (where the speed limit is 20 m.p.h.) at about 40 m.p.h. and so oblivious, I didn't even notice when I overtook a police car. I soon realised my mistake when the blue flashing lights came on. If in doubt, keep on talking – it usually works for me.

'Oh, my God, I'm completely lost! I'm trying to get to Winchmore Hill. Am I near? I'm three hours late and I'm running out of petrol! I thought if I drove faster I'd get further on what's left in the tank. *Please* tell me I'm not far from Winchmore Hill!'

'Calm down, calm down!' the policeman was sweetly saying.

'But I'm *so* late, my boyfriend will be *really* cross! And I need petrol … Where is Winchmore Hill?'

'You're nowhere near it, I'm afraid.'

'Can you tell me which way to go?'

'Well now, Winchmore Hill from here, let's see …'

At first he started to give me some very complicated directions before saying, 'Just follow me.' That kind man got in his car and drove in front of me all the way. Thank God he liked blondes!

I met a really good, lifelong friend (Susan Lewis) at this time. A PA on *The Biz*, she then worked on *Splash* and she says when she met me she was dazzled by the hair, the clothes and the white car; she also thought, this is a girl I really need to know – she's going places. Susan had a flat in Chelsea and I'd end up there after the show. We'd crack open a bottle of wine and she'd tell me all about the characters in her novel and we'd sit up for hours dreaming up wonderful romantic heroes. Afterwards she'd sit at her word processor all night, writing it up.

Sue's first book, *A Class Apart*, has a character based on me: a TV presenter called Ella Marie – except I have never been to

Monte Carlo or sat on the lap of a rich man in a casino wearing no knickers! On the day of publication she and I went to Paris to see it on sale at the airport and took pictures of each other standing next to book displays.

In 1987 we filmed a Christmas Special for *Splash* out in Disneyland, Los Angeles. At the time I was 23, and I really felt this was as good as it gets. Flying to America to work, how cool is that? But when I got home, buoyed up by the fun of the trip, Mum told me that Grandad was in Guy's Hospital. Of course I went to see him straight away. He looked extremely small in the bed, very thin and yellow. How could he have changed so much in the three weeks since I'd seen him? He was really pleased to see me and I made sure my face didn't betray my fear.

'Do they know what's wrong with you, Grandad?' I asked.

'No, they've been doing tests, but they haven't told me anything,' he said.

So I did my usual and got a busy on. I found a nurse and I said: 'My grandad's been here for three weeks and nobody has told him what's going on. He's had lots of tests – they must know something.'

'They do know ...' she said, 'The doctor will be round in a minute.'

'Don't worry, Grandad – I'm back,' I told him. 'I'll sort it out. I'll see the doctor.' I was getting all puffed up and protective, the way I always feel about people I love: I want to make everything right for them.

The doctor called me away from the bed for a chat. 'We thought you knew,' she said, 'Your grandfather has a tumour and it's inoperable.'

All at once a wave of pain hit me, travelling from my toes to my head, then back down again – I'm amazed I stayed upright. But I dealt with that terrible news as I handled all the big things in my life in those days: I went into overdrive, talking as if I'd just been told Grandad had split ends, not terminal cancer.

'How long does he have?'

The doctor said it was hard to know: it was liver cancer and there was no treatment. I told her that I was going home to get the rest of my family together and asked if she could meet them all at 3 p.m. to break the news – I didn't feel strong enough to tell them. She agreed.

I told Mum the doctor wanted to see us, then I called Uncle Jim, but he said: 'Lisa, we *all* know – Nan knows, Alan and Shirley know. We just couldn't tell you or your mum because we didn't know how you would cope. We decided it's best not to let Grandad know.'

Typical of my family: they couldn't face telling Mum and me, so they didn't. What did they think would happen? How would we find out? It's a good example of how we operate: say the right thing for now and don't worry about the consequences.

So I told Mum and she broke down in tears. We held each other and cried together. We'd both had very different relationships with Grandad from the others: Mum had never left home so she'd been in the same house as Grandad for 46 years, and he had brought me up, which was unusual for a grandfather to do and gave us a special connection. Tears streamed down our faces but we resolved to be strong for his sake. Nothing more could be done and so he came home in a very weakened state. I arranged for Marie Curie nurses to come in and the whole family more or less moved into the house – they were all over the place, sleeping on chairs and sofas, all waiting for him to die. Grandad remained himself to the very end. One of the nurses, a big black woman with the loudest, jolliest laugh you ever heard, could talk for Britain – she never stopped.

'If this fucking thing doesn't get me, she'll jaw me to death!' said Grandad.

We had one last Christmas together, at Uncle Jim's house in Buckinghamshire. Jim picked him up in his Bentley and wrapped him in a new sheepskin coat that swamped him – he was so small. We took lots of pictures of us all with him, but to this day Mum and I have not been able to look at them. Darren was there that Christmas – I told him I needed him because I was scared about how I would cope when Grandad died. That summed up our relationship: I told him what I needed and he provided it without question or thought for himself.

I wasn't in the room when Grandad eventually passed away, but when the nurse asked me to get clean pyjamas and his false teeth I knew it must be the end. I remember thinking, I can't be there, I don't want to be scared watching Grandad die. I ran downstairs and said: 'She wants teeth and pyjamas!' Everybody jumped up, all panicking. In the end, Auntie Shirley, Uncle Alan and Auntie Lynn went up to be with him. I didn't want my last memory of him to be his death – I wanted to remember him with his white vest on, a roll-up in his mouth and on a beach at Torremolinos. That was my Grandad.

He'd never seemed very impressed by my career. He always used to say: 'So what's she doing? She can't be doing that well – she's never been on *Blankety Blank*!'

At the time he was dying, I'd recorded an appearance and it was to be shown the next week. When I realised the end was close, I said to him: 'Wherever you're going, you'd better make sure they've got a telly because I'm on *Blankety Blank* next week.'

He smiled.

Grandad was 76 when he died and still working as a messenger for a city firm. He had his own little box of an office where he sorted the post. When Nan and I went in to collect his bits and pieces we found the walls covered in pictures and newspaper and magazine stories about me.

'He was very proud of you,' his boss told me.

'But he always told me to get a proper job,' I protested.

'Oh Lisa, a day didn't go by without him talking about you! We all know everything you've done,' he smiled.

The day after Grandad died, I went back to work on *Splash* although they had told me to take time off – it worked for me to keep busy and not have too much time to think about it. In those days that was how I dealt with things. If you don't stand still, you don't have to face up to your grief. But if you're so scared of losing control, you never know true joy, true love or true anything else, although it's one way to avoid pain.

It was while I was working on *Splash* that Mum did me a great favour. One of the clients at the solicitors' firm where she worked was Malcolm Cook, manager of Alvin Stardust. Whenever he was in the office he would ask her how I was getting on (I don't think Mum was shy about coming forward and boasting). She told him I was doing a kids' show and he said to her: 'The problem with a kids' show, Val, is that nobody watches it *except* kids.

She needs to get herself a press agent – someone who will tell the world about her and make sure everyone knows when she's on. I know a chap called Clifford Elson. She should give him a call.'

So I rang Clifford, who at that time worked with Pat Lakesmith (they were huge in the business, legends). Clifford's nickname was 'The Godfather' and he was the publicist for loads of big stars, including Bob Hope when he was in Britain. I made an appointment, but I was sure I couldn't afford him. In fact I was so worried that I walked in and before he'd had a chance to speak I said: 'I don't really know what you do or what it costs but I'm only a kids' TV presenter.'

To the outside world, anyone who appears on the box is assumed to be making a fortune, but I wasn't earning a great deal at this time. And so I babbled away, and meanwhile Clifford just smiled and put a hand up to stop me.

'I don't normally take on unknowns,' he told me, 'but I see you as a bit of a challenge and we'll have a go.'

'But I haven't a lot of money. What will it cost?' I gasped.

He smiled benevolently again, then said: 'How does £25 a week sound? We'll start at that and we can review it when your career gets busier.'

God love him, he was so kind. I was spending that much on fags and tights – I could easily afford it. So there I was, with the most amazing press agent in Britain, for £25 a week.

It was the best investment I'd ever made and immediately started to pay dividends. The next week Clifford lined up press interviews for me, and from then on, almost every day. In those days coverage was not as salacious as it is now (it was all quite innocuous), but it got my name and my face in front of the public and other producers and directors, too. Would you believe it, my first magazine cover (unless you count *Photo-love*) was for *Amateur Gardening*? I was captured sniffing a rose at the Chelsea Flower Show. Even in these gentle interviews my old worries would surface: I would tell journalists my father had left us when I was just a few years old. It was ingrained in me that my birth was something shameful and I was still covering it up.

Clifford introduced me to the man who was to become my next agent and gave me a new career. I don't understand how he had the foresight to realise that a kids' TV presenter might be good on comedy sketch shows because as far as I know I showed no signs of being funny, but he felt this was the right direction for me. In 1986 I met Mike Hughes, an agent who represented all the mainstream comics of the eighties: Freddie Starr, Russ Abbot, Les Dennis and Dustin Gee. I went up to Liverpool to see him, which in itself was an achievement. Mike had a reputation for being the Wizard of Oz because everybody knew about him but nobody actually saw him: for years he represented some of his acts without ever meeting them face to face and everything was done over the phone.

I liked him straight away: he's a very charismatic man, positive and clear about what he wants. You had to do everything his way or he wouldn't represent you: it was his way or the highway. In a business where many try to run with the hare and the hounds, Mike was always straightforward: he'd never let you down. One of the first things he said to me was, 'I don't have many female clients – they all go off and have babies just when you start getting them really good jobs.'

This one sentence had a huge impact on my life and is probably why I put off having babies for as long as I did: it was career or family, not both. At that stage I cared more about my career than anything else. To be honest, I didn't have any maternal feelings and I wasn't interested in settling down and having kids so I can't lay the blame completely at Mike's door. As far as I was concerned, babies were bad news and only caused shame and heartbreak.

From the beginning of our relationship I had made it clear to Darren that I would never marry him or have a family with him. Bless him, he never asked or tried to push me in that direction. I must have been quite formidable: I knew what I wanted and what would make me happy, so I didn't have any qualms about letting others know, but I never led Darren on to believe we would spend the rest of our lives together. Anyway, Mike's words struck a chord and I felt it would be highly unprofessional to get pregnant in the middle of a series. I was a very blokey sort of girl at this stage – a 'ladette', they'd say nowadays – and I kept my feelings well buried, thanks to my childhood. I didn't even know them myself.

Anyway, Mike went on to say because Clifford Elson had spoken so highly of me, and prophesied I would do well, he was prepared to give things a go. 'If you do things my way you will be a big star,' he told me. From that day onwards for many years I never had to audition for a part; he started to place me in the right vehicles, and with his connections he could easily do so.

There was another major change in my life at this time. Working in property, Darren had heard about a new award-winning development, near Archway. He took me out to see it and I fell in love with the place. We walked into the show house and I wanted everything: not just the house but all the furnishings, too. The minute I said I wanted the house, Darren arranged to buy it: it was the early eighties and we paid £250,000 – a lot of money then, but we easily got a mortgage. The house cost £230,000 and the rest was for the show-home contents.

It was amazing, a private gated mews of converted Victorian warehouses and stables. There was exposed brickwork and metal reinforced steel joists on show; the bedrooms were downstairs and the living space upstairs. On the third floor you could get out onto a roof terrace with a conservatory. There was a balcony with intricate ironwork, the wood was stained green and there was a yellow stable door: it was the 1980s and this was the height of cool.

The other people who moved in were all as trendy as we thought we were. On one side our neighbours were the feminist broadcaster and writer Jill Tweedie and her journalist husband Alan Brien. On the other was a fashionable hairdresser and just along from us lived Sara Dallin from Bananarama. It was like media row and there were some amazing parties there.

This was my first proper home away from the family and I was so proud of it. Mum was bowled over. I hosted Nan's 75th birthday party there and hired caterers to take care of the food – it was a wonderful day.

Soon after we moved, Mike Hughes landed me a major breakthrough, a regular part in *The Les Dennis Laughter Show*. Les had been appearing in a double act with Dustin Gee – they were separate comics until Mike put them together. Tragically, Dustin died at the age of 43 from a massive heart attack, which happened while in panto with Les. I never met him, but everyone spoke of him highly as a naturally funny man. The BBC had decided to keep the format going as *The Les Dennis Laughter Show*.

To replace Dustin, the idea was to have a repertory company of young talent around Les so that he could still do his sketches and impressions. Two others were chosen: Martin P. Daniels (son of Paul Daniels) and Mark Walker (Roy Walker's son). Mike represented us all, so you can see how influential he was – I don't think Les had any say in the matter. This was a venture into the complete unknown, right outside my comfort zone: I'd never done anything like it. The only comedy I'd ever done was onstage and heavily scripted – I hadn't a clue what was expected. I kept on thinking, I hope they haven't made a mistake, I hope they know I don't do impressions. What if they expect me to be funny?

When you've been in comedy for a while you know where your funnies are, the things you do that really make people laugh. You can go to work and, even on a day when you're feeling low, turn it on like a tap. Apart from being the class clown at school, I had never thought of myself as funny.

I was nervous about meeting Les, who was so experienced, so good at his job – a million miles above me. And I knew if we were to work together it was really important we all got on well – I'd never met Mark or Martin before, either. I thought to myself, the most important thing I have to do is let Les Dennis know I'm not going to let him down and let him know he hasn't hired some talent-free zone. If he thought I was a good choice, I could probably deliver and I would learn on my feet, I felt. So it was in a state of high nervousness that I went to the BBC rehearsal rooms in North Acton, a famous place in the history of all TV drama and light entertainment. This was a purpose-built seven-floor building put up in the seventies with 18 large rehearsal rooms. Everyone who was making a BBC programme went there: in the canteen you would bump into every famous face you have ever seen on the box.

I remember once having Francesca Annis and Leo McKern at the next table to me and David Jason, Nicholas Lyndhurst, Ronnie Barker and lots of other big names in the same room. It was probably the closest you'd get in Britain to the old Hollywood studio system, where everybody working for the same company would be in the same environment. I spent a great deal of the next three years of my life there and there was a wonderful warm feeling when the receptionists and canteen ladies first recognised me and said my name: I felt I'd arrived. Sadly, the building doesn't exist any more – it was sold to Carphone Warehouse and eventually demolished not long ago.

Just around the corner in Wales Farm Road was the BBC costume department. This was another place where they got to know me well. It was a treasure trove: you could see the skimpy outfits worn by the dancers on *Top of the Pops* as well as all the stiff period costumes for the big-money dramas.

I'd been to North Acton studios before as a child actor but this was my first time as a grown-up. I found the rehearsal room allocated to the show. It was really difficult walking in – I always prided myself I could go in anywhere, that I never felt nervous, but this was something else. Between 30 and 40 people were sitting round a huge table and I hadn't a clue who they were, but they all knew each other. I was scared they would feel sorry for me if I ended up sitting on my own, so I said to myself: 'They won't want to know you until they know whether you're any good and you won't get to be good unless they give you the chance.' It felt like *Catch-22* and I had a deep conviction that I was going to fail.

The one thing sustaining me was that I knew Mike Hughes had confidence in me, although who knows why. 'She's bloody good and she'll do it!' is what he had told them: if he had the courage of his convictions, I had to live up to them. Oh well, I'll just jump in the deep end and see what happens. I can only sink or swim, and I'm going to try my best to swim, I thought. So long as someone I respect thinks I'm capable, I'll always do my best.

I was introduced to the sea of faces. Each of them seemed to be 'head of' something – head of this, head of that, head of carpets, head of hats, head of anything you can think of … Everybody who was anybody in production was there and they were all sizing me up. I knew they didn't know me. Even if they'd seen me on kids' television, which was unlikely, why would they think I could do comedy? I was bricking it and convinced they wanted me there just to provide some crumpet, a token dumb blonde to be the wife or girlfriend in a sketch.

Les was sweet: he came across and introduced himself, but I could see he was nervous, too. It was his first show without Dustin and he'd been landed with three sidekicks. Martin had been on a show called *Game For a Laugh* and I think Mark had done stand-up, so I was the unknown quantity.

I was used to drama, where you always saw a script before you got to rehearsals, but on a comedy sketch show they're writing down to the wire. All I knew in advance was there would be a sketch called 'The 29 Steps' (a spoof of the famous *39 Steps*), in which I would play Miss Fisher to Les's Richard Pranney. Written by Brian Leveson and Paul Minnet (a brilliant team best known for *My Family*), it would be like a mini-serial running through every episode of the show.

Before I got there I had decided to make Miss Fisher rather posh, with rolling r's and a bit of a lisp (she was first cousin to my *No Limits* persona, but more upmarket). At the read-through, I tried out her voice, and to my amazement people were laughing. Blimey, I've cracked it! That's that out of the way then – maybe I *can* do funny, I thought.

I wasn't needed for any of the other sketches in that first show. After the read-through, the writers and producer went away into a huddle, deciding what to chuck out and what to leave in. I went to the canteen with Mark and Martin, where we talked about Mike Hughes – I remember we were a bit competitive about who knew him best.

'How do you feel about doing an impression of Princess Di?' asked one of the producers after the meeting. They'd had this idea for a spoof of the *Blue Peter* bring and buy, with all the Royals getting rid of priceless oil paintings and jewels.

'Sure,' I said. I'd no idea whether I could do it, but I looked confident – I was doing AFF all over again.

'We'll get you a VHS of Diana. We'll be recording at the end of the week, so you've got two days until we rehearse it,' I was told.

They gave me the tape to take home and for the next two days I didn't move from the TV screen. I watched it over and over, studying every blink, every expression, every turn of the head, the way she pursed her lips and the shape of her mouth. It had to be perfect, and for two days I *was* Diana. If Darren asked me a question, he got Diana answering him. As soon as I started to master it, I didn't want to stop in case it didn't come back.

On the day of the rehearsal I drove to North Acton in character. I was looking at people at traffic lights, then casting my eyes down in that coy way she had. They must have thought I was coming on to them – either that or a madwoman.

When I got to North Acton I walked up to the reception with my eyes cast down, like someone with an eye problem. As I glanced up at the man on the desk, I could see the look on his face: he thought I was a bit touched. I didn't care – I was completely isolated in my Diana zone. Once I got to the rehearsal room I had to do it straight away, and thank God, they loved it. They were falling about laughing. Les was going, 'Oh, this is *brilliant*! Come here, come and see her doing Diana.'

The producer Mike Lego came back with the series producer, John Bishop, saying, 'Look at her Diana, it's hilarious!' People who'd been busy in other parts of the room all came to watch, too. I felt so clever, a genius: it was tremendous to be right outside my normal range but proving I could nail it, a real high. And I learnt something about myself: I was so scared to start off with, but I soon knuckled down and didn't let anyone put me off or take me out of the zone. This has served me well as an exercise for many years. Acting is often highly emotional and things going on around you can take you out of the emotion: in that rehearsal room I learnt not to allow myself to be distracted. What I really admire about impressionists is they can go into a character at the drop of a hat. I was never able to do that – even when I'd got the impression down, I could only do it for the sketch I was working on.

After the success of my Diana they gave me lots of videos to take home to learn other parts. I did Kylie (to Les's Jason Donovan), Julie Andrews and Janet Street-Porter (funny when you think she's famously tall and I'm tiny); I had a fantastic set of teeth, which I used again for Sally Thomsett in a spoof of *The Railway Children*. Even if I was unable to do a perfect impression, I would work out a catchphrase or a signature look and enlarge it a thousand times, chucking it in whatever I could to bring the audience back to who I was.

Les and I did our serial 'The 29 Steps', spending a lot of time handcuffed together. We were the main parts, but there was a wonderful cast around us, including the lovely Jeffrey Holland (Spike from *Hi-de-Hi!*). At Christmas we did a *Raiders of the Lost Ark* special. The budget was amazing. Altogether, I did four series of *The Les Dennis Laughter Show* and we went on location for three weeks at a time every year for filming.

The other two newcomers, Martin and Mark, had their own comedy stand-up spots, but it became more and more about Les and me doing sketches together. He was keen to make it a sketch show and it was a great advantage for me to have had an acting background. Soon the writers were providing material for Les and Lisa – although he was the big star, I was definitely his sidekick.

We became really good mates, going to the pub together after rehearsals and after the show; we have a similar sense of humour. Les has always got on better with women than men, though he and Darren hit it off. He is a sensitive, kind and brilliantly talented actor; also very intelligent and definitely not your typically pushy, boisterous showcasing comic. At the same time as I was doing *The Les Dennis Laughter Show* I did three series of *Russ Abbot's Madhouse* with Les and I was also in *The Joe Longthorne Show* (Joe was probably the funniest man I ever met and just as entertaining offstage).

Along with Bella Emberg, I was part of Russ Abbot's repertory of characters. We all went to Bournemouth to do a summer season, where Les and I shared a penthouse flat. We had the time of our lives, 10 weeks of partying – I was working hard, making good money and enjoying myself with good mates.

Les and I shared so much history that we almost developed a shorthand language. He could make me collapse in fits of laughter. One night in the pub, after rehearsing all day at North Acton, we were choosing something to eat.

''Ave chicken pie,' said Les in his Liverpudlian accent.

'Can you say that again in English?' I said and we collapsed into giggles. I look at the words written down and they're not at all funny but for us, at that moment, they provoked about 10 minutes of uncontrolled laughter. Recently, I saw Les at a charity do. 'Chicken pie,' he said and 20 years just stripped away – all our shared history was there. Nobody around us could see what was funny, but it broke us up.

It was while we were working together that Les's first marriage to lovely Lynne Heseltine (Les's real name is Heseltine) began to unravel, and I was there for him during a very difficult time. Years later, when he wrote his autobiography, he said about me: '[Lisa] is very funny, warm and extremely talented. Lisa and I only have to look at each other to end up in fits of giggles.' In the front of my copy he wrote a personal dedication: 'To my lovely leading lady who became a lovely star. You're the greatest. Love Les.'

Les stayed with Darren and me at our house when the shit hit the fan and the press were after him. We'd sneak out the back way from the rehearsal rooms and zoom off in a BBC car with blackened windows. I thought that bit was quite exciting, but then I wasn't on the receiving end and I know it was a hellish time for the couple. I knew Lynne, too, and their son Philip because they used to come down during filming – they'd hang out with Darren and me.

We didn't take sides, but we were naturally closest to Les when he needed friends. Being a gated development, our house was a good place to hide. Les stayed with us for a few months and then bought one of the houses, so we became neighbours. Around this time he started to see Sophie Aldred (Dr Who's assistant, Ace) and she became part of our gang. Back then it was a buzzing, fun place to live.

# CHAPTER 8

# The Lisa Maxwell Show

Parties in our gated development were legendary: I remember George Michael turning up on New Year's Eve 1989, and Anita Dobson, who was then at the height of her fame as Ange in *EastEnders*. We found ourselves surrounded by other successful young people. Darren was friendly with Jake and Angelo Panayiotou who owned Brown's nightclub, one of the coolest venues in London, and it was through Jake that we met Ginette and Errol Brown. Ginette's a very funny lady and she became a great friend of mine.

We were also friendly with man-about-town Dieter Abt. He threw amazing parties. One Christmas I found myself singing at a karaoke party with Simon and Yasmin Le Bon and Paul Young and Nick Rhodes. Dieter and I became close friends and I played hostess at one of the starriest dinner parties ever, thrown by him. Round the table were Joan Collins, Michael Winner, Jenny Seagrove, Ginette and Errol Brown, Michael Caine, Roger Moore and even Prince Andrew. More importantly Dieter also invited Denis Selinger, one of the most respected agents in the business. Denis represented Michael Caine and Ben Kingsley and was the man who discovered Peter Sellers.

Den loved comedians and we gelled so well that he always asked to sit next to me at dinner parties. One night after I told a joke with all the facial expressions, accents, bells and whistles, he kept dragging people across, saying: 'Lisa, tell that joke! You've got to hear her, she's the funniest woman ever!' He was always suggesting I move to his company: 'Oh, little one, I wish I could look after you!' he'd say.

It was a good time in my life although you could be right if you think it sounds shallow. At work I was dedicated, professional and prepared to put in long hours, but in my own time I was frivolous and up for fun. It was my old philosophy: if I work hard and play hard enough, I need never think about who I am. If I'm 'great fun Lisa', nobody will ask any questions.

I took no interest in the financial side of things: Mum had made sure I had everything I needed when I was growing up and I simply assumed life carried on in that way. Darren made it seem as if it did and so I left it all to him and never worried. To be honest, I didn't know what a mortgage was: Mum didn't buy a house until after Grandad died when she bought our council house so I hadn't grown up with any financial understanding.

I believed I existed in a more colourful, theatrical world, living out my dream, and I never wanted to be bothered by the practicalities. Worry about money, *me* – of course not! After all, wasn't I going to marry Prince Andrew? Meanwhile, Darren and I were still living the yuppie life. He had one of the first mobile phones, the size of a brick, and then a mate of Les's brought some phones into the studio and I paid £700 for one. I remember thinking, I'm doing really well – I can afford a mobile phone. Trouble was, only Les and me could ring each other: nobody else had them! Because I was doing so well I went to see Clifford Elson, who was still charging me £25 a week.

'I'm taking the mickey here, this is daft,' I said when I called him.

'Come in and we'll have a little chat,' he told me.

And so I did, and he said, 'I'm happy with things the way they are.'

'Well, I'm *not*,' I insisted.

'£35 a week any better for you?'

God love him, he wouldn't take another penny.

One of the hottest TV shows at the time was *Noel's Saturday Roadshow*, and thanks to the prominence I was getting on Les's show Noel Edmonds was keen for me to take part. I was appearing every week in *The Laughter Show* as a yuppie (Fiona Filofax) and doing a little monologue written by the brilliant Neil Shand. Fiona was a great success and Noel liked the idea of having her (or someone like her) in a regular slot as one of the people who 'worked' on the *Roadshow*.

I suggested a different character, the sort of overly enthusiastic person you sometimes meet working in television or radio: so thrilled to be part of it, they'd do it for nothing. And so I created Janice, secretary of the Roadshow Fan Club – a bouncy, slightly mad, overly happy woman with a real snort of a laugh, who went around giving signals to the audience to clap and cheer. I wore a short, dark wig and a joke pair of reindeer antlers to show how zany she was.

My agent Mike Hughes had by now moved to London and he and I became close friends. He had an office at The Prince of Wales Theatre, and while I was appearing in Russ Abbot's record-breaking 12-week run at The Palladium Mike would turn up afterwards and take me out to dinner at Quaglino's or Bibendum or one of the other trendy restaurants of the day. Apart from the fact that I liked him enormously, it was also very good for me: if your agent likes you, it counts for a lot. He'll think about you and put you in front of people. Talking to Mike always gave me a terrific insight into what was happening in the business. His marriage had broken up and his family was back in Liverpool, so I think he was happy to have a companion, too. He would take me to the RAC Club and spoil me rotten. It was how I dreamed show business should be: young actress being squired about town by her agent.

Back then you could go to high-profile places full of famous faces and there were rarely any paparazzi outside. Either the restaurants didn't tip them off or there wasn't the same insatiable demand for celebrity as now. Happy days!

My relationship with Mike was always platonic: we were good, reliable mates for each other. In some ways he was a father figure to me, yet he was also like a best girlfriend you can tell anything to. A multi-faceted person, he had more energy and zest for life than most people half his age. He was about 30 years older than me, but it never felt like an unbridgeable gap. We had a few holidays together, going to Hong Kong three or four times (Darren was busy working). I don't know whose idea it was to go there first, but we had such fun and it was there that I fell in love. Darren knew nothing about this, but it explains why Mike and I made so many trips: he was a real pal and he always kept my secret.

I'm really, genuinely, Not That Kinda Girl. In the circles in which I moved I could have had lots of affairs: there were always men who would like to do more than flirt with me. But I'm quite prudish, and when I look back I can count on one hand – well, *one* hand and a couple of fingers – the number of men I have slept with, which must be unusual nowadays. I was always wary of men: when you've had a mum who's been made unhappy all her life because of an affair, you don't forget it, and the whole sex and intimacy thing has to be put in a place that feels safe and secure before you even consider it. Above all else, I value love and respect: without them, there can be no sex.

Even my affair with my first, unsuitable boyfriend was based on him looking after me, adoring me and placing me on a pedestal. But I'm all in favour of women making their own choices and I don't expect anyone else to be the same as me: I don't look down on women who treat sex as a commodity or believe having a good time involves sex. And no, I don't feel superior because of my prudishness – I'm simply stating a fact, it's the way I am. Occasionally a man breaks through my self-protecting shell, and the guy in Hong Kong did just that. An ex-pat, he was living and working out there, and we met by chance in a hotel bar. Justin was blond and tanned, with great hair in a foppish cut. He had the preppy Californian look I love, but at the same time he was very British, ex-public school. He was wild, a real party boy. One night when everyone else had gone to bed we were partying so much I ended up crawling on all fours on top of the bar.

We fell madly in love. Mike and I would go out for dinner but I'd always be waiting to get back to Justin. When he finished working – which was often late – he would take us to the ex-pat bars. About 4 a.m., Mike would peel off and we'd go back to his flat. I was bonkers about him and I know he felt the same way, too. It would have been impossible for us to get together full-time – he had a girlfriend, I had a boyfriend – but I really fell for him. We managed to keep our affair going over five years (he even visited me in America). In all, we probably only saw each other eight or nine times but there were lots of long-distance calls. It was very passionate and the distance and difficulty of meeting made it all the stronger. We talked endlessly about being together properly, but deep down we both knew it wouldn't happen.

Mike enjoyed being part of my secret. I think he loved the fact that I was young, vivacious and energetic and he could keep up with me when we went out – he has the youngest spirit of anyone I've ever known. He and I made friends with a little guy who was on holiday out there. He was smaller than me (which takes some doing), bald with a shiny head that looked well scrubbed. Mike knew he was gay, but always teased me that he was my boyfriend. He kept saying things like, 'You've got hearts in your eyes for him.' In the end, the little man picked up on it and even thought we might become an item. I'd be planning to go somewhere with Mike and when I got down from my room he would be there – it was all part of Mike's evil sense of humour. In the end I had to make it very clear. Even today when I talk to Mike (who can stretch a joke to the moon on a piece of elastic), he'll say, 'So-and-so sends his love and he misses you.'

Years later I went back to Hong Kong with Paul: the colony was handed back to the Chinese in 1999 and we watched the ceremony from the top of the Mandarin Oriental. It proved to me that I'd got Justin out of my system: he wasn't there any more but the place was so entwined with the relationship that I was slightly concerned about going back, but I didn't even think about him at all.

Mike made sure I got good billing at the Palladium for *The Russ Abbot Show* over Christmas 1991 and my face was on the poster (because he also looked after the top turn, he had influence). He and Darren got on so well. Mike once said the part a partner plays is crucial: he wanted total control of his artists, and what got in the way in many cases was the person they went home to. Darren never got involved in my professional life except to be supportive.

I turned down the chance to join the cast of *Something for the Weekend*, another BBC sketch show that Shane Richie joined. He and I hadn't worked together but our paths crossed a lot on various panel shows. As we were the same age and both doing the TV comedy circuit, we got to know each other. At the time my management was keen for me to stop doing comedy rep and work on my own more.

I'd heard a rumour that Geoff Miles, the producer on *The Les Dennis Laughter Show*, told the head of light entertainment at the BBC: 'There's one series I want to do next year, *The Lisa Maxwell Show*. If I can't do it here, I'll do it elsewhere.' The production team on Les's show were all talking about it, even discussing titles: *The Max Factor* was one, *Maxwell House* another. I was excited when Mike called me to his office and expected him to say I'd got my own series. Instead he said: 'The BBC want you to do a show but I think it should be a two-hander. You should work with someone else – Mark Walker would be good.'

Looking back, I can see the brilliant Mike was trying to protect me. He was not keen on me taking the full weight of a show on my shoulders: he was simply covering my arse. If I did the all-singing, all-dancing, full-on *Lisa Maxwell Show* and it flopped that would mean Lisa Maxwell flopped and you don't get a second chance when you've been shouting from the rooftops to that degree – there's no one else to blame. Mike wanted to take the pressure off me in case it all went pear-shaped, but my ego had landed: I was getting used to the idea of my own show and I was suspicious he was trying to promote Mark through me (in the same way he had promoted me through Les). I just wanted to say, 'I've got my own show.' But I learnt a huge lesson: it's not about saying something or having the moment for the moment's sake, you have to think it through.

Up until then, my career had all been AFF: I jumped into projects and everything worked out. All Mike wanted was to give me the toggle for the parachute to open, but in my arrogance I chose to ignore it. As it turned out, I didn't have to reject Mark Walker myself – the production team said they wanted it to be just me. As far as Mike and me were concerned, the damage was done, though. People were saying, 'Your manager is letting you down – he's made the wrong decision.'

So the show was commissioned in 1990 when I was just 27 and simply titled, *The Lisa Maxwell Show*. It was six half-hour comedy slots: I was very excited and happy with the team I had around me. I remember meeting Lenny Henry in the foyer at BBC Television Centre when we were both waiting for cars. When he asked what I was doing next and I told him I had a sketch show lined up, admitting, 'I haven't a bloody clue what I'm doing!' he gave me some good advice: 'Keep a Dictaphone with you at all times. Anything you think of, put it on the Dictaphone. The fact that it comes from you, starts with you, will make it better.'

Afterwards I did as he suggested and at my first meeting with the writers I had come up with all sorts of ideas. I think Lenny was right – for me it felt the most organic and truthful of all the material. The script editors, Paul Alexander and Gavin Osbon, were amazing: they virtually wrote the whole series. There was a terrific buzz and people were saying things like, 'You're going to be the next big thing, you're going to be huge!' Although I was nervous, it was hard not to catch the infectious confidence that we were on to something good.

I loved making the show; I did my own musical numbers and the sets were incredible. Money was spent on everything we needed: for one sketch we built an entire street scene so that I could do an impression of Madonna in the Dick Tracey film – we even had a Rolls Royce on set. The budget for my wigs alone was £20,000: it was the sort of cash unheard of in television today.

We did five days of rehearsals and then recorded it in front of an audience. I did my own warm-up, putting together 10 minutes of original material; I felt it was important to let the audience know who I am. It's different when you're Russ Abbot and already well known. I wanted the audience on my side. This was a completely new experience for me because I had never done stand-up.

We had a launch at the Groucho, where I was introduced as 'the most talented girl ever' and the 'next big comedy thing'. I didn't want to stay and watch the show with the journalists – I'd seen bits of it, but never all the way through. Somehow I knew it wasn't as good as we were all saying it was. Press launches are strange: you have to be very positive about the product, which is awful when you know the opposite is true. You can't say, 'I'm not coming because I've seen it and frankly it's shit,' although I expect most of us in the industry have wanted to do so on the odd occasion.

The series went out on Thursdays at 8.30 p.m. on BBC1, a fantastic slot. Nowadays they 'warm up' a new comedy show by putting it on BBC4, then transfer to BBC2, but I was doing AFF again, straight into a prime-time slot. With a sketch show it's all about the edit: you have to come out of the sketch at the right time, otherwise you'll find yourself exposed, feeling like you're crawling naked to the end of it in the hope that no one's noticed – it's a horrible feeling to see that make it to the screen. Because the writers and producers thought I was a good actress, they wanted to create three-dimensional characters; they were trying to do what Catherine Tate does now. In that way the show was ahead of its time, but it just wasn't good enough. At least there were some good parts, but it was inconsistent. The biggest problem was that I was much too young: I'd only been doing comedy for three years and I needed a longer apprenticeship.

On the first night it went out I was doing summer season in Bournemouth with *The Russ Abbot Madhouse*. I was dashing in and out of the dressing room, trying to see it. The reaction from people on the show was interesting: nobody went overboard. Les said it felt strange, seeing me working with another man. Convinced it was my moment to move on, to be my own person, I felt quite hurt. They were all being gently honest, but I think I wanted to be heaped with praise.

I never understood the decision about the running order of the shows as the second and third episodes were definitely much better than the first: if we'd launched with one of them we might have created a bigger buzz. In one sketch I was a Jerry Hall type of rich celebrity wife and then I did a ballet with Wayne Sleep and another where Victor Spinetti tried to help me play Shakespeare. The figures were very good: we had 7 million viewers. Nowadays, with so many competing channels, this would be an amazing figure. The reviewers praised my talent but said the show was just not funny enough.

The one person who was right, whose judgement I really should have trusted, was Mike Hughes. Although the series was not an out-and-out flop, I'm the sort of person who beats myself up about everything I do and I'm always convinced I could have done better (on *Loose Women* I come off set thinking, I wish I'd said that). If only I'd listened to Mike and shared the responsibility, I might have had another opportunity, or at least I would have been less associated with the series.

I don't think of it as a failure because it wasn't, at least not for the BBC. But when you are the artist holding a show in your own name, you get one chance, and although the series wasn't bad it simply wasn't good enough, so the BBC did not pick up the option for another. It was a time when light entertainment was going through a seismic shift: *The Little and Large Show* on Saturday nights had been axed and we already had *Not the Nine O'Clock News*. New Oxbridge satirists were coming in, and a lot of the old guard were considered nothing more than end-of-the-pier comics. As happens, a lot of good things were swept away for the sake of change.

I always felt I would have fitted into the comedy mould more, had I looked stranger. To me, it seemed all my characters had to be unattractive in order to be funny or to connect with the audience. I remember Russ once saying to me, 'Why do you pull all these funny faces? You spoil yourself.' But in those days I believed that for the women in the audience to laugh, too, I must not be seen as a threat or someone their blokes might fancy. Thankfully, everything is so different now.

It seemed to me that America wasn't the same. My absolute heroine was Goldie Hawn: cute, charming, beautiful, hilariously funny and a formidable businesswoman, too. And so my move to the States, my next and biggest break, seemed a good choice and the right home for me. It happened because Mike Hughes was working with another personal manager, Freya Miller. For many years she had handled Shakin' Stevens, and her aim was to break British acts in the US.

I was working at the Palladium at the time. When *The Lisa Maxwell Show* was not optioned for another series, I never had a sense of 'Will I ever work again?' because my old work with Russ and Les was still there, but Mike wanted me to move on. Again, he was clever enough to see the writing on the wall for our kind of mainstream comedy. He introduced me to Freya, an extremely strong and direct woman. Immediately I felt confidence in her because for Mike to agree to share representation meant he valued her highly and she'd been out in the States for a few years. I can't remember any of her other clients except for a wrestler called Rowdy Roddy. Shakin' Stevens, Rowdy Roddy and now Lisa Maxwell … what more can I say?

Despite her inauspicious client list, Freya was a force to be reckoned with. At our first meeting she said: 'Just come out to

LA for two to three weeks – I'll fix up some meetings.' And so I did: it was my third trip to the USA because my mate Lisa Haddigan and I had been on holiday to Disneyland California three or four years before and I'd travelled to Florida with *Splash*, although this was hardly a complete introduction.

When I was there with Lisa we stayed with two friends of hers: a couple called Bob and John. John was a dancer, Bob was a costume designer and Lisa knew them through friends of friends in the industry. They lived in a lovely bungalow complete with a pool and a beautiful garden in Burbank, the heart of the film world and the Hollywood Dream. When I went back I stayed with them again. I didn't want to stay with Freya – I found her quite scary and it was enough to face working with her. The only other choice was a hotel, where I would have been very lonely. Bob and John were wonderful: they treated me like their little girl, spoiled me rotten and eventually saved my sanity … but we'll come to that later.

In those days the BBC had a God-like reputation in the world of broadcasting, and to have had my own series opened doors. The first thing Freya did was to introduce me to a hungry young agent called Michael Foreman. He had enormous energy and, especially important in Hollywood, great tenacity. Michael set up meetings for me with the vice presidents of some of the biggest companies: Lorimar, Castle Rock, 20th Century Fox and ABC Network – I met so many people, my head was whirling. Among them was Helen Mosler, vice president of casting at Paramount.

I'm good at walking into a room full of people and giving the old spiel and there was nothing to lose: after all, none of these people knew me. Soon I realised that all they had to go on was a showreel of *The Lisa Maxwell Show* and anything I chose to tell them about myself, so I made sure I looked good, with my Emporio Armani suits and Naf Naf dresses, my tan, full hair and make-up – I'd learnt how to do a good job from the artists I'd worked with before in television.

Soon I discovered that in America they always want you to be 'the next' someone: I was the 'next' Tracey Ullman, the British comedienne who had a massive show under her own name in the States and launched *The Simpsons* as a segment of it. Around Hollywood I was introduced in various offices as 'the new Tracey Ullman – but prettier' – their words, not mine. In the US, it seemed, it was an asset to be pretty and I had to learn to stop pulling the funny faces Russ had already commented on.

For my first three or four meetings I talked about myself, but it's frustrating, just banging on – I'm British, we don't do bigging ourselves up. Besides I was always happier in character than being myself. So, for my next meeting, with Helen Mosler, I decided to handle it differently and pitch as if I'd written a comedy series about a girl like me.

I came up with the outline: I was a Cockney kid from the Elephant and Castle who had won a free flight to LA through buying a vacuum cleaner (this at a time when Hoover were giving away free flights to anyone who spent more than £100 – it caused a huge scandal because everyone was rushing out to buy Hoovers just for the sake of flights). So the girl flies to Los Angeles and sets about trying to be 'discovered'. Like Lana Turner, she sits in a soda bar and then tries being Vivien Leigh. My idea was it would be a mock documentary with me impersonating all these big Hollywood names.

'Right, this is a great idea but I'm not the person you should be talking to,' said Helen, after I'd pitched it to her.

'Who should I be talking to?' I asked.

She looked slightly taken aback, but I could see her thinking, why not tell her? So she told me I had to see Dan Fasse, the head of comedy at Paramount.

'Great, so when can I see him?' I persisted.

I could see this high-powered Hollywood woman was looking more than a little bemused by the pushy Brit kid, but she was also intrigued enough to pick up the phone and set up a meeting.

'He'll see you on Thursday, 11 a.m.,' she told me.

I didn't realise this was anything special until I told Michael Foreman. 'My God, I've been trying to see that guy since forever!' he said. 'How did you do it?'

This time Michael came to the meeting with me.

'Do we have a treatment?' he asked, before we went in.

'No, I just made it up,' I answered, truthfully.

Dan Fasse had a woman with him at the meeting (a head of something else at Paramount), but I didn't take this in. I did my schtick again, and at the end he leapt up and shouted, '*Great*! Right, what are we waiting for? Let's *do* it!'

I don't think I've ever been to a meeting where everyone was so positive. Secretly, there was a voice inside me, saying, 'Do *what*? I haven't a script or anything,' but I was also thinking, don't worry: we'll deal with that later.

'We'll be in touch – and I *mean* that, we really *will* be in touch,' said Dan as we left. Meanwhile, Michael was so excited that he could hardly keep still: 'In all my years in the business,

I've never felt such energy in a meeting!' he told me. To be fair, he was only young and so he can't have been that long in the business. However, the very next day he received a holding offer from Paramount. A holding offer is when they put a sum of money on the table in return for you not going anywhere else. Of course as soon as they made an offer Michael used this as a lever to see other people and everything started to go crazy. Hollywood is an extremely paranoid and insecure place: they think if someone else wants you they may be missing out. I was blagging my way through the meetings and there was a sense of great satisfaction that it was me who was making it all happen.

Castle Rock told us they had just done a deal with the British actress Morwenna Banks (who later did sketch show comedy with Harry Enfield and Paul Whitehouse), or they would have signed me. They said they wished they'd seen me 10 days earlier but felt they couldn't sign two of us doing similar things. Meanwhile, Fox and Lorimar both came in with a bid.

John and Bob couldn't believe it; I was a stranger to the Hollywood machine but they knew it inside out and they'd never known anything like this. They had had other aspiring youngsters staying with them but the reaction from the studios was unique.

I phoned Mum and Darren and both were thrilled although, like me, they didn't realise how special it was – they thought it was what happened to talented people in Hollywood. Then I spoke to Mike Hughes, but he was not as enthusiastic as I would have expected. We were drifting apart: I had been his baby and I think he felt I was growing up and away from him. America was not his patch and he had handed me over.

With three deals on the table, we had to make a decision. Michael Foreman told Paramount about the other two offers and they remained passionate about signing me. It was their commitment and interest that swung things their way, so we went in and I signed to them.

I signed to Paramount! You know, I can still hardly believe it as I write this: Lisa Maxwell, a kid from the Elephant and Castle, 'Father Unknown', signed to one of the biggest Hollywood studios.

# CHAPTER 9

## Life in LA

I had only spent 10 days in America and I'd signed to Paramount for a year. What's more, they lined a job up for me straight away, a TV drama. Sadly, I didn't have the right paperwork – I was there on a holiday visa so I wasn't allowed to work. The studio wanted to fly me out to Mexico to sort out my visa and bring me back in, but even then it would have held up production for too long so I flew home on my economy ticket. From then on it was Virgin Upper Class all the way as part of my deal. Flying home, I was still little Lise, quietly hugging my amazing success to myself among the holidaymakers with their Disney souvenirs.

By the time I was back, the fax machine at our house was chattering out documents, all with the impressive Paramount heading. Everyone I told was over the moon, telling me it was an incredible opportunity. At the back of my mind was the stark reality: I will be leaving everyone who loves me, moving to a place where I know nobody. As usual I was adept at living in the moment and pushing the big thoughts out of the way, though.

Darren was as excited as I was and looking forward to coming out to see me; he himself wanted to get back into the industry and had a script to get off the ground.

Because the break had come so easily, I didn't appreciate it – I had no idea what it meant. In fact the stakes were high and I was playing a massive, powerful game I knew nothing about, which could make or break me, professionally and psychologically. Other pros who had worked for years for such a break knew how important it was; for me, this was just my next step up the ladder, and I had taken it with ease. Why wouldn't it continue to work out?

I didn't fly back to Hollywood straight away: it was six months before everything was sorted out. In the meantime I was in demand for work here and busier than ever. *This Morning with Richard & Judy* was *the* daytime show, and they booked me to appear in regular segments called *Pardon My French*, which were filmed in France (I was teamed with Philip Franks, who had played the love interest of Catherine Zeta-Jones in *The Darling Buds of May*). The idea was that we learnt, and taught the viewers, basic French. Philip, who was considerably more intellectual than me (not hard!), could already speak French, but all I could remember from my classes at Italia Conti was '*Madame Souris a une maison*', which means, 'Mrs Mouse has a house'. Altogether, we spent 10 days in France, with me blagging my way through and having a really good laugh. Philip was very different to me but we shared a camp sense of humour. The series was a success, with a successful book and a video, so straight away we were sent off to Spain to do *Pardon My Spanish*.

I also made two pilots for Noel Gay Television, a hot company owned by Charles and Alex Armitage. I'd met Charles before when auditioning for *Me and My Girl* in the West End but they gave the part to Jessica Martin, who had been working with Bobby Davro and doing the same kind of sketches as I was doing with Russ and Les. Charles was a very knowledgeable man, whose company I enjoyed, and who later met up with me out in LA. A good friend of the horror writer Stephen King, he wore shirts designed for him by his friend in bold prints.

When they rang Mike Hughes to say I hadn't got *Me and My Girl*, they said: 'We think Lisa looks too young, but tell her to come back in a year.' 'Well, I hope she's not going to bloody age that much in a year!' said Mike and put the phone down. If ever there was a part I would have loved to do, this was it.

The first pilot I made was a comedy drama, *Once in a Lifetime*, with Pam Ferris, Maria McErlane and Kate Robbins. Carlton had just acquired their franchise and commissioned six pilots, which they broadcast and then awarded a series to the one with the best viewing figures (*The Brighton Belles* won). In our pilot I played a Yorkshire Goth, with black eye shadow, dark clothes, the lot … The other pilot was for a game show made in a studio in Norfolk. I was the all-singing, all-dancing host, very glamorous, wearing red tights and black leather hot pants. The game was to work out the real person doing a real job. The format didn't work here, but I think it was picked up abroad and did well. On both these pilots the director was Sylvia Boden, and years later she was a producer on *The Bill*. I loved the fact that I was never pigeonholed by comedy: here I was doing straight drama and also being a full-on game-show host.

I did two really fun jobs before going back to the States. One was *Gibberish*, the very last show that Kenny Everett made (tragically, he was already ill from an AIDS-related condition and died three years later). An improvisation show a bit like *Whose Line Is It Anyway?*, it went out every morning, five days a week, and you really had to think on your feet. I worked with a team of actors Kenny had gathered around him, including Danny Baker, Lesley Joseph, Keith Barron, Jan Ravens, Carol Vorderman, Derek Griffiths and Lynda Bellingham, who now shares the *Loose Women* table with me (it was the first time we'd ever worked together).

Kenny was lovely: I was in the throes of passion for Justin in Hong Kong and ran up a big phone bill from the production hotel. At the end of the shoot I was presented with a massive bill, but when Kenny heard about it he somehow waved his magic wand and made it disappear (he loved a bit of gossip and had enjoyed the details of my affair). He was a very sweet man and his early death robbed us of an enormous talent.

The other job was a real career highlight: the chance to work with Rik Mayall and Ade Edmondson on their massive cult hit series, *Bottom* (I was in the very last episode of the last series). Apparently Rik wanted to work with me so they sent the script to Mike Hughes.

'Do you think they know who you are?' he asked.

'If they've asked for me, they must know who I am,' I insisted.

'You have a look,' he said, handing me the script.

'Is Patricia Routledge not available?' I asked, after reading it.

The part was a woman called Lily Linacre, who was in her mid-50s and ran a dating agency, Lily Linacre's Love Bureau, to which Rik and Ade turned in their desperate quest for female company. There were some great lines but my instinct was to say I couldn't do it: this was a sitcom, not a sketch show, and I was a 27-year-old, size 6 blonde being asked to play a middle-aged woman. I genuinely thought they might have made a mistake: I knew Bella Emberg had been asked to audition for a Bond movie and when she got there they realised the actress they wanted was *Kelly* Emberg, so mistakes can happen.

The fact they insisted it was me they wanted made me accept the role, but there was still a part of me that wanted to see their faces on the day I turned up for rehearsals and they realised I wasn't the actress they had in mind. They gave no clue on the script about how I should play Lily – all I knew was her age and her job – and so I decided to make her a Northerner, someone who thought she was a little bit better than she was, the sort of woman who would have her colours done and 'knew' she had to wear mauves and heathers. I wanted her hair to be hot-brushed (all the thing then), but not brushed out so the big rolls of the brush showed; I was sure she would have a hot brush in her desk drawer and would wear one of those watches where you could change the colour of the dial. She would be plump with a large bosom that caused her shoulders to round, and I developed a way of carrying myself, with my elbows under my boobs to push them out.

When I went into this stance at rehearsals I must have looked odd because I had no padding or make-up. I was praying for the costume and wig to be ready (I knew the costume people well and they were following my specifications). I chose a nice maroon suit for Lily and a silky blouse with a tie at the neck to hide any crepiness. All the while, I was walking around with this strange physicality that I need to get in character – I'm border-line obsessive about details and I can't bear it when wigs and costumes are not right. I'm seriously anal: sometimes on *Loose*

*Women* we all have to wear terrible nylon wigs for budgetary reasons, and I hate it!

In those days, money was no problem – we could have anything we needed in terms of costumes, prosthetics and complete body suits. I worked with an amazing make-up artist called Jan Sewell, who did the prosthetics for French and Saunders and once made a Robert Maxwell bodysuit for Les which was so good it could have been anybody inside it: make-up and costumes can make or ruin a performance.

Rik and Ade never once made me feel I was badly cast, even though they must have wondered what I was doing until they saw me in full rig. Before we started recording, Rik told me how nervous he always was – he said this, I'm sure, to put me at ease. Lily had some of the best lines in the show. The boys had wanted to meet Michelle Pfeiffer, but as she wasn't on Lily's books she introduced them to Lady Oblomov Boblomov Dob from Moldavia, played by Helen Lederer. It was a very funny episode.

There's a school of thought that it's never good to resort to farting or toilet jokes, but *Bottom* was this all the way through. The audience fell apart when a huge farting sound was heard just a couple of minutes into the episode. *Bottom* was a huge hit, especially with younger people, and because a lot of the humour was visual it sold well around the world. I had no idea at the time, but one day Lily Linacre would come to my rescue.

At the back of everything I did was the knowledge that I had the American deal and it was well known in the industry: Clifford Elson made sure it was big news. He even arranged a magazine shoot where I was dressed as Uncle Sam with star-spangled banners behind me. There was a feeling of 'Watch this space, this is the beginning of something interesting'. Saying this now feels ridiculous, but I really thought I was going to be a big star in the US. I was sucked in by how much it had all fallen into place without too much effort on my part, and I felt this was the pattern. Back in Britain I kept in touch with Michael Foreman, my agent out there. I asked how the idea I'd pitched was being developed, but he said nothing had happened.

'Do they still want me to do it?' I persisted.

'Lisa, they've got lots of other ideas for you – there are writers and producers making pilots all the time and they're really interested in getting you involved. Don't worry,' he told me.

Michael then said he had parted company with the agency he worked for and was working independently. He still wanted to represent me, and because I liked him and felt comfortable with him I agreed. I had the good sense to ring Denis Selinger, though: 'I have a problem – I have an agent, but he's no longer attached to an agency,' I said.

Denis again told me to come over to his company. I was still with Mike Hughes in England but the American deal really had been the final nail in the coffin. I was proud of myself for going out there on my own but I suspect that was part of the problem for Mike: he liked to be in control of his clients. He was so downbeat when I spoke to him that I remember thinking, don't take this away from me, Mike – I worked hard out there and I've got this fantastic opportunity. And so before I left for the States we decided, amicably, to call it a day. Afterwards I spoke to Denis and agreed to move to ICM, one of the biggest players in the industry (Denis had sold his own company to ICM, but was still a director with enormous clout).

So I said goodbye to Darren and Mum in 1993 without too many qualms. I was much too excited to feel sad, but I kept on telling them to come out and see me. I knew Mum wouldn't because she is scared of flying and Nan was getting old, so I didn't think she would make it either. Then I was picked up by the Virgin limo service and whisked off to the airport. On the flight I chatted with Stephanie Beacham, who was very hot at the time after her role as Sable in *Dynasty* – it all felt like part of my new life.

The deal from Paramount was for a year's contract with an advance of $80,000 (£52,000), a red Ford Mustang fleet convertible and the services of a top immigration lawyer in the States to sort out my visa. After a few weeks my agent found me an apartment in Studio City, North Hollywood, but at first I moved back in with Bob and John.

The first few weeks were full of meetings set up for me by Dan Fasse and Helen Mosler. As a new signing, I had to meet every director and writer on the Paramount lot, an amazing place: there were painted chalets dotted about, all very quaint, housing the high-powered offices. The first time I was impressed by the huge front gates, and after a while it became as familiar as going to East Street market.

I had a meeting with Sylvia Gold, head of television at ICM, set up for me by Denis. Sylvia was an amazing woman: a dynamic Jewish New Yorker, about 4'1" tall, with hair piled up on top of her head – very high maintenance. She looked like Dr Ruth and was extremely open and direct.

'I'm seeing you because of Denis – I'm very fond of Denis and he tells me good things about you. I'm looking at you, I know nothing about you: tell me about yourself,' she told me (imagine this in a nasal Brooklyn twang).

So I went into my spiel and then she surprised me: 'Denis tells me you're great, so I'll tell you what I will do. I love your shoes. You give me those shoes and we have a deal!' So we swapped shoes. We were both small and so they fitted. Mine were a pair of flesh-coloured ballet pumps with white spots in suede. They came from Maud Frizon (a shop in Bond Street that isn't there any more) and looked French, chic – they worked well with my tan. Sylvia was a woman who wore high heels, so I tottered out on a pair of life-threatening pink stilettos with a new agent and a new pair of shoes. Bizarre!

After that I parted company with Michael Foreman – sadly on both sides, although he understood. Michael had been so good on my first trip, like a Rottweiler on my behalf: he followed everything up with phone calls and kept on pushing. I don't know where he is now, but I hope he's happy and successful because he deserves to be. 'Lisa, you've got a fantastic opportunity, you need to be with a big agency,' he told me.

It was Sylvia Gold who contacted me about the role that could have changed my whole life. Every actor can tell you a similar story, but mine is for real: handled differently, I could now be a multi-millionaire, living in a huge pad in the Hollywood Hills. But you know what? I'm glad it went pear-shaped because if I'd stayed in America my personal life would never have turned out as happily as it has done and I'd never have persuaded Mum and Nan to move out there.

So, what was it, my huge, missed opportunity? Sylvia told me the studio planned a pilot for a spin-off from *Cheers* (to be called *Frasier*) and they had a role for me. Freya was now working with Sylvia and she told me the part of a girl called Daphne Moon had been written into the scripts just for me and they had made her English (she was to be the housekeeper for Frasier's father). Helen Mosler herself rang to say they really wanted me for the role. Freya faxed over what the Americans call 'the sides' – pages from the script. They covered the story of how Daphne first meets Frasier. I read them and saw that she was supposed to come from Manchester, so I rang Freya.

'Yeah, yeah, yeah,' she said, 'they've no idea where you're from. Manchester, schmanchester … It's *you* they want, so don't worry!'

I can do a Manchester accent but it seemed to me if it made no difference it might be better if I played it as a Londoner. So I looked at the script and in my usual way did a bit of work on it: in England I was used to putting my own stamp on things. The scene they wanted me to look at involved Daphne going for the job interview. She rings the bell and Frasier answers the door and catches her straightening her bra strap: 'Oh, you caught me with my hand in the biscuit tin!' she says.

I didn't get the joke but it was no big deal – I just thought if they wanted it to sound authentic (and I'd learnt that the value of truth is comedy), there had to be a better line and I really thought they would want my opinion. So I went along to the meeting and, as usual, a group of execs was sitting on leather sofas and chairs around a table. I'd met them all previously on various meets and greets after I'd signed the contract and it felt to me exactly like going into a script meeting for *The Les Dennis Show* – I thought I was there to play the part and to help them get the script right. They asked if I had any questions.

'Yes, two,' I said. 'Is the character from Manchester? Only I'm a Londoner. I can do a Manchester accent if you like, but it might sound more comfortable if I do it in my own accent.'

'Sure,' they said, 'do it however you want. Is there anything else?'

'Yes, it's about the first line Daphne has, "You caught me with my hand in the biscuit tin" – I don't really understand what that means.'

'Would you prefer to say "cookie"?' one of them asked. 'Only we thought "biscuit" would sound more English.'

'I'm really not bothered whether it's "cookie" or "biscuit", I said. 'That's not what confuses me. I just don't know if it's a funny thing to say – I don't get it. Maybe it's me, but it doesn't seem funny …'

'Try "biscuit", said one of them. The whole thing degenerated into a discussion about 'cookie' and 'biscuit', which wasn't what I was trying to get at. So I read the part for them and then left. I still thought I'd been contributing to a script meeting, which was no big deal for me – I assumed they would go away and get the tricky joke better. But I was completely oblivious to how big the moment was: I'd had no hardship in my career and I just assumed everything flowed naturally.

'You didn't get the part,' said Sylvia the next morning.

'*What* part? I didn't go up for a part!' I said.

'Yes, you did – you auditioned for *Frasier*. And actually they gave it to the girl who came in after you because she didn't assassinate the script.'

'But I didn't know it was an audition. Everyone suggested I had the part. Now you're telling me this was an audition.'

'Honey, *everything* you do in this town is an audition. *Everybody* auditions, *everybody*!'

I was devastated. It could so easily have been mine, had the information I'd been given been better. I'd never walk into an audition trying to change things – I genuinely believed it was a done deal, that I was part of the team. I never cried over losing a job before, but I cried over that one.

Jane Leeves was a former Hill's Angel, but I don't think she appeared in either of the episodes I was in. She has made a fortune out of the role of Daphne because the success of *Frasier* meant the regular actors landed incredible deals. It was a huge lesson for me, shaking my belief that amazing things would happen for me in LA – I couldn't work out why they were auditioning others for the part if it had been created for me. It made things more difficult with Paramount, but they kept trying to find things for me. There were conversations about a series as a nanny but that was soon ruled out because Fanny Drescher was already doing one.

'Do you still have chimney sweeps in England?' asked a studio creative. 'Could you be a little chimney sweep?'

Tim O'Donnell, the guy who created the *Uncle Buck* series, was brought in to come up with a sitcom based on me being one of 'God's Little Helpers', an angel who comes down to Los Angeles in various guises to infiltrate society and spread goodness and happiness because, as one of the producers said, 'LA is hell on earth!' They all thought it was very funny – I was rapidly beginning to see what he meant. We made four pilots for the series, but it was not taken up.

Although they could not find a suitable slot, Paramount were reluctant to let me go and twice renewed my contract, so in the end I stayed out there for nearly three years. It was part of the studio paranoia: they were worried that if they let me go another studio would find the perfect vehicle.

The shine had begun to come off my stay in LA and I was increasingly homesick. At first I wrote to Mum every single day, a diary of what I was up to, and posted it to her at the end of each week. In the beginning my letters were full of the excitement of my new life, but after a few months I found myself forced to sound happy, fun, amazing. I used to go to the cinema a lot – there was a buzz about seeing all the hot films weeks before they hit Britain – and at least it gave me something to write about.

The place my agent had found for me was a two-bedroom apartment with a communal swimming pool and underground parking. There were security gates for the block and a gym in the basement. I think the studios used it for their people – I noticed some of the other residents sitting round the pool, reading scripts. The apartment was unfurnished but in America you can rent anything, even your furniture. I rented my fridge and washing machine but I also had some furniture given to me by Bob and John. I loved the new Californian vogue for white furniture – it didn't exist in England when I left – so I had cream curtains, cream sofas and the chairs were rattan. I think I chose furniture most people put in their gardens.

The apartment was open-plan with stools, which John and Bob got me from the IKEA at Burbank, around a bar separating the kitchen from the living area. Although my agent found the flat for me, I paid the rent myself. The studio didn't provide a support system and thank goodness I had Bob and John – I don't know how I would have survived without them. They gave me a *Thomas Guide* (the LA version of an *A to Z*) and so I drove to all my meetings. More importantly, they introduced me to another friend of theirs, Ron Siegel. Ron did studio liaison at a fashion store in Sherman Oaks in the San Fernando Valley and Bob used to get clothes for the actors at Warner Brothers from him.

Ron, who came from Philadelphia, became a great mate. He had a fabulous East Coast sense of humour and it always lifted me to spend time with him. His nickname for me was Lilian La Flunkin'. Together with Bob and John, these three were my support system. Ron loved socialising and I was a good mate to go out with. Neither of us fancied the other but we became very fond of each other. He was extremely image-conscious and would never leave the house without 'fluffin' and puffin', as he described titillating his hair.

It was a difficult time. I always felt I had to be out on show: perfect, in case the big offer came along. Also, at that stage of my life I didn't have the honesty to face up to my own low mood and so I fought it by never giving in. Looking back, I clung to the guys more than I realised at the time. I went on holiday with Ron to Carmel and Bob and I took a cruise to Mexico.

Another friend of John and Bob's that I met was Guy, who was dying from AIDS. He had been a dancer with Bob and they had travelled the world together, having raucous times. HIV had only recently started to spread: highly controversial, it was referred to as 'the gay plague' and ordinary people were frightened of it, with undertakers refusing to bury AIDS victims and families forced to bribe doctors to put other diagnoses on death certificates. There was a huge stigma surrounding it.

John and Bob went to Guy's flat every day to prepare his food and give him company. When they were going away I volunteered to do it, but I'm ashamed to admit that I did not fully understand the disease then. Guy had not been able to cut his nails for a long time, he was too weak; when I was sitting next to him, he inadvertently scratched my leg with his toenail and it started to bleed. I was scared this might mean I had contracted AIDS, although I didn't consult a doctor. Today I'm ashamed of my ignorance but I'm glad that I was able to help Guy a little in his last days. My cousin Samantha was staying with me for a couple of days and I took her with me to see Guy in hospital. I remember she too was wary and I had to reassure her. When Guy died, Bob and John gave me some of his furniture.

Samantha wasn't my only visitor from home: Darren came out for a few days. He was driving my red Mustang with the roof down back from dinner one night. We'd had a few drinks and were whooping with delight at the fact that two kids from London were in Hollywood. Then we took a sharp left-hand bend, Darren lost control of the car and we ended up in a tennis court. Because we were both over the limit, we simply abandoned the car and scuttled home on foot, sneaking back the next day.

I knew Bob Halley, who was Elton John's business manager at the time from London days, and when Elton was appearing at the Hollywood Bowl I rang to see if I could get tickets. 'Sure, where do you want to sit? How many tickets do you want?' he asked. So I asked for five seats: for me, Bob, John, Ron and Michael, my first agent out there. On arrival, we were ushered through the VIP area to some amazing seats, but when we got to them a black guy and another guy were playing tonsil tennis.

I was getting a real busy on – I may only be 5'2", but I can be quite formidable and all I could see was two people where they shouldn't be.

'Sorry,' I said to the two blokes, 'these seats are reserved.' I said this really loudly and they moved apart – one of them actually cowered a bit. They apologised and moved away. I looked at John and Bob with an expression of triumph, only to see them looking back, slightly shell-shocked. 'Do you know who that was?' Bob eventually said. 'That was Luther Vandross and you've just thrown him out!' Well, he was in our seats …

At the beginning, lots of people wanted to be my friend and I was taken around to various parties, where I was always introduced as, 'This is Lisa, she's signed to Paramount.' 'Lisa-signed-to-Paramount' became my name: it meant I was someone worth knowing as I might have a glittering career ahead of me. There were so many hangers-on in Hollywood, people desperate for a break, so someone with a deal was a very minor celebrity. I teamed up with a talent booker, Eileen Bradley Goldfarb, and we went out a lot together. Looking back, I can see she was another single lonely woman and it suited her to pal up with me just as much as it did for me to be taken under her wing. She knew lots of people, and at the beginning, when I was a good proposition (Lisa-signed-to-Paramount), she got a buzz from being my friend.

Eileen was another East Coaster. I found their humour much closer to our British sarcastic, cynical, self-deprecating irony and I think that's why I connected so well with her and Ron. I enjoyed the parties, where I met a couple of English actors and one or two famous people. I even met my childhood idol, David

Cassidy. What a disappointment! It was a very short conversation between two very short people – he didn't seem interested in talking to me. He didn't seem any taller than me either (which means *small*).

I had visitors out there: Freya had other performers coming out to see her, and because I had supposedly put myself on the right road straight away with my Paramount deal she recommended they ask me for tips on how to handle things. Both Bobby Davro and Les Dennis came out, too, but this was well before things started to go wrong for me.

When Les came out, he had just begun seeing Amanda Holden and he was very excited and happy about it. He put me on the phone to talk to her and we chatted away (she seemed nice and bubbly). Afterwards he asked my opinion.

'She seems lovely – I've never see you so happy,' I told him.

'But what do you really think?' he persisted.

'I don't bloody know. I've only spoken to her on the phone!'

He put her on to me again the next time she rang. 'It's really important to me that you like her,' he said. Over a boozy lunch with him and Mike Hughes at Geoffrey's restaurant in Malibu he kept asking for my opinion – I don't know what it was, perhaps because she was so young and Les was such a good friend and I was worried about him getting hurt, but I said: 'I don't know what this girl is doing, but she is making you happy, Les. Just be careful you don't get hurt again. Be careful she's not working you.'

I didn't know Amanda but I knew there were strong, ambitious women in our business and they might use Les as a stepping-stone. I was so fond of him and I didn't want anything like that to happen. Later, he said that he had told Amanda what I'd said and asked her if I could be right. It's not surprising she never warmed to me! After this episode we didn't see as much of each other, although we stayed friends.

I'd begun drinking quite a lot in LA: it started on my first trip to the States when I was staying with John and Bob. I'd have a little nip of vodka before going to a meeting just to give me a bit of Dutch courage. In the end it became a ritual, and when things were going well I was superstitious about breaking it; a shot of vodka was helping me perform. As none of my LA plans materialised, I came to rely on it more and more to get me out there, pretending to be bright, breezy and funny. I still had to walk into meetings with the same enthusiasm, even though I was now feeling jaded and tired of all the waiting around for something to happen.

Before I left Bob and John's house to live in my own apartment I was topping up their vodka with water, and if they ever suspected, they were too kind to say anything. Living on my own, I'd buy a bottle at the local supermarket while picking up my groceries (sometimes the vodka would be all I'd buy). Los Angeles is a place where lots of people pretend not to drink – they sip water over their business lunch. Before they left home many of them had a stiff drink, so I wasn't the only one doing it. For me, it became a dangerous habit … and not the only one acquired in America.

# CHAPTER 10

## *Meltdown*

As well as drinking too much, I also developed an eating disorder while in LA: I became bulimic. I think the main trigger was the *Frasier* rejection – I knew, logically, the reason why I lost the job, but I still started to wonder if maybe it was something to do with the way I looked. The deal with Paramount allowed me to go after jobs with other studios (I appeared in episodes of *Murder, She Wrote* and *Acapulco H.E.A.T.*) and each audition involved waiting in a room full of other actresses, all exquisitely beautiful and very thin.

At first I thought, as I always did in England, that I didn't need to be perfect because I was a funny girl (back home it had always seemed a disadvantage to be pretty). After all, I wasn't selling myself as sexy and gorgeous so I was allowed to be quirky and flawed, but in the end I could no longer convince myself. It wasn't as if I was overweight – eating disorders are not usually about that – it was in order to be perfect, to be in control of my body. My life seemed to be spiralling out of control and this was a cry for help. I was living in a foreign country, nothing was going the way it was supposed to go and I had nobody to turn to, I felt.

Desperately lonely, I had too much time on my hands but I didn't want Darren to come out and see me either. I could remember all the fanfare made about me going to the States and I felt embarrassed about the fact that I was hanging around, going nowhere. Also, I felt I was letting people down: Mum, Nan, everybody back home who said I was going to be the next big thing. As always in my life, I was looking at everything through the prism of how I felt it would impact on others; I believed everyone would love me more if I became a big success in America. Of course it all came back to my childhood again: I had to prove not having a dad didn't matter. If I could blind everyone with my success, no one would care about my background.

After a few months I started making myself sick after eating. I knew perfectly well what I was doing – don't forget, I'm a stage-school girl who grew up surrounded by girls who were very conscious of their physical appearance. I'd heard the sounds of vomiting in the Italia Conti loos; maybe because of that, I was good at hiding it. Desperate to keep it a secret, I didn't let my friends Bob and John know because I knew they had contacts back home and friends who came out to stay with them. In LA, vulnerability has to be hidden at all costs; it's a world in which careers are launched on self-confidence, and I had to exude this. I'm an actress, so I managed to do this, but it was all an act. I even managed to convince myself because I've always been scared of showing weakness and I wasn't about to start now. Learning to accept that vulnerability is not a bad thing has been a big life lesson for me, one of the biggest.

I was living on Shredded Wheat, skimmed milk and Equal sweetener. I used to put 10 packets of sweetener on my cereal – it was the only thing I could eat without making myself sick afterwards. In company I'd eat normally, then throw it all up afterwards. Sometimes I'd order a Chinese takeaway, then vomit. If I felt hungry, I'd have cereal. Often I'd drink after a load of food. Drink makes throwing up almost acceptable: you can pretend, even to yourself, that you were sick because you drank too much. I was never formally diagnosed with an eating disorder and I never weighed myself, but I know my weight went down to a real low: probably just over six stone or even less. As I'm only 5'2", seven and a half stone is about right for me.

Bulimia has other side effects as well as weight loss: it causes your hair (never my best feature) to drop out and I may have had to have more fillings than normally because it damages the enamel on your teeth. I was lucky not to have any permanent after-effects, though. For me, it was a way of taking control: in that moment when you are being sick you are doing something physical and there's no time or space for anything else – it shuts out all the real problems. I never asked for help and I never told anyone. Mum will only find out the extent of my bulimia when she reads this.

The gym at the apartment block became one of my main haunts, and I exercised frenetically; I also spent hours by the pool topping up my tan. Interestingly, most of the women in LA were pale – perhaps they already knew about the damage too much sun can cause, but more likely they stayed in the shade because pale skin looks better on-camera. Having a tan still made me feel more confident. It was like a body mask: you can hide your size and shape with it.

My drinking extended to large glasses of vodka when I was at home on my own. In my mind it was never out of control, but I always had a drink before I left the house and climbed into the car. Most of the time I was driving with alcohol inside me; I never seemed drunk but I kept my level topped up.

I was stopped three times altogether by the police for speeding but never, thank God, for drunk driving: they are tough on drivers who are over the limit. The first time I was in downtown LA when a cop jumped out and waved me down – the red Mustang was very noticeable. I put on my best Penelope Keith accent.

'Oh officer, I'm from England! I'm just trying to find my way around Los Angeles but I'm afraid I'm terribly lost. I don't suppose you could put me on the right track?' I said.

'Ma'am, did you know you were going very fast?'

'Oh dear, was I? I don't know the roads here. I do have an international driving licence – I am allowed to drive here, aren't I?'

'Yes, ma'am, but you were going too fast.'

'I'm so sorry, officer …'

He let me off, but about six weeks later I was stopped again and was about to go into the same routine when the policeman peered through the car window.

'Oh God, not *you* again!' said the same cop.

He must have enjoyed my cabaret because he let me off once more, but this time with a stern warning. Unfortunately, the next ones to stop me were not so friendly. A couple of months later I was travelling along the freeway and the first thing I did when I heard the sirens and saw the flashing lights was to pull over and get out of the car. I didn't know that in the States you are not supposed to do this (it always seems polite over here), but they are worried you may have a gun, run towards them and start shooting. So I heard them yelling at me through what looked like an electric megaphone: 'Get back in the car, get back in the car!' Panic-stricken, I froze for a moment before I got in, which may have worried them.

This time they weren't impressed by my daffy young Englishwoman act, and I was booked. I had to go to Traffic School – they ran classes for naughty drivers in the States long before we had them over here. What's more, you could choose what kind of school you wanted to attend, so I chose Traffic School with Humour (there was also stand-up school and you could pick your comic). There was something for everybody, loads of different schools; I remember single Hispanic mothers being another.

The course, which lasted eight hours and was held by a professional comedian, was hilarious for all the wrong reasons. I can see why he did it – the only way he'd ever get a laugh was if you couldn't escape. I had to keep pinching myself to stay awake: if you nodded off, you had to do the whole thing again. We were all laughing away. It wasn't at all funny but we daren't look bored or as if we weren't paying attention.

While I was away I didn't have any relationships. I may have been lonely and craving attention, but I didn't look for love in the wrong places. I've never been the kind of girl who finds solace in the arms of a man, regardless. From time to time I was propositioned, and Justin visited me once, but Darren was my secret weapon and I wore him like a 'Danger, Keep Out!' badge. I had my own weaknesses, drink and bulimia, but I never saw casual sex as a solution.

Looking back, Los Angeles was an awful, lonely time. It's almost like seeing another person and I can't believe I endured it for as long as I did. Today I would realise the magnitude of my problems, I'd understand myself much more; I'm grounded now, honest with myself. Back then I was young and still pretending to myself that my American dream would all work out one day – just one more meeting, one more pilot …

It was my thirtieth birthday, 24 November 1993. It was also Thanksgiving weekend when the whole of America departs to spend time with their families. Los Angeles emptied out, but I had nowhere to go. As always, I was waiting to hear about a meeting. One or two people had half-heartedly invited me for the break but I knew this was as special to the Americans as Christmas is to us and so I didn't want to intrude.

My friend Eileen was going off to her family for the holiday weekend, but she gave me the names of some people who were going to be around. I ended up phoning complete strangers and persuading them to come to my birthday party; I bought sushi and champagne, trying to make it a great place to be. What it really came down to was a bunch of freeloaders getting pissed out of my pocket. I tried my best to enjoy myself; I was the life and soul of a rather odd party where I didn't know anybody. I drank a lot, too, which was my recipe for stopping myself thinking: what am I doing, who am I kidding?

'Oh, Mum, it was amazing – a house full of people! Shame you couldn't be here, you missed a fantastic party,' I told Mum the next day over the phone.

'Listen, don't worry about me. As long as you had a good time that's all that matters! You're doing so well, Lisa. I'm so proud of you,' she told me.

'Thanks, Mum.'

When I put the phone down I could barely swallow; there was a huge lump in my throat. Suddenly I felt so isolated and scared at the realisation there wasn't anyone who could help me, no one really knew or understood what was happening to me. I hadn't been able to be vulnerable and tell the truth to anyone, not even John, Bob or Eileen. I can't do this, I thought. As someone who hardly ever cried, I felt that 30 years of tears were fighting their way out and this time there was nothing I could do to control them. 'I'm going home – this isn't for me! Who am I actually doing this for? Everyone else seems to be getting much more out of this than me,' I told myself.

This light-bulb moment was to unravel quite a few deep-set questions later on. Was all this for Mum? Was I still the same little girl whose mission in life was to make the man who left us regret it? Was I doing all this so that Mum could feel vindicated and say to everyone who had been around at the time of my birth, 'Look, you all thought I'd made a mistake but just look at her now!' Possibly.

Darren was the only one who had a clue that things weren't perfect: he'd had to send me some money by Western Union, but we didn't talk about it. The physical gulf between us was too great – he couldn't get inside my world in Hollywood any more than I could understand his in London. He didn't tell me about his financial difficulties and work problems, and I didn't tell him my own problems.

I hadn't paid the rent on the flat in Studio City for months. Like I've said all the way through this story, I never paid any attention to that kind of thing. So when the money began to run out after two years I did a typical me: burying my head in the sand and ignoring it. I didn't pay the rental on the furniture, either – I was in a real mess.

Towards the end of my time in the States, Les Denis asked if he and Amanda, who was now his wife, could come and stay. My flat was tiny so I said they could have it while I stayed with Eileen. She was a good friend, even when things weren't going my way. Eileen was the only one who noticed how thin I'd become: 'You gotta eat, Lisey. You gotta eat 'cos you look like a fucking bone!' She lent me a few dollars here and there, while I waited for Darren's money to arrive.

Like everyone else in London, Les thought I had a good life out there and things were happening for me. I was delighted to hear from him because it meant we were still mates. One day he rang me and said: 'We've just had this man knock on the door about the furniture. He wants to take it away.' 'Oh, it's all a mistake: it's been paid. You know how hopeless I am. I just forgot to pay, but it's all taken care of,' I said to make light of it.

And so I covered it up, all the while feeling extremely uncomfortable and dreading the next phone call to say the fridge had been repossessed or the landlord had changed the locks. I'm deeply embarrassed now about the state I was in, but I can see how people become homeless: things just build up, you shelve responsibility and suddenly it's too late. The fact is, I was a failure and I should have been able to face it, to tell Mum and Darren, 'Do you know what? I went, I had an amazing opportunity but it didn't work out. I may have let you all down and let myself down, but my sanity is at stake here.' But it takes an awful lot for me to acknowledge there is a problem. Eventually, I knew I had to come home. I had an impending sense of doom; I would crash the car while drunk, have a breakdown or get arrested for not paying my rent and debts. If I stayed, something terrible would happen, and I couldn't cope any more.

The decision to leave America, once I'd made it, was easy. In one way it was a massive change to my whole life plan, in another it felt like the most natural thing in the world. I dressed it up to everyone that I was homesick and needed to see them all, then slipped back home without any fanfare.

It takes a certain type of person to survive in LA, and my circumstances were particularly difficult because I was mostly on my own with little support. Out there, you have to eat, drink and sleep the industry, and probably the one thing that saved my life is that I was simply not that ambitious. I've always loved my career and wanted to do well in what I'm doing, but if I'd been consumed with ambition the rejection would have been much harder to take. For me, it had never been about proving I was the best actor, the funniest girl or whatever, it was just a matter of showing that I was worthy to be on the planet, I was someone who deserved to be loved. That was my driving force.

When I was a kid at stage school I never had a clear idea that I wanted to sing, act or dance better than everyone else – it just seemed the best way of getting myself accepted. When I did things well – presenting, impressions, acting, dancing, singing or comedy – it seemed people loved me and I thrived on that feeling. I didn't know I was lovable in myself, I always felt I had to earn it; if I could be good at things, it took away any feelings of shame about my existence.

I flew back to London Economy, using the air miles collected from my Virgin Upper Class flight. Dennis Selinger, my agent, was terrific: 'At last, you're back! Finally, I can do something for you,' he told me.

When I finally made the decision to return home, nobody at Paramount was bothered and no one at my agency tried to stop me – it was all too easy to let me go. For ages it had been, 'We're just setting up this meeting …', stringing me along as if something was about to happen. But the writing was on the wall and they too accepted nothing big was around the corner.

My big Hollywood career ended with a whimper, not a bang.

# CHAPTER 11

## *Coming Home*

Feeling nervous, I walked into the audition at the Dominion Theatre. It was a few months after America and I was up for the job of Marty, one of the 'Pink Ladies' in *Grease*. Not the lead, not even the second lead, but a good part and one that I needed very badly for my self-esteem, to re-establish my name in London … and for the pay packet.

When I returned to England things had changed. In my mind I would slot straight back into the house and pick up where I'd left off, but the first thing Darren had to tell me was that our house had gone. His business had collapsed, through no fault of his own, like so many at the end of the property boom. Like the good yuppies we were, we'd overstretched ourselves and everything had gone. All our possessions were now in storage but I was so relieved to be home that I didn't pay too much attention. I didn't take in that our house had been repossessed (I thought we must have sold it); I remember thinking we would one day get some money from the sale when everything was sorted out.

I didn't blame Darren because he had told me about the repossession, but as usual I was in denial. I have knack for blanking out inconvenient things and I often choose to put my head in the sand.

Darren and I were genuinely pleased to see each other again, although there was now a huge gulf between us: I'd kept my problems in LA from him and he had kept the financial difficulties back home from me. We'd had fragmented transatlantic phone conversations, but we'd both been kidding ourselves we were coping. He'd told me a bit about our house going, but I hadn't really taken it on board until I was back.

We fell back into our comfortable relationship, like putting on a favourite pair of shoes. Darren was still in the property business; he had a flat in Regent's Park, which belonged to a friend of his, but he was able to stay there and so I split my time between him and Mum. We drifted along, more like a brother and sister, and somehow we didn't spend much time together. I have no idea if while I was away Darren had started seeing other people – he'd only be human if he had, and I don't blame him – but neither of us was the kind to sit down and have a long talk about where our relationship was going.

Mum and Nan were both thrilled that I was back and nothing was ever said about my lack of success in America. Until I was with them again I didn't realise how much I'd missed them; I'd pretended to myself that I didn't need anyone. Back home, I now realised how wrong I was – not that Mum and I got along any better, we still had fiery rows. We didn't argue about the big issues between us, they were never addressed, but we'd have a flaming row about the weather, anything.

Luckily for me, and it was a real lifesaver, I was soon working. My agent, Denis, put me up for the part in *Grease*. It was a year's contract in the West End and he wanted to see me make that level of commitment to work and to staying in England. I loved going for lunch with Denis every fortnight at Langan's Brasserie, where he always had the same table, the first one on the left-hand side.

*Grease* was being produced by Paul Nicholas and David Ian – I'd known David from panto, years ago. We were in *Goldilocks & the Three Bears* together, with me as Goldilocks and him as Hank, the circus owner. He was then at the beginning of his career while I was fairly established. It was strange having to audition – it felt as if I was back in the days immediately after Italia Conti. The choreographer was Arlene Phillips (lovely, very professional) and the assistant choreographer, Tony Edge, had been a dancer on *The Lisa Maxwell Show*. It could have felt odd, but he was very sweet and made a point of telling me that everyone, even the leads, had auditioned. I've always believed if you are nice to people on the way up, they will be good to you when you're down – I've never had a problem with anyone I've worked with, partly because I've always wanted people to like me.

It was an audition like the ones you see in films: a bank of five or six people sitting in the darkness with a little light over a desk so that one of them can write notes. I sensed people might be wondering about me, thinking I'd come down, but as you know if you've read my story this far, I'm not the kind of person who spends hours thinking about myself and my problems. To walk into the audition I had to swallow some pride, but the simple truth was I needed the job.

Auditions for musicals are tough: they want to see you singing (and that includes songs in different tempos), dancing and acting, so there are a lot of hoops to jump through. When it came to my acting scene, I changed it a little from the script and put a spin on certain words, making Marty more affected than she was on the page. Out from the darkness came a ripple of laughter and I felt a wave of relief: I had the part! And I still had the ability to make people laugh, to put my own stamp on a role. I'd wanted that part so badly that I almost cried with relief when they confirmed it was mine.

Shane Richie was playing the lead of Danny and we became really great mates on that show. Adam Garcia was also in it, and Steve Serlin, who played opposite me as Sonny – we were a couple in the story, an unusual physical combination as Steve is much taller than me and ridiculously thin. We had to jive a lot and it was like jiving with Stretch Armstrong as he'd fling me around and outwards; I felt I'd hit the other side of the stage before he whisked me back in again. Don't get me wrong, though: Steve's very talented, there's nothing he can't sing.

Adam was only 22 at the time and it was his second job in the UK. No one in the show doubted this boy would go far. He was compelling to watch. I've never seen other cast members stop what they're rehearsing to run in and watch someone else rehearse. It was a fantastic cast: Linzi Hateley was playing Rizzo, and she's one of the best West End performers ever.

To this day Shane, Adam and Steve are three of my closest friends. It was a good time: everyone partied hard that year, which suited me fine. I was still drinking heavily and still bulimic. Darren once caught me making myself sick in the bathroom, but I made light of it (I'm an adept liar).

'You've been sick, haven't you?'

'I've got an upset tummy – I knew I was going to be sick so I just made it happen quicker. I think it was something I ate last night,' I told him. 'I'm feeling better already.'

I don't know if he suspected the truth but he didn't say anything. Anyway, I soon stopped being sick; I was just too busy doing eight shows a week and running a mad social life, so I needed all the energy I could get. Looking back, I'm so grateful that I escaped from an eating disorder as well as I did – I know they can go on for years, wreaking havoc, and I was very lucky. During *Grease*, our social life was so hectic that I can remember being on stage thinking, I wish this bloody show would end, so I can go out and party!

I'd get back to the flat or Mum's house at 3 a.m., sometimes 4 a.m. Darren never asked any questions. Sometimes he would come and join me at the party, and as usual he fitted in easily and well with my showbiz friends. I love to work, and in those days I validated myself through work. That's why America had been so tough: I don't know who I am unless I'm working, or at least I didn't back then. Without work there was not a lot left of Lisa Maxwell, I felt.

Chances are, in the industry I chose to work in there will be times when you won't be busy, so to only feel complete and a real person through work means you're on a hiding to nothing; it's bound to lead to misery. Why couldn't I be happy just being me? It had a lot to do with my drive to be a success, to stop people digging deeper into my life and my background. I was always trying to prove to an absent father that I was worth sticking around for, worth loving. And also for my Mum, to make her feel all the sacrifices and loneliness were worth it. If I kept busy, making things right for other people, there was never time to stand still and say, 'But what about you, Lisa? What are we going to do about *you*?' This was becoming harder to ignore, and I knew I was suffering beneath the façade. But don't open Pandora's box; you can't possibly deal with what's inside.

I didn't treat Darren too well at this time. I wasn't good at dealing with the big stuff, I never had the emotional tools to sort things out. Having him around suited me and I think maybe it suited him, too: he liked mixing with my friends and would join in the party. From time to time, when I was out with my crowd of friends from the show at a nightclub, I'd bump into him with his friends. It was bizarre, looking back; we were still supposed to be an item but we had no idea what the other was doing. I always felt good when I saw him there, I knew he'd got my back, but it was unfair on him and actually bad for me. It was time for me to stand on my own two feet. Darren deserved a girlfriend who was one hundred per cent there for him.

Like America, my relationship with Darren slowly petered out without any huge drama. For a great deal of the time we avoided each other, although we started to become niggly. The dinner party circuit we'd been on before I left the country had completely broken up, everyone had moved on. Now I was back to being a jobbing actress, working every evening. I did tell him we ought to end it, but I didn't say so with any great conviction. After all, I was Queen of Denial and happy to let things limp on. Ending didn't make any sense. I couldn't imagine being with anyone who would understand me as well as Darren, and we'd had 13 years of shared history. He'd also been there for me when Grandad died. All I could think was, it isn't *that* wrong.

But there were problems of a different sort to the ones I had with my first boyfriend. Darren's business had not only folded under him, it had folded under me too, because my name was on a great deal of the paperwork. Not just for our house in the gated development, but I had also signed for a mortgage on another flat in my name. Of course, I'd been told what I was signing, but as usual I wasn't interested, so I only realised I owned it when it had to be sold. I'm not blaming Darren: he didn't do anything underhand and he definitely told me what I was signing. Only I didn't listen to the scary stuff, did I? I know it sounds insane but I just took no notice. When we were together, our money went into the same pot and as long as I had what I needed (and Darren more or less made sure I had anything I asked for), that was fine by me. It turned out we had considerable joint debt and the shit was about to hit the fan. I should have made myself understand more instead of passing on the responsibility and complaining about it afterwards. After all, what did I expect when I couldn't be bothered to find out more in the first place?

Darren and I had whole lists of creditors and in the end we had to set up an IVA (Independent Voluntary Arrangement). Again, I didn't take it in: all I knew was that out of the £1,200 a week I was making from *Grease*, £700 went straight to our creditors. After saving for tax, I was left with little more than pocket money. Even then I wasn't worried; I just felt something would turn up and make it all right. I was a bit concerned about my possessions (which were still in storage) because among them was the only picture of Nan and Grandad on their wedding day, a lovely old sepia print. Darren reassured me we'd get everything back when we had somewhere to put it all.

To my surprise, it was Darren who finally ended our relationship before I left *Grease*. Late one night we had an argument in the street after we'd both had a lot to drink (I can't remember what it was about).

'I can't do this any more,' he told me the next day over the phone. 'I don't think you want it any more.' I wasn't heartbroken: I think I'd been trying, subconsciously, to bring it all to a head myself, but I was surprised. I never expected Darren to be the one to end it, but I'm pleased he did own the decision to call it a day. It may sound childish, but ultimately he put a lot more into the relationship and I'd been selfish in taking what I needed from it. Afterwards I wrote him a letter, telling him how much I appreciated him. He had been a sweet, kind and loyal man at a time in my life when I must have been a bit of a handful and he'd always been nicer to me than I was to him. I wanted him to know that I was aware of what he had to put up with and was sorry to have caused him any pain.

The break-up came near the end of my time in *Grease*. One side effect was that I had to move back in with Mum and Nan. So there I was, 32 years old and living like a teenager with nothing to show for all the years of work and my successes. Meanwhile, I was paying off debts and driving around in the little Fiat Punto Mum had bought for me (she was really there for me when everything went wrong, too). My career had started so well, with such high hopes – I couldn't work out what had happened. But you know me, I didn't even try to work it out. Instead it was all keep busy, go out, flirt with bartenders, feed my ego … All to validate myself. I was not in a great place.

\* \* \*

But then the happiest, most amazing day of my life arrived. Think of any other adjectives for 'amazing' that you can and stick them in! This really was the big turning point and I don't have enough language to express what it meant to me.

Not that I recognised it immediately. It was about two weeks before the end of my year in *Grease*, and as usual I was happy to be invited along to a party after the show. Someone I knew owned the Sidona Bar and he rang to ask if any of the cast would like to come to a party to launch the new modelling arm of the famous IMG management company. And so a few others and I went along – it was just the sort of thing we did after coming offstage, to unwind and enjoy ourselves. The champagne was flowing, and all was good until a photographer who had taken some pictures for the new model book decided to chat me up.

He was very persistent, turning round everything I said to make it sound like I fancied him. I started out being charming and nice, gently giving him the brush-off, but he didn't seem to take the hint. I'm going to have to let this bloke know in no uncertain terms because he's so thick-skinned, he's not picking up my vibes, I thought to myself. While all this was going on, I clocked the absolutely gorgeous bloke standing with the photographer and I can remember thinking, Wow! I've *got* to make this guy like me. He was exactly my type: tall, preppy looking, with a great head of hair. I like that blond Californian look: Robert Redford, the young David Cassidy …

He was wearing a trendy black suit and one thing that struck me was that when he was amused he laughed and talked at the same time. And he was definitely amused by my efforts to get rid of his persistent friend. I don't remember which of my sarcastic remarks finally got through to the photographer that he ought to try his charms elsewhere but he did move on, leaving me with the man I wanted to talk to. And talk we did: we talked and talked and talked – and we have not stopped talking since. I knew very quickly that I had met someone who was going to be important to me. I don't suppose in that crowded bar I really felt a premonition that this was the meeting that would change my life, but I like to think I did. And if I didn't know it then, it didn't take too long for me to find out either.

Paul Jessup was the creative director on the model book produced by IMG, and that's why he was at the party. I can't remember our first words to each other, but I do remember that I danced, wiggling my derrière in front of him, trying to make him really fancy me. I'm becoming a bit predictable, aren't I?

We soon realised we had the same sense of humour and even in that packed, noisy bar we were making each other laugh. Afterwards a crowd of us went on to another nightclub and we ended up having breakfast at seven o'clock the next morning in Café Boheme in Old Compton Street. It was a favourite haunt for night owls, mostly people who don't want the evening to end for one reason or another – I certainly didn't.

Over our full English fry-up, Paul and I just talked – which sobered me up after a night's drinking. Like me, he had been in a long-standing relationship, with a girl he met at art college. They were together for eight years, then got married and within weeks had broken up. With hindsight, that wonderful gift that allows us all to put a shape on our lives, he could see that he'd gone along with the wedding because his father was ill and his family were very fond of his girlfriend; he wanted his father to see him get married. Soon after they split, his father had died from a heart attack.

Paul had been very close to his dad, and when we met, six months later, he was still trying to adjust to it. Unlike me, he was able to confront his grief and allow himself to feel it. It would take some time but it was from him that I would learn the importance of looking honestly at my own life and facing up to things rather than pushing them away, out of sight and out of mind. It's important to feel things, even if the feeling is painful, I've discovered. I can't remember now how much of our life stories we shared on that first night, but I do remember the talking, the laughter, and there was nothing more – it would be two weeks before Paul and I kissed. I simply could not believe how beautiful and open he was, how he gave a straight answer to every question.

Paul is a rare breed, someone so comfortable in his own skin that he doesn't have to put on an act. In contrast, I'm one of those people who always thinks about what to say to make themselves more interesting, dresses everything up and sells it to make it sound better than it really is. In the world I inhabited everyone did the same: jazzing things up, embellishing the truth, doing whatever necessary to come over better. None of this would ever occur to Paul: he is never rude or tactless, but he gives honest answers to questions. Early on I realised he doesn't mind if people don't like him, and consequently everyone likes him, they are drawn to him. He's not the all-singing, all-dancing dinner-party guest, but people gravitate towards him. Paul's the most secure human being I have ever met.

He's also the only man who has ever truly known and understood me. Even to this day he can see when I'm reverting to the old Lisa, the one who buries her head in the sand to avoid issues or puts on a suit of armour to prevent herself from being hurt and at the same time prevents herself feeling anything, even the good things. 'We need to deal with this. Let's not pretend it's something else, let's sort it,' he says when he sees me doing this. Paul has changed me, brought me home to my real self, laid my ghosts for me … Although much of this would be in the future, I think I knew from the first day we met that he was the man who was going to heal me.

Initially I fancied him because he seemed well travelled, cultured, intelligent and funny. Also, he must come from a different class to me, I thought, but I was pleased to find out we were actually very similar. I'm not sure if I could have pulled off posh for any length of time! Paul's father came from North London and his mother was from Welwyn Garden City, which is where he was born before the family moved to Dunstable, where he grew up. After the local comprehensive, he went to Camberwell School of Art to study graphic design, then sculpture. His family background is so solid that it has helped make him the grounded, secure individual he is, with a clear sense of right and wrong.

Paul is a terrific judge of character. While I'm busying myself trying to make people like me, he is watching and listening, coming to his own opinion. I've learnt so much from him and I'm more observant now. That morning, after we first met and shared breakfast, my one major decision was to give him my home telephone number. Now this was a big deal for me: I *never* give it out, I always take other people's numbers so that I can call the shots. Crazy and as drunk as I have been at times in my life, I was always sensible enough to control who I allowed across a certain line in my life. After just that one night I knew Paul was going to be allowed in, though.

He felt as keen on me, I knew: when we parted, we had already arranged to meet back at the same place for supper that evening. Of course, once I got home I began to wonder if the drink had made me exaggerate how much I liked this man. Was I making a big mistake?

From the moment I got back from America, I had picked up my friendship with Mike Hughes again. He was no longer my agent, but still a close mate, and we enjoyed each other's company. So I rang Mike and told him my predicament. 'I've met this gorgeous man – at least, I *think* he's gorgeous, but I had been drinking a lot of champagne. It could have been the beer goggles talking. I've arranged to have dinner with him, and if he turns out not to be the way I remember him and I've got it horribly wrong, I'll be stuck with him for an evening. And I've given him my phone number …'

Mike said he would come along to Café Boheme and breeze in as if by chance. If I needed to be rescued, he'd be there. Meanwhile, Paul and I talked on the phone for about two hours that afternoon. I took a lot of care with my appearance that evening, wearing a red V-neck sweater with white piping round the neck and three-quarter-length sleeves, a matching little hipster skirt and big, white patent high wedge loafers to add vital extra inches as I couldn't remember how tall he was.

As I bowled up to the front of Café Boheme in my Fiat, Paul was standing outside wearing a tailored leather jacket and jeans and I knew all my instincts were correct: he *was* bloody gorgeous! I felt peculiar: my stomach was flipping away and my legs were weak. When we sat down at a table, he was doing that laughing and talking thing at the same time again and running his fingers through his hair because it kept flopping forward. I knew he was everything I had ever wanted and the feeling of wanting him was a deeper, more passionate feeling than I'd had for any man.

The whole meeting was so exciting, stimulating, brilliant … Paul had the looks, the honesty, the humour, the strength of character, the intelligence – everything I could ever want. I was in sensory meltdown.

Mike arrived as planned and carried off the casual bit. 'Hi Lisa, fancy seeing you here! D'you mind if I sit down with you for a drink?' He and Paul started talking and clearly got on well. After a little while, Mike said, 'Are you eating? I might stay for a bit of dinner myself.' I shot him such a look, signalling with my eyes that I was perfectly happy and he should piss off. Although I know him well enough to realise he had picked up on my silent message, he simply chose to ignore it and stuck around with a twinkle in his eye.

In his usual nosey way he gave Paul the third degree, but he was also being protective of me. He knew me well enough to know my reaction to Paul was unusual – I didn't fall in love with every other man I met. I think he even asked Paul about his intentions towards me on our first date! He questioned him about his job, what car he drove, where he came from. Paul gave straightforward answers and didn't seem at all phased. 'What I like about you is that if I ask you a question you only bloody answer me!' Mike told him (he was used to showbiz people who would have turned every answer into a performance). He and Paul would go on to become firm friends and I'm glad about that because Mike's opinion was, and still is, important to me.

But I'd have done anything to get rid of him that night. I expected him to have one drink and, on the nod from me, disappear. At least after the meal he did show a bit of sensitivity and left first – he probably thought we were going to have a bit of a kiss and a cuddle. Paul said goodbye and promised to ring me the next day. I stood by my car, watching him walk away, and I'll never forget it: he has ever so slightly turned-out feet and he walked with a bit of a bowl. He looks like a really happy man – I hope he *is* happy, and happy he has met me, I thought to myself.

I then experienced that strange feeling everyone knows when something huge and significant has happened: I watched the other people in the street and I thought, they don't know, they've got no idea what's happened, they're carrying on as if the world is the same place it was 24 hours ago – but it isn't!

Meanwhile, my world was forever changed.

# CHAPTER 12

## Falling in Love

Paul and I were talking on the phone every day: long, epic conversations. It felt as if I could say anything to him and all I wanted was to hear his voice – we could not bear to end our chats. We were seeing each other whenever we could and I was trying hard to be sensible, not to rush things. I didn't want to frighten him off, but I knew I was feeling something stronger than I'd ever felt before. Finally, I knew what the words 'in love' meant.

One night when he dropped me back at Mum and Nan's house he came in for a cup of tea. It was late, so they were both in bed. Paul liked the fact that I lived there with them and I loved them both so much. At first glance I may have seemed to be a girl about town, but that wasn't the real person. Paul loved the fact that I was very down-to-earth.

When we first met it was quite difficult for me to go through my life story with him. I didn't want to sound like the big 'I am', neither did I want to say I was a failure. But Paul wasn't interested in the show business me: he was looking for the real me, the one I had worked so hard to keep hidden. To me, the most amazing thing was that he actually liked the real me. I still wrestle with that knowledge and even now I'm sometimes insecure about it; I do have to remind myself that I'm worth loving.

There was one subject I wouldn't be drawn on, however: my age. I had a feeling he was younger than me and I decided not reveal how old I was until he knew me well enough not to be put off.

The first time we kissed was after a night out and it was magical but we didn't take it any further. We were like a couple of American high-school kids, slowly working from first to second base and beyond. A week later we made love at Paul's flat in Muswell Hill. We both knew the first time had to be significant because we were very special to each other. Neither of us wanted to trivialise it, just doing it for the sake of it after too much to drink. We'd been out, probably to a club.

We went back to his flat and, without planning it, started to kiss. I was desperate for our lovemaking to be good; I felt so much for him and I didn't want either of us to be disappointed. The craving for him was so enormous it was only ever going to be fantastic, but we both knew it had to be perfect. And it was: we waited and made love in the morning when all the effects of our night out had worn off. We really wanted to savour it. After a leisurely morning in bed, he asked what I wanted to eat and I said fish and chips. We went out and got some, then sat in his garden eating them.

Paul drove me into town – I told him not to take me all the way home (I think he had a meeting to get to). He gave me one of his sweatshirts to put over my lace dress but I must have looked odd walking down Marylebone High Street in broad daylight in a figure-hugging, ankle-length dress, high heels and last night's make-up. When you are madly in love you don't care what other people think, but it did take me an hour to find some way to get home. In the end I had to get a cab and Mum paid at the other end.

Mum knew from the first time I mentioned meeting someone that Paul was special. I was locking myself away in the bedroom like a 14-year-old schoolgirl, laughing and giggling on the phone all day. So when we decided to go away for the weekend to Bournemouth and he arranged to pick me up from home, I knew Mum and Nan were desperate to get a glimpse.

'Please don't make a fuss, *please* don't hang out of the windows gawping at him – just stay indoors!' I pleaded with them. Of course they couldn't resist taking a peek from behind the curtains when we heard his car draw up. 'Oh my Gawd, in 'e 'andsome?' said Mum.

Somehow I managed to get myself out of the house and into the car before either of them had the chance to rush out and say hello. I don't know why we chose Bournemouth, probably because it wasn't too far and it was by the sea, plus it gave us an excuse to share a room in a hotel. So, off we set and the wonderful thing I discovered about Paul is that I can talk a lot, but he gave me a weekend off. I remember walking along the front, a bloody long walk, and he started talking at the beginning and was still going at the end. 'Do you always talk this much?' I asked.

He thought it was a problem for me, but it was wonderful. Usually I work hard at being the life and soul, keeping the conversation going, so it was lovely to be in the passenger seat for once. He was still teasing me about my age: I knew he was 28 and I think I may have admitted to being 30, no more.

When we got to the room we couldn't keep our hands off each other. I knew I had fallen in love, but all my old cautious instincts were still there. I had never surrendered my feelings to anyone, never before in my life – I always protected myself from rejection. With Paul, it was different: I remember thinking, Oh fuck it! D'you know what? I'm going to tell him I love him. I'm going to move in with him and he can take the piss if he wants. Maybe he'll be off next week, but I don't care – I'm going to risk it.

Making myself vulnerable was a big deal but in the end I told myself, to coin one of Ron Siegel's favourite expressions, 'You've got to shit or get off the pot!' So while we were cuddling on the bed I said the words, 'I love you.' Then I added, 'I know it's too early …' But Paul didn't let me carry on with my excuses. He simply said he was glad I'd said it because he felt exactly the same way. Being me I didn't believe him – I thought he was just saying it back because I'd said it first. I was waiting for him to take advantage in some way because I was emotionally vulnerable, but he never did … and he never has.

From the beginning, I was honest with Paul about my financial problems and the fact that Darren and I had been paying off our debts through an IVA, but I was increasingly worried about our possessions in storage. It was the photograph I wanted more than anything – I didn't care about anything else. Every time I contacted Darren about it, he told me not to worry, he was taking care of it all. Eventually I became concerned so I arranged to meet him and took Mum along with me. He finally admitted that we had not been paying the storage fees and we owed thousands. The storage company, who had not even been paid for the removal, were now threatening to sell our possessions. 'They say it's all going to go, but don't worry. I'm going to court over it and I'll negotiate with them. I'll make sure we keep it all,' he said.

It was at this point when I thought someone has to get real. Throughout our time together I'd been happy to leave the business side to Darren, but finally it dawned on me that I had just as much responsibility as him, and I should get involved.

'No, Darren,' I said, 'I want to know exactly where it all is.'

'Honestly, Lisa, don't worry – we'll negotiate a deal, pay them what we can.'

Something inside me snapped. 'Can we just accept these people want their money? We haven't paid a single penny and they're pissed off,' I told him. 'They are holding my stuff to ransom – they can sell it tomorrow. Why should they accept less money? We can't do a deal with everyone. Sometimes we just have to pay what we owe.'

'OK, if you want to take it over, fine!' said Darren, and he gave me the name of the company. I rang them and was shocked by the amount: £2,300. There was no way I could pay and I was heartbroken at the idea of losing Nan and Grandad's picture. It was only a few weeks into my relationship with Paul, so I was certainly not about to ask for help, but I unburdened my unhappiness. Paul immediately took over and agreed to pay off the storage company on condition that I severed all financial ties with Darren and that I sold what we could not fit into the flat to pay off the IVA. As he says, I was not a cheap date … But what an amazing tribute! We'd been together such a short time but Paul is generous and would not stand by and see anyone lose something so valuable. At last I had Nan and Grandad's picture safe and sound. I also had a great deal of furniture, some of which we squeezed into the flat in Muswell Hill and the rest we sold. Paul's mum organised a garage sale and I took control of my money for the first time.

Four weeks into our relationship, Paul had a holiday in Thailand with two mates. It was booked before we met and we were so in the throes of love that he didn't want to go, but he said, 'Pop round to check the flat's safe for me, and if you want to move a few things in while you are there, that's cool. Actually, it would be great if you could be moved in by the time I get back!'

While he was away we ran up huge phone bills. I was thrilled when he said he had told his mates all about me – it's a big thing for a bloke to do and they said I was clearly very important to him from the way he was behaving. So when he came back (a few days early because we could not bear being apart) I had already moved in. When we'd been together six months it was my birthday and Paul booked a surprise holiday in Marrakesh. Afterwards he came round to our house and Nan said, 'Where are you taking her, then?'

'To Morocco, really just to get a look at her passport and see how old she is,' he laughed.

'You could have just given me the money! I'd have told you she's 33,' said Nan.

I aged four years in six months but he didn't care about my age – he's always said he doesn't like younger women – and because it's Paul I don't think he's only saying it just to be nice.

\* \* \*

I couldn't wait to introduce Paul to Shane, Adam and Steve, my old mates. I knew he was right for me and Mike Hughes had already given his seal of approval but I wanted the rest of my buddies to meet him and know why I was so head over heels. First of all, I took him to meet Shane and Coleen and they were wonderful, very friendly (Shane has always said I'm the sister he never had). I was 'Little Lise' to him and the other two guys and they wanted to make sure no one was taking advantage. Then I invited Adam and Steve to the flat in Muswell Hill and they both got on really well with Paul.

I met Paul's mum and his sister Lynne soon after we started going out. It was a lovely moment when he said that he wanted to introduce me because it was a sign of his commitment. The meeting with Chris didn't start too well, though. When Paul told his mum I was an actor, she apparently said: 'Oh dear!' His family are so normal and I tried to be on my best behaviour, but Paul told me afterwards I chain-smoked and probably swore a bit, too. Thankfully they liked me, and I later discovered they were pleased that I was so down-to-earth, not a luvvie. Chris is a lovely lady, very generous, loyal, and she's been a great mother. She and her late husband Ron must take a good deal of credit for the way Paul and his sister turned out.

It was rather different when Paul met Mum and Nan. Both adored him and he liked them, too, but I don't think he had ever met a family like ours. Rows and verbal fights are an Olympic sport in my family, something everyone can join in with. I remember him driving me, Mum and Nan for a pre-Christmas dinner at Uncle Jim's, just six months after we met. As usual, Uncle Jim and Auntie Wendy had laid on a lavish do. Elvis Presley was on the CD player and everyone was talking in raised voices, trying to cram as many swear words into a sentence as possible. They even put them between the syllables in a word: abso-fucking-lutely. It was Paul's first taste of my fiery family in full flow, whereas to us it was all normal, family fun. On the way back after a bit to drink, Mum and Nan started to wind each other up. Nan was talking to Paul and Mum said something.

'Shut up, Val! Go on, Paul, what was you saying?' said Nan.

'It's fine, it doesn't matter,' said Paul, trying to keep things upbeat.

'No, go on, *say* it! Don't take any notice of her,' Nan gestured towards Mum.

'Honestly, Rose. It's fine,' said Paul.

'*See*? He doesn't want to say anything!' said Mum.

'*You* can shut up and mind your own business! *Go* on, say what you were going to say, Paul,' Nan persisted.

'I was only going to say it should be a clear run home …'

'*Oi*, don't talk to me like that!' Mum told Nan.

'Will you let him *fucking* speak, Val?'

'I'm sick of you talking to me like that!'

'Oh, you, you, *you* …' Nan was getting more and more in a state, 'you c\*\*t!'

I sat frozen with a Rodney Trotter face on, and I'm convinced if Paul could have abandoned a moving car he would have leapt out the door. They say if you want to see how your wife or girl-friend will turn out in 30 years, take a look at the mother. Well, after such a display from both generations of the Maxwells I'd have packed me in there and then.

\*　\*　\*

After our first two or three dates Paul asked if I wanted children. I had never wanted them. Having babies was associated with the shame and misery of my own birth and I'd taken on board Mike Hughes's warning about not mixing motherhood with my career. Deep down, I was frightened because I didn't think I would be any good at it, but I was intent on keeping Paul.

'God, yeah – I'd love to have kids! I want about eight,' I told him.

When you say something to Paul, he believes you. He tells the truth, so why wouldn't I? It was early on and this might have been a deal breaker. I didn't want to take that chance.

'Great, because I really want kids, and if you didn't, that would be a big problem for me,' he said.

I'm so glad I told him. It might have been a lie, but it put my life on the right track.

After *Grease* I went through a long period when I had no work and it got to the point when I actually thought about other jobs I could do outside show business. I was completely broke and still owed money, Mum used to bung me a few quid here and there and Paul was very supportive. Luckily for me, a cheque came in for the repeat fees from *Bottom*. It was a complete surprise and a real lifesaver; it was several thousand pounds, enough to pay off my debts. Good old Lily Linacre to the rescue! Even so, I did think that maybe I should still give the whole thing up.

My friend Lisa Haddigan (sister of the actor Mark Haddigan) told me about a friend of hers who was selling a new American skincare product, 'New Skin', and she was going great guns. So I went along to a meeting and I thought, I could do that. I signed up, hired a room at Soho House for £50 and invited lots of people. I gave a little speech about New Skin and it all kicked off really well, with lots of people volunteering to be agents. Paul was there, and apparently he was thinking, she shouldn't be doing this.

'I'm not giving up acting, I'm still an actress!' I told him. 'I'm only doing this because I'm *really* interested in skincare and beauty products.' I made it sound as if it was just a bit of fun, to convince myself as much as Paul. It wasn't what I wanted to be doing – I just needed to earn some money. In fact, I only did it for a couple of months – it really wasn't right for me.

Paul still says to people, 'D'you know, when I first knew Lisa she was selling beauty products? Can you believe it? She's so bloody good at acting! How could she ever think of doing something else?'

So my life was falling into place, apart from work. There was nothing lined up, and before I left *Grease* I made a list of everybody in the industry I knew. I wrote letters to everyone and I made lots of phone calls and went to meetings. It was gratifying some really important people made time to see me and I was given some great advice. Nigel Lythgoe, who had been the producer on one section of *The Joe Longthorne Show* (made for Central TV back in 1988), was by this time head of light entertainment at London Weekend. He made time for me and we talked through which direction I should go in. I wasn't asking for anything other than advice.

Paul Smith at Celador also knew me from *Gibberish*, the show I'd made with Kenny Everett. Altogether I saw five or six top people, including Paul Jackson at the BBC, and they were all happy to see me, told me I should not give up the business because I was too talented, explained television was tough at the time (budgets were low) and because I hadn't been seen onscreen for a long time it would be a struggle. No one was able to offer me work but they were all very kind and didn't fob me off politely without seeing me. 'You will get back – cream always rises,' was one comment I particularly treasured.

One of them offered me seats for several *An Audience With …* shows. My initial reaction was, 'Ooh, that's a sorry state of affairs when all I can get is a seat in the audience!' but I went to loads and they were fun events that made me feel I was still connected, even if I wasn't actually working.

During my time in *Grease* I had met a new agent. Denis Selinger was lovely but he was used to representing big stars, not people who needed to have a lot of work put in on their behalf. I wish I could have lived up to his expectations but he was too big for me. Stan Dallas (Shane's agent) regularly watched the show, which impressed me; he also knew the background I came from because he represented a few comics. He himself had been part of the Dallas Boys act so he understood the business inside out.

Stan was very friendly. He once told me that before I joined the cast of *Grease* he always used the bedroom scene (where the Pink Ladies sing 'Sandra Dee') as his cue to go to the loo but I turned it into one of the funniest parts of the show and so he had found himself a different toilet break! It was positive feedback after my confidence had taken such a knock. If your agent is a fan, you know they'll always try to promote you.

Stan got me a meeting with Andy Harris from Granada, who was casting *Cold Feet*. The part I read for the TV series was the one that eventually went to Fay Ripley (Jenny Gifford), playing opposite John Thomson. I was so nervous, I wanted the part so badly, and I ended up doing the worst audition of my life.

Nerves were new: I'd never had to cope with them before when I was younger. I've always believed if you show how much you want a part, you won't get it (I think you can smell desperation and it puts people off). I walked out knowing I hadn't got the part, feeling I never wanted to audition for anything ever again. It was a very low point for me when I seriously believed I didn't have what it takes to stay in the business. When I read the script for the audition scene, I knew I didn't feel anything; I now know that to be a good actress you have to be truthful to yourself, and at this stage I was only beginning to accept the truth, to allow myself to feel my own emotions, and my emptiness showed through at the audition. Meanwhile, the happiness I did have – and I *was* very happy – all came from being with Paul. That was the most important thing to me, and I started to question why I was even trying to keep going with my career.

Paul's career was going well. His design business was doing well and he had plenty of work to keep him busy. We were friendly with Jake and Angelo Panayiotou, the brothers who owned Browns Night Club, the scene of many a late-night party crime for me. I'm proud to say I'm the only girl to be barred from there twice, for trying to get in when they were closed. On one occasion I sneaked in through the staff entrance when they were bringing the bin bags out, crawled along the floor and jumped up from behind the bar. Jake and Angelo were mates and they commissioned Paul to design a logo and re-brand all their companies, including the chauffeur hire company. He ended up moving his premises to a studio above Browns.

So Paul's business was going from strength to strength and he was looking after me. It wasn't something I was used to, and to this day I still don't feel comfortable being completely dependent on someone else financially – I like to feel I have my own choices. Having your own money gives a feeling of independence; you don't have to explain when you treat yourself. In the end, when you're with someone you love your goals merge and you want to spend money on the same things, anyway, but I wasn't used to not contributing. From the age of 11 I'd been earning my own money. Paul loved taking care of me but he also knew I wanted to work and he was totally supportive of all my efforts.

At this time there were a few of us with nothing to do, and Shane came up with the idea of doing *Boogie Nights*, a musical set in the 1970s. A gang of us went along to a rehearsal room at Pineapple Dance Studios in Covent Garden to workshop it. Shane took the lead role of Roddy, I was his girlfriend Debs, Steve Serlin was also in on the idea, Claire Dallison and Peter Piper. We sat around talking it through and improvised bits, which we then videoed. Somehow, with the help of writers Jon Conway and Terry Morrison, we pulled a show together. We chose the name, *Boogie Nights*, because that was the nightclub where a lot of the action would take place.

By complete coincidence, the year we launched the musical the Hollywood movie of the same name came out. We had to decide whether to change our name, but we didn't, and as we got there first they couldn't force us. It was great fun working on the musical, and quite quickly Jon Conway had a completed show to produce. The première was in Bromley, November

1997, around my 34th birthday. It was a great time – I was with my old mates, I made new friends and the show was packed with really good seventies' music. Also, I got to sing 'I Will Survive', and what could beat that? It brought the house down every night.

I always worry about my voice when I'm in a musical. When I was at school I was a mezzo-soprano, and it was a good strong 'chest' voice. It has since slid down the scale, thanks to years of drinking, smoking and partying. I don't think bulimia was any good for it, either! I love singing, but the first thing I did every morning was check it was still there. I think a lot of people in musical theatre do the same.

After good reviews, we took the show around the country. I was working and on a payroll again, which made me feel good. Paul, bless him, followed the tour around the country. He'd pack up work on Friday and hit the road. During this time he became great mates with Shane, who is one of the best, most loyal friends you could ever have – he always looked out for me. I know the break-up of his marriage to Coleen resulted in bad publicity for him, but he's always maintained a dignified silence and I can only speak about the Shane I know; as far as I'm concerned, he's one of the good guys. The three of us really bonded through some pretty low points during the tour as Shane's marriage was on the rocks. Shane's PA, Chris Gosling (known to everyone as 'Gos'), became another great mate and really kept us going for our three months on the road.

I've seen so many relationships founder because of tours – I'd been there myself, remember? But Paul and I were rock-solid. He was smart enough to know we needed to nurture our love, and besides, we couldn't bear to be apart for more than a few days so he made an enormous effort to be with me. All the time when he wasn't there I was dreaming of the day when he would arrive. Everyone liked him and he fitted in so well, he became part of our touring company.

We had a lot of laughs. The unattached boys in the cast could be quite naughty and I remember coming out of a nightclub in Bristol to see one of our lads driving away with a girl in the car. Meanwhile, a big Bristolian was clinging onto the roof, shouting, ''Ere, that's my bird he's got in there!'

When the tour was over we went straight into the Savoy Theatre in London for 12 weeks. Reviews were mixed but we played to packed houses, and that's what counts. The audiences were mostly women and they would stand up, screaming and shouting, whenever I sang 'I Will Survive'. But I didn't create a stir – I don't think any of the critics remembered me from my brief period of celebrity before the States. My big opportunity to set the world on fire had gone and I'm glad it didn't happen. Really, I don't think I had enough drive in me because my motives were always dubious; I wasn't doing it for the sake of the work itself, it was to prove something. Looking back, I felt relieved that I had come a cropper before anything bigger happened for me.

Most of all, I felt so relieved that I hadn't stayed in America and missed the chance of meeting Paul. Being with him felt more right than anything ever had. I'd come home at last. So it was natural and inevitable that I would start to want everything that went with a full life with Paul: a baby. I don't think I ever had that broody thing some women experience where they go round peering into prams, I wasn't a maternal person, but I wanted a baby with Paul, a part of him. For the first time in my life I was with someone to whom I could make myself vulnerable and admit to making mistakes, a person who loved me for the parts of me which weren't successful, who loved the real me. But the one thing that held me back from saying 'yes' to a baby was an overriding fear: 'I'll fuck it up.'

'You'd be a great mum,' Paul told me.

He must have been the only person in the world to see me as a mother. Everybody in my family believed I was still a kid, too scatty to look after a baby – and I believed them. After all, this was someone who was scared of dealing with grown-up stuff like money, and having babies was about as grown-up as it gets, but I decided to go for it. When the run at The Savoy was over, *Boogie Nights* went back out on tour. Neither Paul nor I wanted to be apart like that again, and we'd made the big decision. I left the cast to start a family.

Two weeks later, I could tell something was happening. My period was late, but it was more than that: there was a definite feeling of something being different about my body. It was far too early for there to be real signs, but I knew. While Paul was at work I bought a pregnancy testing kit, and when he came home I wee'd on it but didn't tell him. Coming back, he found me perched on the back of the living-room sofa, head in my hands.

'What's wrong?' he asked.

'I've just done one of those pregnancy thingies …'

'*And*?' he said, gently.

'I don't *know*, I can't bring myself to look at it! Will you check it? It's in the bathroom.'

And so Paul knew I was pregnant before I did, for he came back beaming. It wasn't the last time he would get in there first with life-changing news but I wouldn't have wanted to find out any other way, I must say.

Paul always has this wonderfully patient way of filtering information and presenting it to me in the best possible way. I hope I know him well enough to do the same for him these days. On this occasion I don't think he was consciously filtering anything, he was just thrilled, and the feeling was contagious. We cuddled, hugged, cried a bit. With Paul the way he was, it didn't seem right for me to be anything but overjoyed. But I was scared because I didn't know anything about babies; I didn't have any real parenting role models. Mum, Nan and Grandad had all been there for me, but it hadn't been a conventional family. I had no idea what fathers do either; coming from a generation who believed babies were women's work, Grandad had not been hands-on when I was little. How would I cope?

After a week or two I rang Mum to tell her the news, but I made the call with trepidation. I didn't want to burst our happy little bubble. After I'd told her, she went quiet. 'Is that good?' she asked (I could tell she didn't know what to say for the best and she really didn't know whether I would be happy or desolate). In her experience, it could be the worst thing that's ever happened. I rushed on and said, 'I feel great. Paul's over the moon – we're both delighted!' I threw a wall of happiness so tall at her, she could not break it: 'This is happy, this is *good*!' I was saying. 'Take on this message and behave like normal people. Celebrate the news!'

# CHAPTER 13

## *Beautiful Beau*

I might have been able to make a positive case for my pregnancy to Mum, but inside I was really, *really* scared of childbirth. I once read an interview with Helen Mirren in which she said one of the reasons why she does not have children is she was almost phobic about the idea of childbirth, and I know where she's coming from.

It was actually an easy pregnancy: there was no morning sickness, no real discomfort. I was very healthy, eating sensibly and not drinking at all. The minute I suspected I might be pregnant I gave up smoking, too. I knew I would be 35 when I gave birth, and this worried me, particularly after an obstetrician described me as 'an older mum'.

Paul was totally understanding and committed to making me as happy as he could. We're both NHS people all the way through our lives and I'm a huge supporter, but he said to me, 'If you are scared, we will go private and then you will have someone you can ring up at any time, whenever you have anything bothering you.'

So I booked into the Lindo Wing of St Mary's Hospital, Paddington. As he said, we were doing one of the most important things of our entire lives and the cost was no more than a luxury holiday – wasn't this a much better way to spend the money? And he was right about me having someone to phone: by the end of my term the staff all recognised my voice on the other end of the line. Whenever I saw anyone there who looked remotely medical, I said the word 'epidural' – I wanted them all to know I don't do pain. I'd have had the epidural in the cab on the way to the hospital, if I could.

We knew we were expecting a girl because we had a gender scan. Right up to the moment when I was told she was a girl, I thought my baby might be a boy. I think this was because Mum had always said she would have loved a son. 'Boys look after their mums,' she told me. Maybe that's why it was in my head that I needed a boy for her. I was completely taken aback to find out our little one was a girl. I loved seeing her on the scan, looking so cosy and with her little hand up to her nose.

I remember having slight reservations about telling Mum I was expecting a girl – I think part of me wanted it to be different from her own experience. What I said was, 'I'm having a girl, like you.' By this time she'd got her head around the fact that it was all good news and she said, 'That's wonderful! Brilliant, darling.' I used to lie on the bed to relax and if Paul was around he would come and lie down with me, but he would soon get bored and play war games on his PlayStation 2. 'We're under attack, we're under attack!' was all I could hear as I tried to think peaceful thoughts. 'Bloody hell, this baby will come out armed to the teeth and ready for action!' I told him.

\* \* \*

I didn't work through the pregnancy. I didn't want to, I wanted to concentrate on this wonderful thing that was happening. Also, I knew myself well enough by then to realise that if I took on a job I would get so distracted and immersed I'd convince myself nothing else was happening and then I'd have an almighty shock when the baby was born. I needed time to get my head round it, to absorb every part of it and share it with Paul. The old Lisa would have been in denial, but since Paul came into my life I was so different: I didn't want to sweep anything under the carpet.

But I did get myself a new agent when I was five months pregnant. Stan Dallas had been great; he'd got me a good opportunity (which I'd blown) in *Cold Feet*, but his main interests were light entertainment and comedy. Being pregnant had forced me to prioritise everything in my life and I had no intention of leaving this baby unless it was something I really wanted to do. I'd always intended to get more into drama. Maybe, as I didn't care so much whether I got the jobs or not, I should only go for the ones that were really special to me.

Mark Thrippleton, one of the mates who had appeared with me in *Boogie Nights*, recommended his agent Derek Webster, so I switched. I told Derek I didn't want to work while I was pregnant or immediately afterwards but he was so cool about it and still took me on.

It was Paul who kept my fear of the birth under control; he was with me for every scan, the antenatal classes, read all the books and made a fuss of me for the whole nine months. It made me realise how different it must have been for Mum, trying to conceal her pregnancy for as long as possible, always ashamed

With Linzi Hateley, backstage at the Dominion Theatre, after a performance of *Grease*.

Hitting the Champers after the final performance of *Grease*.

With Shane Ritchie.

The night I met Paul. It's surprising he got a word in edgeways!

Early days with my gorgeous partner Paul.

Simon, Paul, Shane and Spud.

On the *Boogie Nights* tour with Shane and Steve Serlin.

Meeting the Queen with Christopher Cazenove.

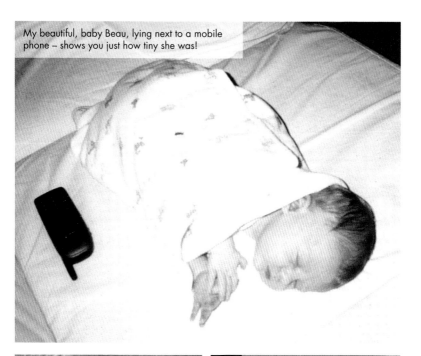

My beautiful, baby Beau, lying next to a mobile phone – shows you just how tiny she was!

Looks like she got the posing from her mum!

This is one of my favourite pictures of me and my gorgeous little girl.

Part of *The Bill* family.

Dressed up like old coppers.

A night on the red carpet with *The Bill* girls in blue.

Filming a scene for *In Deep*. This is what I look like dead!

The photo of himself that my dad gave Paul the day they first met.

My dad as a young lad with his mum and his nan.

My great-grandfather on my dad's side.

Paul and his beautiful sister Lynne.

The day I won the mum's race at Beau's sports day.

Another favourite picture: me and Beau on the beach in the Maldives.

Paul on the beach.

Paul and Beau snorkeling in Hainan Island, China.

Four generations of Maxwell women.

A picture Beau painted of my nan.

Opening the door to our Cotswold dream.

Sometimes all the hard work pays off. Here I am with the BAFTA *The Bill* won in 2009 for Best Serial Drama.

With Adam Garcia.

On the set of *Loose Women*.

and alone. During those months I felt for her and I really appreciated what she had been through to bring me into the world.

Once we knew we were having a girl I started buying all the gear we needed: the pram, car seat, cot … It was all in the spare room and I would lie on the bed and imagine one day a baby would be there. I'd lie there, looking at the baby things, having a foot massage from Danuta, our Polish cleaner, and think, innit lovely, my life?

We began the quest for the right name, lying side by side on the bed and coming up with ideas. After going through a couple of books, nothing really spoke to us. For a time we thought of calling her 'Frankie' after Frank Sinatra. We wanted something strong, not too frilly or girlie, and we didn't want lots of others with the same name in her class. It was Paul who finally came up with it. 'How about Beau Jessup?' he suggested. It was perfect, Beau being the first four letters of 'beautiful'. We agreed to reserve judgement until she was born, just in case she didn't look like a Beau, though.

The birth started on Saturday, 9 October 1999, just a week before my due date when I went to the loo for a wee, finished and then had another one immediately afterwards. Weird, I thought, so I rang the Lindo Wing. 'Hello, Lisa, what now?' said the nurse, not even waiting until I said my name. 'Do you think your waters have broken?' she said, after hearing about my little wees. But there was no great flood and so she told me, 'Just keep an eye and call us later or come in.' By Sunday my double wees were continuing, and when I rang again they said to definitely come in this time. My waters were probably leaking rather than gushing away, and without the water around the baby there's a risk of infection so they wanted to induce me.

The worst part of the whole experience was having the epidural. They told me it could hurt and said: 'Don't be frightened to swear or yell, or whatever you want.' I think I broke the world record for the amount of 'shits' anyone can say in a short space of time. Paul, who was outside the room, said all he could hear was me going, 'Shit, shit … Shit, shit, shit … *SHIT*!'

They put me in bed and then I had to wait for everything to happen. I remember watching the MTV awards, eating Terry's Chocolate Oranges (one of the nurses suggested we call her Terry when she was born). Very serene, I was feeling nothing but aware the contractions were starting. When the obstetrician came in to see how I was getting on, he told me everything was on course apart from the fact our baby daughter had her head down but was in a strange position on her back, which wasn't ideal. He said some doctors could do a Caesarean, but he would rather wait a while to see if she turned on her own. If she's lying in the same position as me and I turn, maybe she'll turn, I thought. So I lay on my side, and a few hours later when he came back she had turned. Meanwhile I couldn't feel a thing, thanks to the epidural.

'Are we ready to do some pushing?' he asked.

'What do you mean?' I said. 'I don't think you understand. I've had an epidural, I'm not doing the pushing!'

'You still need to breathe, Lisa.'

'No, I'm not doing the breathing, I've had the epidural!'

'You still need to breathe.'

'I'm breathing, but I'm not doing the puffing or pushing – I've had the epidural!' I insisted.

'But Lisa, how do you think I'm going to get the baby out?'

'Can't you just pull her out? I've had the epidural …'

Honestly, I didn't realise that I would still have to do some work even though I wasn't feeling the contractions. All those antenatal classes, all those books … somehow I'd missed the point. I thought the epidural would take away all the work, too.

'All right, I'll push! How long do I have to push for?'

'Maybe three hours.'

'*Three* hours! I'm not doing three bloody hours!'

I was knackered; my body was still going through labour, even if I wasn't in pain. I'd had a shaky moment when I felt cold and my teeth chattered, but apparently this can happen after an epidural. I kept telling Paul I was cold and the heating was faulty, but of course it wasn't. So I decided to take control of this pushing business.

'Right, let's get on with it!'

'When I tell you to push, push!' said the midwife.

And so I did: I got up on my haunches and screamed the place down, pushing with all my might. It paid off because I popped her out in 45 minutes, at 4 a.m. – I almost popped my tonsils out at the same time.

Beau emerged with both her arms outstretched in front of her face as if to say, 'Here I am, world!' They gave me a choice to hold her or have her cleaned up first. Because I'm squeamish, I asked them to clean her up. I still didn't know how I would feel when I saw my baby for the first time, and as I knew I wasn't a maternal person the last thing I wanted was to feel squeamish about the way she looked. When she was handed back to me, all clean, I put her straight to the breast and looked down at her fuzzy little soft head: 'Hello, I'm your mummy,' I told her.

She was the most beautiful thing I've ever seen. She was perfect. All those maternal emotions I didn't think I had came charging in. I never wanted to have her out of my arms, not ever again. It was the weirdest thing, a huge surge of wild happiness. I was amazed, I'd never expected it. Why would I be a natural mother? Everyone said I wouldn't be; only Paul had faith in me. But, lying there with Beau on the delivery bed and introducing myself as her mummy, I felt such pride. Paul was watching over us. He never took his eyes off us; he was in love with us both. We started calling her Beau straight away – the name was perfect for her.

Beau weighed in at 6lb 13oz, a normal weight. She was put on a preventive course of antibiotics because of the risk from my leaking membrane before the birth. This meant we had to stay in hospital for five days, which was great because it gave us time to get to know each other. We existed in our own little bubble: Beau, Paul, the nurses and me.

We didn't sleep that first night after the birth – we were both so high from the thrill of it. At 6 a.m., Mum, Nan and Paul's mum Chris all arrived to coo over Beau, and by eight o'clock Shane and Steve walked in. They were on tour with *Boogie Nights*, but had driven overnight from Blackpool to be there. We'd already decided Shane was to be Beau's godfather; he'd told us so himself, the minute he knew I was pregnant.

'How's my godchild coming along?' he'd ask, every time I saw him. While I was pregnant, Paul and I made a pact that we would make our little girl smile every day of her life and so it was no surprise we chose Shane. He's been such a good choice, always getting it exactly right and genuinely caring about her. And he's taught her some very valuable life lessons, too: she was the only five-year-old who could make it look like she'd taken out one of her eyeballs and popped it into her mouth so her cheek stuck out like a lop-sided hamster (if that doesn't get her on in life, I don't know what will). Some years later Shane was to return the compliment by asking Paul and me to be godparents to his first baby daughter. Adam has also been a big part of her life; he lived with us for 10 months and they became really good friends. Steven has been trying to beat Beau at Xbox since she could hold her own controller. She adores all three of them: Shane, Adam and Steve.

For the first few days Paul had a little bed in our room, but after a couple of nights he had to go home. He said it was strange going out into the outside world; he wanted to yell at all the passers-by, just as I had on the day we met, 'Do you know what's happened? Do you know the most massive thing has happened and you're all just carrying on like normal?'

She was the prettiest baby, with a lovely shape to her head. Some newborns have squashed faces from the birth, and it doesn't matter because it soon rights itself, but Beau's face was perfect from the start. Her nose was ever so slightly crooked, but corrected itself in a couple of weeks. She was amazing, in every possible way. The funny thing is when she was tiny she slept with her hand up exactly the way she did before she was born when I saw her on the scan. I suppose it's only natural that babies do the same things outside the womb, but it was still touching to see.

I came home from hospital to packing cases and a certain amount of chaos although Paul did his best to shield Beau and me from the move. We were still living in his two-bedroom in Muswell Hill but during the pregnancy we'd looked for somewhere bigger. Amazingly, a house came up just three doors away. It was everything we wanted because we loved the location and it was similar to the flat, which was simply a house divided into two. The owner told us that she had bought it when she was pregnant with her first child, which seemed like a good omen.

The sale of our flat and purchase of the new house were going through while I was in hospital with Beau – Paul was popping out of the Lindo Wing to make calls and arrange money transfers. I remember him walking back into the hospital and announcing: 'We've got a house!' As all these wonderful things unfolded before me, I felt delirious with happiness. We had a baby, a beautiful house and a perfect relationship.

Two weeks after I got home, we moved in. Mum stayed with us and she was brilliant: she was doing the washing and the shopping, and we muddled through those hazy, milky, timeless days. My other great help was Danuta, and when I had trouble breastfeeding she took Beau's tiny head and stuck it to my breast until she latched on – I learnt so much from her.

The house move was organised by my Uncle Alan. He'd followed Uncle Jim into the haulage business and turned up with a van. A lot of our stuff could just be carried down the street, but the heavy things went in the van. Of course we didn't have enough furniture at first and the new house felt massive after the flat. Meanwhile, Paul and I used to spend hours lying on the floor in the back sitting room, just gawping at our wonderful baby.

I breastfed Beau for six weeks to give her a good start, and the day I stopped feeding her I started smoking again – terrible, isn't it? I never smoked in the same room as Beau, but taking that first drag after all those months felt good. Six years ago I gave up again and managed to stay off for four years. Then I foolishly decided I could have 'just the odd one', but it doesn't work like that. So I gave up again in 2010 – I used Allen Carr's *Easy Way to Stop Smoking*. I was too scared to read the book in case it worked, so I gave it to Paul (who got halfway through and quit). This time I'm sticking to it.

In the April after Beau's birth, when she was six months old, Paul and I got engaged. I don't know why or when we decided we were getting married, but it seemed right. What with the birth of the baby and moving house, the wedding was put on hold – it was all too much at one time – but we wanted to get engaged, to make the public commitment. A friend of a friend of ours, a jeweller who sources diamonds for Cartier, came round to the house with envelopes full of diamonds so that I could pick the stone I wanted. I was amazed and honoured when Paul insisted I have the diamond I fell in love with: a three-carat, princess-cut flawless blue stone – it cost a lot, but it's forever. We decided on a simple platinum setting, nothing to detract from the beauty of the diamond, and Paul had the date we were engaged engraved inside. I have small hands so a cluster of stones would have looked wrong. This is the most perfect ring in the world.

We had a party to celebrate our engagement, just a few friends. Mostly, Paul and I just love being on our own with Beau – we like retreating into our own space. For so many years when I was with Darren I was half of a couple who only functioned well in public when we were a winning team, part of the cabaret. But me, Beau and Paul, we are good as a unit; we don't have anything to prove, the three of us are fantastic together.

For the first 18 months after Beau's birth I told Derek Webster that I didn't want to work at all. When I was ready, I said to him, 'I don't want to work outside the M25 area and I don't want to be onstage doing eight shows a week.' Poor man, ever since he'd known me all I did was tell him what I didn't want to do, which is the exact opposite of most unemployed actors. He was very lovely about it, but extremely happy when he rang to tell me about my first job: 'Lisa, it's what you want! It's television, it's being shot in Hertfordshire, just up the road from Muswell Hill – you'll *love* it!'

*In Deep* was a cop drama starring Nick Berry, who I'd known since I was 16, and Stephen Tompkinson (*Ballykissangel* and later *Wild at Heart*). Jake Wood (Max Branning from *EastEnders*) was also in it, and Michael Maloney, a heavyweight actor most familiar from his role in *Casualty*. The director was Paul Marcus, a highly respected and revered director (he directed the first *Prime Suspect*), so I was keen to do it. But I was worried because I felt I didn't have the right body of work behind me for such a dramatic role. The story was that Nick was an undercover cop, so deep undercover his whole life was overtaken by the subterfuge. I was up for the role of his wife, Pamela Ketman – a part with harrowing scenes and great tension attached to it.

Unlike the *Cold Feet* audition, I was relaxed. I didn't expect to get it. I'd heard they had a couple of Shakespearean actresses up for the part. As for me, my home life was perfect, couldn't have been better; I wanted the part, but if I didn't get it then I had the rest of my life to fall back on. So, I indulged myself. They asked me to read a highly emotional scene and I just got right into it. By now, I was ready to feel everything and I was in touch with who I was, which helped me get in character. So I did my AFF routine, plunged into freefall and made the most of it.

It was so easy, reading opposite Nick. After our teenage encounters, I'd seen him on and off over the years and heard about him through friends of friends. Before the audition he said, 'Are we going to get the pictures out?' (He was now a parent, too.) 'Don't get me started!' I said. And so we chatted about having babies and agreed it was the most amazing thing that had happened in our lives.

He gave such a lot to me. It helps to read with someone you know and he held eye contact and kept me rock-steady throughout. I loved it, and driving away afterwards I remember thinking, well, even if I don't get the part, I've had a blast. My priorities had changed so much and I genuinely did not mind whether or not I got the part: Beau and Paul came first and my career was way down the list. Probably for the first time since I went to stage school I was in a healthy relationship with my own career.

The audition tapes were sent to Mal Young, head of drama at the BBC. To my surprise and delight, I was asked to take the part. After the initial exhilaration, panic set in: could I do a serious acting job? It was one thing pulling out all the stops for an audition, but could I sustain it?

On set, everyone was very supportive although it still felt strange to be leaving home for work. I'd left Beau for short periods, but to be doing long days of filming felt as though a part of my body had been amputated – I was so used to the weight of Beau in my arms, they felt positively empty. We had a day nanny at home looking after her and Paul was around as much as possible. The two grandmothers, Nanny Chris and Nanny Val, were also very supportive; Beau was a first grand-child for them both. They adored her and spent as much time with her as they could. But you know me: I soon got stuck into the work, *really* stuck into it.

Pamela Ketman, my character, was emotionally drained and mentally scarred. She was trying desperately to hold her marriage and her two children together while leading a double life because of her husband's job as an undercover policeman. Paranoid and insecure, she was on the verge of losing the will to go on. So I did what Lisa does: I got myself into the zone and stayed there all day, even when I wasn't on-camera (it was a bit like my first impression when I did Princess Diana). I've since learnt to switch on and off more easily, but on day one I was so keen to get it right that I became Pamela, even during a five-hour break!

One of my first scenes was with Jake Wood and I remember he came to my caravan during the break, probably just for a chat. What he found was this strange woman, who was numb and completely withdrawn. He must have thought it very odd because I'm normally bubbly and you can't shut me up. I bet he left thinking she's a bloody basket case! But I was just feeling my way into real drama: I was relying on instincts and desperate to get it right. I think I did all right, though, because after my very first scene the crew clapped and the director, the lovely Paul

Marcus, said in front of everyone, 'That was ace!' I felt amazing: for me, this was virgin territory, and the fact that someone as experienced and brilliant as Paul had been prepared to cast me was a huge accolade. Now there he was, praising me in front of everyone.

The series was shot in 10 days and my agent was right about it being easy for me: driving north out of London in the opposite direction to the commuter traffic was no problem, and so I wasn't away from Beau for too long. It was a success and a second series was commissioned. In this one I was murdered – well, it was nice while it lasted! It was to be a powerful, disturbing exit (poor old Pamela is hung from a loft ladder by Michael Maloney's character). I'd never died in anything before and was excited when the make-up designer said I'd need ligature bruising on my arms and made me all blue and dead looking. When my character's husband (Nick Berry) came home, he walked along the landing and suddenly there I was, dangling in front of him.

I took a Polaroid home to show to my family. 'Here you are, this is what I look like dead!' I announced cheerfully. Mum was a bit upset, but I think it was better that she was prepared rather than just seeing it on screen. Paul was much more relaxed – 'I wish I'd been there to enjoy the moment,' he said. We'd been together long enough now for him to be making ''Er Indoors' jokes.

In between the two series of *In Deep*, I had a part in *The Bill* as the wife of a gangster (played by Michael Elphick). When *In Deep* went out, I was called in by Louis Hammond, casting director of *The Bill*, for something else: a meatier role playing Paul Usher's sister-in-law, who was leading a vigilante group against a local paedophile. I was offered the part but when someone checked the records they saw that I'd been in the programme within the past 12 months (they have an absolute rule that no actor can be used for different parts within this time frame). Louis was disappointed, and when he rang my agent to tell him he said: 'I'm sorry we can't use her this time – I think she's absolutely brilliant and I'm definitely getting her back.'

But before my next visit to Sun Hill, I was asked to play an unusual part in a docudrama. *Get Carman* was about the famous barrister, George Carman (played by David Suchet). My agent rang to say they wanted me to play the part of Gillian Taylforth, the *EastEnders'* star who, with her partner, had been involved in a case with Carman (she had tried unsuccessfully to get the programme stopped). I was being asked to play her from the original transcript of the court case.

'I feel a bit weird, being offered the part of someone who is in the same business. It doesn't feel right,' I told Derek (I'd never met Gillian, but always heard nice things about her).

'Look, I know Gilly – I'll give her a call,' he offered.

'Tell her if it's going to create hell for her I won't do it,' I said.

When he spoke to Gillian, her reaction was, 'Look, someone's going to do it! I'd rather it's done well. Tell Lisa to go ahead – and tell her I really appreciate her asking.'

Later I worked with Gilly and she said the same thing; she was touched I'd taken the time to find out how she felt about it. She's a great lady – down-to-earth, upbeat, a real joy to work with. I swear to God, if she hadn't wanted me to do it, I wouldn't have, though. *Get Carman* was broadcast after I took the call about a job that was to impact not only on my career but on my personal life more than any other: *The Bill*.

# CHAPTER 14

## Being DJ Sam Nixon

The call to another casting meeting at *The Bill* came and I was delighted, hoping they had another meaty role in mind. When I got there I was taken in to see Louis Hammond and Paul Marquess (a top writer and producer who had worked on *Coronation Street* and *Brookside*). Paul had been brought in to save *The Bill*. The show had been running since 1984, and although it had a faithful audience, the ratings were dropping and he faced an ultimatum: get the figures up or it's coming off. Not that I knew this at the time when Louis introduced us.

Earlier in his career Louis had been an agent, and we knew of each other. To my great surprise he was aware of everything I had done in the past before I dropped off the radar and vanished to America. 'She's had a phenomenal career,' he told Paul and recited my CV better than I could have done it myself. He couldn't have been more generous.

After Louis gave me my build-up, it was Paul's turn. He began to explain in clear terms exactly what his plans for the show were. 'I love strong female characters,' he said. 'My favourite characters in *Coronation Street* are the strong women, the ones who can sustain a role for 30 years or more and still find a lot in it – we need to get the female audience back to *The Bill*.'

He asked what I thought of the show and I knew it was better to be honest than gush about it, although I hadn't seen many episodes. I enjoy getting to know what makes characters tick and so I said I'd like to know a bit more about the policemen as people rather than just the collective face of the Met and their rules. Maybe that's a female thing. Somewhere along the line it occurred to me this wasn't the usual five-minute chat about another part.

Paul then told me he had a strong female character he wanted to bring in. At that stage her name was Jackie Maddocks (she went through a few name changes before Sam Nixon finally hit the screens). He gave me her background: 'She comes in as an acting detective inspector, she has a degree in criminology and she wanted to be part of the Met's profiling team, but she didn't make it. She believes she was the victim of sexism and she's got a big point to prove. And we find out she has a dark past …' When he asked, 'Is this something you'd be interested in?' I thought, why are you even asking? What I said was, 'She sounds fascinating – I'd love it.' Then it was all, 'Great to meet you, that was a really interesting chat,' and we said goodbye.

'Leave your phone on,' Louis told me when we got out of the meeting. Of course I phoned my agent straight away and told him there was a great part on offer, a regular character, but I wasn't sure if they were seeing lots of others for it. Derek told me they wouldn't tell him what it was about before I went there. 'I'll let you know the minute I hear anything,' he promised. But I'd hardly had time to get into my car before he rang, literally within 10 minutes of leaving the meeting. 'You've got it!' he said, 'It's a big part and they want you on the show for two years.'

I was chuffed to pieces. But two years? It was a huge commitment, and although I wanted to work I really enjoyed the downtime between jobs to be with Beau. Straight away I rang Paul and said, 'We need to meet for a chat.'

Beau was at nursery, so Paul and I met at Café Rouge in Highgate.

'So, how did it go?' he asked.

'Really well, but something weird has happened – they want me for a two-year contract!'

It was a lot for us both to take in: that morning we'd been thinking I was going for another part that would span one or two episodes, and this was something so different. It wasn't just the time commitment I had to think about, but also my anonymity. I could walk around being Mrs Paul Jessup, Beau's mum, but a lead role in *The Bill* would put my face back on the screen but also in magazines and newspapers again. Paul, as ever, was completely supportive: 'It's a great opportunity, and whatever you decide we'll make it work – but it's up to you,' he said.

Paul has never told me what to do with my work; he's creative and passionate about the work he does, and one of the things he loves about me is that I don't do things by half.

'You've always wanted to act on a regular basis and that's what they're offering you. This is as good as it gets! You choose, you can always ask if you have to commit to two years,' he suggested.

So that's what I did. I rang Derek and said yes, but can you ask if it has to be for such a long time. He got back to me straight away: they wouldn't shorten the contract. So we agreed as a family that I would sign for two years, and DI Sam Nixon was born in April 2002. I think her name was changed to Sam so that she could, from the beginning, insist on Samantha – it immediately painted her as a bit of a control freak. She was a fascinating character and I quickly felt at ease with her.

I soon felt part of *The Bill* family: Roberta Taylor (Gina Gold) had just started, Diane Parish (Eva Sharpe) joined at roughly the same time as me and Scott Maslen (Phil Hunter) had not been there long. There was an explosion of new people and quite a few of the old familiar faces had gone. Every producer makes his mark, and Paul Marquess was determined to fulfil the brief to get the figures up.

I know some critics have said that during Paul's reign *The Bill* became too soapy, but it certainly wasn't like that at the beginning. He simply gave more depth and personal stories to the police officers, not just to the characters involved in the crimes they were solving. He gave the audience a reason to keep tuning in. I also know later on the private lives of the police characters did start to dominate over the crime, but ultimately it was this added layer – their private lives – that pushed the viewing figures up to their highest ever. Paul did what he was asked to do: he saved the show and kept a lot of people in employment.

My first director was Jamie Payne, who went on to direct *Ashes to Ashes*. On the first day he said to me, 'People don't realise the potential of comics as actors. I've just worked with

Bradley Walsh and I'm a big fan of his – I think the two of you have similar backgrounds. Comedy is much harder than drama, and comics have a tremendous quality to bring to drama.' Thank God he doesn't think he's been landed with a naff turn, I thought.

I vividly remember my first scene: Carl Collins had to bring me in and Simon Rouse, playing Jack Meadows, was to introduce me as a new acting DI and profiler. Talk about introduction – they lit me like something out of *Dynasty*! The viewers saw the back of me first, then I turned round and introduced myself. I made a speech that was full of psychobabble, the psychology of this and that, and took an age over it. When I look back at it, I think: for God's sake, Lisa, get on with it! In my defence, I did improve over the years as Sam.

Meanwhile there was no time for nerves as we went straight into filming a heavy storyline with Hywel Bennett as one of the main characters. My character, Sam, was always intrigued by the minds of killers or potential killers and eventually the storyline emerged that she had a child by a murderer, although she didn't know it at the time. She was obsessed with finding out if there is a genetic predisposition to murder because she was worried about her kid, Abi – later to be brilliantly played by my dearest little mate Georgia Moffett, who at the time was only 17. When she joined *The Bill*, Georgia already had a son – Ty – and I was in awe of how she coped as a young mum. She's now happily settled with her partner David Tennant (who, like her dad, once played Dr Who).

We worked at Merton, south-west London. At the beginning the schedule was workable, but it soon built up. We all drove ourselves to work, but later on a rule was introduced that if we did more than 14 hours straight we could have taxis (14-hour days were not uncommon). In reality, I frequently worked a six-day week. After we checked with Equity, we found they could actually work us every Sunday, but they kindly agreed only three out of four. I would leave at 6 a.m. and get home at about 8.30 p.m.

The first thing I did when I got home was to drop my bag and go straight upstairs to Beau's room to read her a bedtime story and tuck her in. She'd be awake, waiting for me. Afterwards I would go downstairs, kiss Paul 'hello', grab something to eat and start reading my dialogue for the next day – I had to be in the make-up chair by 7 a.m. In those days I was Sam Nixon far more than I was Lisa Maxwell. It's a bittersweet situation on a long-running show: you want the writers to like you and your character, to write for you, but the more they write for you, the less time you have with your family, and this can be tough, particularly if you're a mum.

At first I rolled with the punches, thinking, this is all right, I can handle this. In fact, I thrived on it and loved the chance to flex my acting muscles. I learnt a lot and had a great time with the other regulars. Everyone was terrific, and although the work was challenging I enjoyed being able to do it; there was a definite buzz from holding my own on such a demanding show. As the schedule became busier and busier, I got sucked into it, and when Sam became a permanent DI, I found myself in almost every storyline. As a senior officer, she had to deliver briefings at the beginning of each episode: it was a device to bring the audience up to date with the storyline but meant learning as much as 15 pages of dialogue for one scene (we nicknamed it 'News at Ten').

When I started, the show was on once a week for an hour, but doubled to twice a week. At any one time I could have eight different scripts in my head and be working with four or five different film units. And as time goes on and you become a reliable member of the company, you are entrusted to take care of business without much support. Which is absolutely great, but with it comes a certain amount of pressure.

The hours were becoming unreal. I hardly saw Paul; we had no time for a conversation, but we always seemed to find time for an argument. The work–life balance was completely wrong: I was doing nothing but working. When I'm working, I'm frighteningly committed, I can't dabble in something: I have to be focused. It's a selfish trait because I had two people who loved me and who I loved, and they suffered because I was not always there.

Children were not allowed to visit us at work so Beau had no understanding of what I did. Once when she did come to the set (she was only three years old), a security man yelled at her, 'Oi, where do you think you're going?' She froze and burst into tears so I couldn't even share my work environment.

During one of Beau's Sports Days I realised the old Italia Conti competitiveness had never left me. Beau had been keen for me to run in the mothers' race on sports day. I was working flat out on *The Bill* and was worried I could not get the time off again. I had a break between scenes and ran off the set, still in costume, and jumped into a cab. The driver was excellent and got me from location in South London to Highgate Wood in North London just in time. I went straight over to the field to join in the fun. Some of the mothers were taking it seriously and others just having a laugh.

I took Sam Nixon's shoes off and went to the starting line in bare feet, intending just to make Beau proud that I had taken part. Some of the others were doing stretching exercises and everyone was jostling to get to the front of the huddle of competitors. The headmistress, obviously a bit alarmed at how seriously it was being taken, appeared with black bin bags filled with balloons and told us we all had to run with a balloon between our legs. She'd tried to take off the pressure by turning the whole thing into a joke, but now I was wound up and ready to go; also slightly disappointed. I was going to be Zola Budd, the barefoot runner – but how could I do that with a balloon between my legs? I don't know why I cared – I didn't even know if I was a good runner.

When the race started, some of the women immediately popped their balloons while others held them in their hands. It was clear they were there for a race, and a race it was going to be. I kept my balloon in place for a lot of the way, but then when I saw they were running flat out I thought, I'll have some of that! So I dropped the balloon and pelted towards the finishing line.

'Run, Forrest, run!'

Beau's friend's mother, a tall lady with legs about as long as my whole height, was the only one left in front, doing one stride to every three or four of mine. And that's when the old Conti win-at-all-costs ethic kicked in and I whizzed past her like the demented roadrunner in the cartoons, right on the finishing line. I felt such relief and exhilaration you'd have thought I'd been in the Olympics. When the headmistress was presenting the prizes I remember she joked, 'The naked determination on the face of some of these mothers was frightening …' We all knew who she meant …

Beau was thrilled I'd won and that was what mattered most. But I turned up, ran the Mums' race, won it and then dashed back to work. It was insane but I felt I just had to win because I couldn't be part of the whole day.

About a year after I started on *The Bill*, I was filming a scene when I realised the actor playing opposite me was not holding my gaze: he was looking behind me. What's wrong with him? This isn't very professional, I was thinking, until I realised everyone else on the set was doing the same. I was so distracted, I messed up my line and asked the crew, 'Can we do that again?' 'No, there's no time to do it again …' said a voice to the right of me and I turned round to see Michael Aspel with the big red *This is Your Life* book.

Oh my God, they're doing *This is Your Life* on somebody! I thought, and stepped aside to let him get to whoever it was he had come to surprise. Then he said the famous words, 'This is Your Life, Lisa Maxwell,' and I said, 'Oh my God!' again.

Everyone clapped and cheered as Sue Green (the producer on *TIYL*) stepped out to whisk me away. 'But we haven't finished the scene,' I protested. Someone had to explain to me it wasn't a real scene, just something specially written to get me in the right position so that Michael Aspel could appear behind me. 'Great, so I've spent all morning working on a load of nonsense! Why didn't you give me a later call?'

Sue took me away because the actual show could not be recorded until 10 o'clock that night – the cast of *The Bill* had to be able to finish work, get changed and travel to the studios. 'Where shall we go?' she said. 'I'm taking you to lunch.' I chose Wimbledon Village because it's quite near the studios. In the car she told me they'd been trying to get me for ages, which was very flattering – especially as I'd been away in America and not appeared in much since then.

'They've only gone and got me on *This is Your Life*!' I said when I rang Paul from the car.

'I know, darling – I know all about it! Didn't you notice all the photos have gone from round the house? Thank God you work so hard!' he laughed. And it's true: by the time I got in from work, I'd be lucky to notice if there were walls in the house, let alone pictures.

'Have you told my mum?' I asked.

'Lisa, just go and have a lovely lunch. As if your mum doesn't know …'

'But what am I going to wear?'

'Your new cream suit,' he told me.

A couple of weeks earlier we'd been to Emporio Armani to buy an outfit for me, which I thought was for a friend's wedding. I remember being really touched that Paul came with me, thinking: he really doesn't like shopping – it's so lovely he's come.

I found a cream suit: it looked like a tux from the front but had a large cut-out shape in the back of the jacket. 'This is the one! It's got really nice detail on the back,' said Paul. Of course I had no idea that Paul, a creative perfectionist, was thinking on *TIYL* there would be lots of shots of me from the back. The suit was really expensive but he insisted we buy it. But now, when he said that was what I should wear, I told him, 'But that's for so-and-so's wedding …' 'Lisa, go and have lunch and I'll see you later!' he laughed.

Sue was also telling me to get off the phone because I was asking too many questions. We had a long boozy lunch and then the car took us to Teddington Studios, my old stomping ground, where I was virtually locked in the dressing room for the evening. Thankfully, Chrissie (the dresser who worked with me on *The Bill*) was more or less locked in with me, so I had good company.

The show was wonderful, with so many old friends there. As I walked onset, the first person I spotted was Paul. Russ Abbot, Nick Berry and Stephen Tompkinson all filmed tributes. Shane, of course, was there and was very funny and lovely; Laura James and Bonnie Langford came on to talk about Italia Conti. Todd Carty and Perry Fenwick told how we had all been child actors together. Jeffrey Holland and Bella Emberg made an appearance, and all the cast from *The Bill*. Mum was the first guest to come on, and Nan entranced Michael Aspel and loved her big moment, singing 'Put a Little Treacle on Your Pudding, Mary Ann' on national TV. For me, the highlight was Beau coming on at the very end: she was three years old at the time and they had filmed her singing and wearing a police hat so I was really surprised when they said she was there in person. As the sliding doors opened, she was standing there on her own, looking so serious and lovely. She reminded me this really *is* my life: Beau, Paul and me, it was a fabulous night.

Paul went through a terrible experience when I was on *The Bill*, one that shook him and his mum to the core and something they will never truly recover from. I am deeply ashamed of the fact that I was not there for him as much as I should have been – how I wish I could turn the clock back. Paul's lovely sister Lynne was only 36 when she died of cervical cancer. It was diagnosed in January 2002 and she died in the August, a few short and terrible months for her family.

Years earlier, some dubious cells had been detected and she was told she could have a hysterectomy but she hadn't met a man she loved and she was keen to have children one day. Instead she opted to have six-monthly check-ups. Sadly, she had four miscarriages, and while the doctors were investigating this they found a tumour the size of a tennis ball on her cervix despite regular smear tests.

As you will know by now, anything pivotal and profoundly emotional in my life has been swept under the carpet. In my family the unspoken motto was, 'Don't make an issue of it, get on with it'. If you pretend it's not as bad as it is, it may go away. And if it doesn't … well, shove it to one side and get on with the next thing! Going into overdrive with the practical stuff was all I knew, so I took Lynne to Paul Edmonds in Knightsbridge for a beautiful new haircut and when it became clear that she was going to lose her hair I took her to a company who make all the best wigs for stage and TV. She looked stunning; no one would know it was a wig. However, despite the fact that Paul had taught me to be more open and to accept my feelings I was tired and overworked so I'm afraid I reverted to type. At one stage during Lynne's illness I actually said to Paul, 'We don't have to keep dwelling on it, do we?'

Now I cringe when I think of it. Paul and his mother both knew the only way to face their terrible grief was to go through it, not over or round it. What he needed most was for me to listen, to find time to be there. Instead I was scared by the magnitude of his grief and shied away from it. I think that was the beginning of the problems in our relationship. Paul made a lot of allowances for me being busy at work and rightly thought I should have given him priority at that time. He could not offload his grief on his mother because she was coping with her own sorrow and consoling Lynne's husband. Meanwhile, Paul was floundering and I was a lousy partner. I didn't have the tools to deal with it, but I really should have tried harder. We have now worked through this together, talked about it and I have apologised. Paul, bless him, has forgiven me. I should have been his rock because even when things have not been good between us I love him more than I ever knew it was possible to love someone.

Paul was broken after the death of his sister and needed time out. I was still working fourteen hours a day, six days a week, so he was looking after Beau more and more and doing everything without me. Rather than run his business badly and leave Beau with a nanny Paul decided to set up a studio at home and work when Beau was at school. My money was good and this meant Beau would always have one parent there for her.

On one occasion when I was filming on a Sunday (which I always hated), Paul was taken ill. As usual, I'd left home at 5 a.m. so I was unaware he was unwell. I knew I had another 14-hour day ahead – we often filmed the driving sequences on a Sunday when the roads were quieter. I was working with Gary Lucy (who was playing a trainee detective constable). At about 11 o'clock my phone rang and it was seven-year-old Beau. She never rang me (she didn't have a phone of her own) and so I knew it was something important. This is something awful, I thought, as soon as I heard her little voice.

'Daddy's not well, Mummy,' she told me.

'What do you mean, darling?'

'He just slid down the wall in the bathroom.'

'OK,' I said, trying to keep the panic out of my voice. 'Can I speak to Daddy?'

But Paul hadn't the energy to come to the phone. Instead he told Beau: 'Tell Mummy you've already rung Nanny Chris.' But I knew his mother lived a long way away and it would take some time for her to get there.

I'm so ashamed of myself, but I didn't know what to do. Most people would have said 'I'm out of here!' and gone home, but my work ethic kicked in. If I went home, we had wasted a whole day's shooting, I told myself. It was unfair on the crew and on Gary, too (he and I were the only actors working that day) – everyone would have to make it up on another day. So I went to the director.

'Paul's collapsed, he's very unwell,' I told him. 'Beau can't tell me what's wrong, but she's too young to look after herself and I need to know he's OK.'

'Right, what do you want to do?'

He put the ball back in my court and I dithered. In retrospect, I think he should have said 'Go!' Like me, he was probably putting the show first. And so I went into Maxwell mode and thought, am I making a mountain out of a molehill?

'I really don't know what to do. I can ring Paul's mum and find out what's going on,' I suggested.

'By all means,' he said.

I could see he was thinking about having to abandon a whole day's shooting, too. As I went to make the phone call, I told Gary what was going on.

'What are you doing here?' he said. 'Why aren't you halfway home by now? You're not packing parachutes here, it's only a TV show. Go home, now!'

'I don't want to let you and the crew down …'

'Will you just shut up and go home!'

Gary was only about 22 at the time and just starting out on his career, yet it was such a grounded response and I was impressed. As soon as he said 'go' I knew he was right, and I took myself off home as fast as I could.

Paul was really ill; some kind of parasite had got into his system. He made a full recovery but I should have known from the moment I heard Beau's voice that this was something important: Paul would never bother me at work about anything he could handle. Once again, I came close to not being there for him – it was taking a long, long time for me to learn my lessons. It hurt a great deal when I realised Beau had phoned Nanny Chris before me. Strange how we instinctively know who can be relied upon to help, but sad I was not the top of the list for my own family.

But you can't keep a good entrepreneur down. On Beau's first day at school she came home with a little teddy dressed in a replica school uniform (they were given out to new pupils to help them feel at home in their new surroundings). Paul could see this was a great idea with potential, and over the next few months he had set up a factory in China, making and supplying bears to over 3,000 schools. The idea was that he could still do this around Beau's school hours and only in term time, but it really took off. The Great British Teddy Bear Company is now a multi-million-pound business.

# CHAPTER 15

## Running on Empty

Before I went into *The Bill*, Paul and I had had conversations about wanting another baby and we agreed on extending our little family. We were happy to put our plans on hold for my two-year stint, though. I wasn't worried about it and I didn't feel the old biological clock ticking to tell me to get a move on. Neither Paul nor I thought about my age: I've always looked young, acted young, felt young, we didn't think getting pregnant would be a problem (remember, I got pregnant with Beau within two weeks of us deciding we wanted a family). That's how my body works. I'm obviously very fertile – we can pick and choose when we'll have the next one, I thought. We took it for granted there *would* be a next one, no issue about it.

Two years crept up and now I was in year four. By this time Paul was gently reminding me we should start trying for our 'next' baby and that I was needed at home, but it was a very busy time at work and Scott and I were about to go to Romania to film two episodes. 'Can we just get Romania out of the way, maybe wait a bit longer?' I asked.

By this time I was losing the plot for sure. In a long-runner you're surrounded by people who always put the show first and you absorb that feeling. I was spending far more time with my *Bill* 'family' than with the real thing. Scripts were coming in later, we never wrapped early, we always went to the wire … Most of us agreed to the extra work because we were imbued, possibly even brainwashed, into thinking the world would stop turning if we didn't get the next episode in the bag. Somehow I had lost touch with my priorities. Beau always came first and any spare time I had was devoted to her, but Paul was missing out. I think my reasoning was he's a grown-up, he understands how much pressure I'm under at work and he knows I want to be with Beau – he'll understand.

And he did understand, to some degree, but it was unfair because all he got was the dregs of me. On my one day off a week I was so tired, I didn't want to do anything – I was fit for nothing after the best of me had been given to the programme. But there was only so much he would put up with and so he agreed to wait until after Romania, 'but', he said, 'then we must try for our second child'. So we did, but this time nothing magical happened after two weeks … or two months, or six months, even nine months. It seemed odd after having Beau so easily; maybe I was lucky with her, but I'd assumed this would be the same. I was 42 by this time and obviously the odds were stacked against me, but I didn't feel old or even older and so I'd arrogantly assumed I could choose my own time.

\* \* \*

We went to see Professor John Studd, a top gynaecologist I'd known and trusted for years. I told him we were there because I wasn't getting pregnant.

'Are you worried?' he asked.

'Sort of.'

'Well, you *are* getting on a bit – you don't make as many eggs as you get older. You might need to consider IVF.'

Naively, this had never occurred to me. I thought he would tell me something reassuring and we would walk away and make a baby, but now I said to Paul: 'Let's go and see what's involved, then we can decide.' Neither of us felt desperate but, looking back, I can see we were keen enough to consider it. So we went along to the Lister Hospital in Chelsea to see a colleague of Professor Studd's and he explained what was involved. It sounded horrific: IVF would be painful, there were no guarantees and the success rate was not even high. I'd be poked and prodded, while Paul's contribution would be done pretty much alone.

I know it works for some couples, and I know for some it's their only chance of having a child and I understand why they do it – I'm certainly not criticising anyone for going down that route. It just wasn't for us and we both knew it there and then in the room with the expert. We looked at each other and I could see Paul felt the same as me. Afterwards he said, 'That's not how we want to make babies.'

We both knew we were already blessed to have Beau, and it might have been different had we been childless. The other really good thing was we were in agreement: it was not as if one of us was pushing for it while the other was resisting. I began to reappraise my own arrogant attitude. 'Who the hell do I think I am? Just because I want another baby doesn't mean I can have one! Anyway, I'm being greedy – I've got my perfect daughter. Instead of thinking how lucky we are to have her, I'm asking for more. We think it's our God-given right to have another one, but d'you know what? Sometimes it's not!'

I think Paul was having a similar rethink. This was the stage when our relationship was at its worst and it was nothing to do with the baby we couldn't have. It was all to do with *The Bill* and the all-consuming demands. And we weren't the most functional of couples – we could have split up several times during my seven years on the series. From always talking things through, we'd now become a couple who had almighty rows and there was no chance to heal them – I'd be up at the crack of dawn to get to the studio. When I came home, Paul would (as usual) be pushed into the background while I spent my precious spare time with Beau.

I was permanently tired and not at the peak of fitness, eating hurried meals of the wrong foods. No wonder I couldn't get pregnant, I was running on empty. It's frightening how hard they can work you on shows like that; I knew a lot of the fault was mine and we both realised that we had to change if we were to survive as a couple. I tried hard to be sympathetic about the fact that when I got home from work there wasn't a lot left of me. We talked about it and both decided to make a big effort to save our relationship. Not just for Beau's sake, although she was of paramount importance, but because we loved each other deeply even if at times we were not communicating this very well.

So, the Christmas after our exploration of the IVF route was crucial. After a hectic celebration with the usual round of relatives and friends in 2007, we took ourselves off to one of our favourite boltholes, a beautiful hotel apartment in Lamorna, Cornwall. Whenever we had the chance we always escaped from London, and our two special places were Cornwall and the Cotswolds – we'd try and get away for breaks at least two or three times a year.

It was a lovely time, with Paul and me making a real effort to talk, making time to cherish each other and get back to what each of us really loved about the other. Beau was always blissfully happy when we were all together and we loved getting her away from the slightly materialistic life of a London kid. She and Paul would sit for five hours fishing on a rock and she never once mentioned Claire's Accessories! We did a lot of walking in the fresh, cold air, watched the sea, ate lovely food, slept, and there was no stress. All the pressure to make a baby had gone, and so when we made love it was purely for our own pleasure and to affirm our love for each other. And that's why, I'm sure, I became pregnant.

It was our happy little secret, which we hugged to ourselves, telling nobody but loving it so much. Everything between Paul and me was good and our dream was coming true. I knew straight away, just as I had with Beau. This time I knew first because I wasn't afraid to look. It was wonderful to see the word 'PREGNANT' emerge on the strip: we were back on course as a family.

The only cloud on my horizon was that I was not speaking to Mum. Ridiculous as it sounds, I can't even remember what triggered it, but I know we didn't talk for seven whole months. Sadly, this meant I wasn't able to see Nan either. I understood why she supported Mum – it would have made life very difficult for her otherwise. Also, when Mum and I had our rows they were usually over the phone and Nan only heard Mum's side of the conversation.

Nan was always a peacekeeper and tried to sort things out, but I think she felt that if she shouted at me as she did when I was little, then I would toe the line. But I was a mother myself by this stage and for the first time I could see how dysfunctional we were as a family. I didn't want to be the third generation of Maxwell women to live like that. They both said some hurtful things to me and they didn't think it mattered. In my family, upsetting people and having a flaming great row is just sport, and in sport you are allowed to say anything you like. 'It was only said in anger,' or 'It was only said in drink,' they will say to excuse themselves, but I'd learnt once you've said it and it's out there you can't get it back.

When I was first with Paul I used to say horrible things I didn't mean when I was upset, but he taught me to stick to the truth and not to say things just to score points. Nan blamed me for the row with Mum and said, 'I don't need this at my time of life.' I felt I didn't need it either – I was very worried about the effect our mad and often destructive relationship would have on Beau, who was now old enough to take a lot of things in. I thought we would be better off without them in our lives. I still had enough life ahead of me to change the way I dealt with things, but I didn't believe they would ever change.

From the moment Beau was born I was determined never to put the madness of my relationship with Mum onto her and never, ever would I lie to her – I never want her to have to struggle to find out her own family history. This is one of the reasons why I'm telling this story: no more family secrets. Beau will read this one day when the time is right, so I was always honest and open with her and I made sure Mum was, too. I spelt it out to her that I wasn't going to perpetuate any family myths about my birth just to protect her, and Beau would only ever hear the truth. Mum agreed because she adored her grand-daughter so much. Once when Beau asked why she doesn't have a grandad Mum explained: 'Nanny Val loved your mummy's daddy, but she couldn't be with him because she didn't know this at the time but he was married to someone else so Nanny Val has never had a husband.' It took a lot of courage for her to say it like that and I wish she could have told me when I was little.

I'm very proud of the way Mum has behaved as a grand-mother. Whatever her shortcomings in the motherly stakes, she has done a very good job in Beau's life. That's why it was sad when during our stand-off Beau said to me, 'I can't be friends with Nanny Val if she's being mean to you.' I hadn't said anything to her and I'd tried to hide my sadness but she'd picked up on it – she's an extremely sensitive little girl. So this was the situation when I became pregnant again: I could not phone my mum up and be happy with her because she was not part of my life. Anyway, before Paul and I told anyone something dreadful happened.

Paul was away on business in China and I was not working that day. I'd been out, but when I got home I found I did not have my door key. In the end I rang the bell at our neighbour's house and asked if she minded me climbing over the back fence with a ladder and getting in through the back door that was already open. She said she couldn't climb herself because she was pregnant. 'It's funny you said that, so am I,' I told her.

So our neighbour was the first person I told. In the end I found my door keys: after upending my big old bag, all sorts of junk fell out. Among it were the missing keys. I let myself in, went to the loo and then I saw blood. I knew immediately what it was. All I could think was, you're supposed to lie down. So I lay down on the bedroom floor, not daring to move or do anything. I had my phone with me and so I rang the obstetrician who had delivered Beau. A nurse told me to get to bed and rest. 'It may not be anything sinister,' she said.

So I crawled along the floor, staying as flat as I could, and got on the bed. I had a strong sense of wanting to keep everything inside and that if I didn't stand upright it couldn't come out. I didn't know who to call or what to do. I didn't want to ring Paul – he was in China working and he'd worry himself sick. After all, the nurse had said it might be OK. I was supposed to be having lunch with a girlfriend and I called her to cancel (I didn't tell her it was a miscarriage, just that I wasn't feeling well).

'Are you OK? Do you want me to come over? I'm sure you've got loads of people looking after you …' she said.

I was actually on my own but I was able to call Paul's mum and arrange for her to collect Beau after school. Chris was wonderful: she moved in for a few days. I was still losing blood and when I spoke to the obstetrician he said, 'It sounds to me like you are losing the baby.'

I was, and I did. It's strange when you have an early miscarriage because there's nothing to show for it. One day you have a baby inside you, the next you don't, but nobody knows because the pregnancy was so early, still secret – you don't even have to go to a doctor. It's as if it never was, as if it didn't count, as if that blue mark on the pregnancy test kit was a mistake. Nobody draws a line under it because there's nothing to draw a line underneath; there's nothing to say: 'This was nearly something very special.'

For me and other women in the same situation it's a huge, secret grief but there's nothing to symbolise it and society expects you to get on as though it hasn't happened – which is exactly what I did. I didn't take time off from *The Bill*: in my mind, I thought I was lucky it had happened when I had two days off so nobody need know. So I seized the moment to push the pain away, not wanting to think about it (my usual tactics), and I didn't have Paul there to stop me. I couldn't wait to get back to normal, which for me meant work.

My main worry was how to tell Paul, and when I did he was devastated. He'd had some time off in China and had apparently been wandering around looking at baby clothes, feeling as smug and excited as we had felt when we were expecting Beau. We both thought getting pregnant was the difficult bit; having achieved that, it never occurred to us it could still go wrong.

Paul tried to make me acknowledge my grief. He held me close and we cried together for our baby that never was. He has taught me to find my own reactions to the big things in my life, even the unhappy things; he knows how to access the feelings I try my best to bury. Even so, we did not grieve properly but we consoled ourselves with Beau. Thankfully, she knew nothing about what had happened – only that Mummy had been unwell for a day or two.

I was still not talking to Mum so she knew nothing about my miscarriage. Thank God, I had Chris, who almost filled the hole in my life – almost, because there was still a bit of me that longed for Mum. I picked up the phone many times to call her, but how can you say, 'By the way, since I last spoke to you I've had a miscarriage'? It was too big, too important to summarise in a conversation so I kept on telling myself: 'Not everyone has a close relationship with their mother, I'm just not a person who has a mother in their life – it's not my lot. Get on with it!'

So Paul and I were getting on with our family life and feeling grateful for what we had. By then I was 44 years old and we were pretty sure our chances of becoming parents again were over. But then another minor miracle happened: I lost the baby in March 2008, but by the July I was pregnant again. We were so excited but more cautious this time – Paul wrapped me in cotton wool. We didn't tell Beau although this time we came close to it, but I remember Paul telling her not to jump on my back (I think he pretended I had a bad back or something).

This time I hung on to our unborn child for a bit longer. I was just about to go for the 11-week scan when I miscarried. We'd already been to the doctor, we'd heard the heartbeat and we were dying to see the scan. Also, I was getting noticeably bigger – I don't think anyone would have realised I was pregnant, but they might have thought I'd eaten too many pies because Sam Nixon's suits were becoming tighter and I had to leave the top button on her trousers undone. I felt brilliant, really healthy, really well – I couldn't believe I had put off having a baby for all sorts of reasons and I knew this was what I wanted more than anything else. And I felt blessed that at my age we were being given another chance.

I was filming with Patrick Robinson (Jacob Banks). The scene we were shooting was in front of Sun Hill and it was light and fun. As it was written on the page it was fairly prosaic, but we both knew how to add sparkle. That's what I love about acting – when the players bring something really special to a scene. It was easy for Patrick and me to work together although we were only just on the right side of corpsing each other.

We rehearsed it, blocked it (worked out where we would stand for the lighting guys), and then went away for a break while they put the lights in place. I went to the loo and there was blood soaking my knickers. I felt a terrible wave of emotional pain similar to the feeling I had when I heard Grandad had cancer. It shuddered through me and almost knocked me off my feet. A bit of the old Lisa, the one who buried momentous events, kicked in because I remember thinking, what a shame – I won't be able to get back the light, giggly element we rehearsed. It was my old, unhealthy reaction deeply embedded in me. Back in the dressing room, I rang Paul.

'There's blood in my pants,' was all I said.

'Come home,' he told me.

'Let me ring the obstetrician …'

'Ring the obstetrician and then come home, Lisa!'

His tone of voice suggested, 'Don't even begin to think you can work today – that would be insane, wouldn't it?' He was trying to stay calm with me, but he knew me well enough to know that's what I would be thinking. So I rang the obstetrician, who said it could be OK, some people bleed all the way through a pregnancy.

'What do you want to do?' he asked.

'I could stay at work …'

'It won't do any harm if you stay at work, but equally, if you want to go home …'

So the decision was back with me. Doctors assume you can go with your instincts but mine were warped and I was trying to convince myself, for the sake of everyone else on set, I should stay at work. I told Paul what he had said.

'Lisa, *listen* to me! You tell your producer *now*, and you come home *now*!'

'Let's just give it a while and see what happens …'

Paul put the phone down and rang my agent, telling him he had to contact my bosses. 'This is her second miscarriage. She worked through the first and she didn't take time out to look after herself – I don't want her to do that again!'

I went to see Roberta Taylor, who was in the dressing room next to me. She was very kind and sympathetic and she said without argument, 'You are going home! Tell the producers, get yourself home!'

'It's nothing to do with them and I can still work …'

'You'll fucking kill yourself and then who will thank you for working? I'm going to tell the producers if you don't! You stay here and rest while I speak to them.'

She was extremely worried and she finally made me realise I had to put myself first. As it turned out, the producers already knew because my agent had been on the phone. Tim Key, the series producer, came to see me and said, 'What do you want to do? I think you should go home.'

It's a difficult one for other people to know how to react. Outwardly, I didn't look any different to the way I'd looked half an hour ago, but my world was in a completely different place. But now, once I'd faced up to the fact that I had to stop work, they were very good: I was given a month off, although I did go back in after 10 days just to tie up some loose ends with the scenes I'd already filmed (Paul grudgingly allowed me to go). They asked if I would like to see scripts for the episodes I was missing as they would be very good for my character; they really thought that if I saw them I'd rush back to work. 'Absolutely not,' I said. 'It would make no difference whatsoever.' Unbelievable, but in telly nothing else matters.

Physically, this miscarriage was much more painful than the first and made it feel much more like losing a baby. Again, Paul and I clung to each other and tearfully said this was obviously the way it was meant to be: Paul, Beau and me. We were lucky because we had our special little unit and when anything big happens we can close ranks, pull up the drawbridge and simply be together.

My greatest medicine is just being with Paul. In his reaction to things I can see the truth of a situation. If he gets sad, I love him so much that I try to think about what it is that's so bad, and in so doing I myself can face up to things. It's like looking in a mirror, only it's a mirror that shows me how I should be, not how I am. I look at Paul and know exactly what I should be feeling and if I'm already feeling it – which, in fairness, I usually am, even though I might have suppressed it – I can find those feelings, give them space, recognise them. It has never been a matter of me not feeling things, always about burying them.

Apart from the trauma of the miscarriage, it was lovely having a month off and getting my life back; being there for Beau when she came in from school. And we made a decision, Paul and me: I wouldn't go back to the life I had before – I was giving up *The Bill*. After seven years, Sam Nixon was checking out of Sun Hill.

Paul's business was doing well so the financial pressure was off. Besides, money was not the most important thing; being together was what life was about. If there was a glimmer of hope that I'd have another baby, it would not happen while I had such a punishing workload, and although we were realistic we hadn't completely given up. We were philosophical: we both felt it would be great if I got pregnant again, and if it happened we would take a lot of care during the pregnancy, but if we were destined to have only the one child, Beau was as good as it gets.

It was the release of pressure when we made the decision for me not to go back that helped me with another huge area of my life that was not right. It was while in Cornwall, that beautiful, spiritual place where we were recovering from our loss, that I picked up the phone to ring Mum. Paul encouraged me; he'd been trying to get me to ring her for the whole seven months, but pride had been stopping me. Why should I make the first move? But this is stupid, nobody is winning here, I suddenly realised. In my family winning the argument is what it's about and it doesn't matter how much hurt everyone suffers.

I wanted to talk to Mum; also I wanted to see Nan. I was very aware that my nan was an old lady now, her best years probably behind her, and I wanted her to have as much time with Beau as she could. I badly missed Nan and Mum. Because of our stupid row, Mum had missed two of the most distressing times in my life: the miscarriages. Time to end the madness, and so I rang her.

'I don't want to not speak to you any more,' I told her. 'It's making me miserable. I'm too unhappy, in too much pain.'

'Oh Lisa, I've missed you!' she said.

In someone else's book there would be a happy ending: we've missed each other, we're back together, we'll never let it happen again … And it didn't happen again, but it wasn't over because there was still a lot of resentment to deal with. Why did *I* have to pick the phone up? Why couldn't Mum have taken care of the situation? The sad thing is you stop expecting someone to do the right thing to protect yourself when they don't – you can't be let down if you don't expect anything. I've done that on so many occasions in my relationship with Mum. But when we weren't speaking I was walking round with a big cloud over my head, so it was clear to me that we had to do something to make our relationship better.

I suggested we should have therapy. I'd been thinking about it for some time and I felt we needed an outsider to help us piece together our relationship. For a long time I'd thought that all Mum's problems and all the difficulties in our relationship stemmed from what happened in 1963 and had never been addressed by anyone properly equipped to understand, someone who didn't have an angle. Whenever I tried to do amateur psychology on her, I was always coming at it from the point of view of her daughter, someone caught up in it all. At one time if I'd suggested this, I don't think she would have agreed, but over the years therapy itself had acquired a better name. Mum had also been frightened by the fact that we'd gone seven months without speaking.

I had a feeling if we went together she would eventually peel herself away and then be willing to go on her own. It was probably going to be a long road but it was at least worth starting out on it. I was conscious of not wanting to take over so I suggested Mum find a therapist and I would pay. She found someone who practises in Covent Garden, which was easy enough for both of us, so we started going. The first few times I did all the talking, giving my perspective on our problems. Eventually Mum opened up, and after several sessions we started going separately. I went two or three times on my own, Mum went more. She still goes occasionally, I think.

One of the biggest things I learnt, and it's a mind-blowing, earth-shattering thing to face up to, was that I'd never felt truly loved until I met Paul. It was a bitter pill for Mum to swallow, she was aghast – even the therapist looked mortified on my behalf. I explored how my experience of her love for me was so wrapped up in shame: on the one hand she loved me, but on the other, she was ashamed of my existence. These mixed messages meant that I learnt never to trust love because it always came with strings attached. Even Nan and Grandad, who idolised and spoilt me, were also ashamed and it was their attitude that made Mum feel that way, too. So, in my young life, love came with shame. And when I got older, until Paul taught me to surrender to my feelings, I put on a suit of armour to protect myself from feeling anything, even love. I always had to be in control, and if anyone told me they loved me I assumed this to be a convenient lie because that's what my family did: told lies.

Mum was very upset. She *did* love me, of course she did – she couldn't see it from my perspective. In some ways she loved me too much, but her love was always conditional, which is why I always felt I had to be a success, for her.

The therapy has made a huge difference to Mum – I can't begin to say how much. She has broken the conditioning that made her negative. She's taken hold of her own life, her own feelings, and she's blossomed. It has put our relationship on a much better footing.

I'm glad we didn't tell Beau I was pregnant: she was too young to understand it then. We've since told her and it was easier because it was in the past and there was no chance she would feel we had lost an actual baby brother or sister. We wanted her to know because we don't believe in family secrets, we want everything to be open and honest, but we're glad she didn't live through the agony of our loss.

I needed to tell her because I didn't want her to find out from someone else. When I left the show I gave a series of magazine interviews in which I revealed that I'd had two miscarriages; I gave this as my reason for leaving, which it was. But it was bigger than that – it was more about drawing a line around it on a public level so that I too was forced to deal with it and not allow it to become another family secret; this happens to people, it has to be talked about and it helps. I never read my own interviews so there was no shock at seeing it in print, but it's all out there, online, and Beau could come across it. After my own childhood, no more fibs is one of my biggest things – I certainly didn't want veiled allusions being made in Beau's presence so she was left trying to put two and two together and making 104 as I did.

Telling her happened easily: Paul and I were chatting and we looked at each other, both realising this was the right moment. First of all, we told her what a miscarriage is and then carefully explained that it's not a dying baby, it's not like having a baby who dies – I didn't want her to feel a sense of loss. She would have loved a baby brother or sister, but like us she accepts this is not to be.

I'm glad, too, that I went public about the miscarriages; it may have helped other women in the same situation to cope. It was also part of my healing process to talk about it, to acknowledge the place in my life those two short pregnancies have. I've worked so hard to get myself into a place where the things that happen to me don't destroy me, so I deal with them and absorb them into my life.

Paul and I are sad that I never got pregnant again. When I think back to how I lied that I wanted loads of children … well, I would have settled for just one more, but it was not to be. We've talked about adoption because we feel we have a lot to give to another child, but we're scared. We've been good parents to Beau but we wonder if that's because she's ours and we love her so much. Could we ever love another child that much? We also think it might be very disruptive for all three of us. We've got these romantic notions that one more child would make life perfect, and maybe it wouldn't, maybe life is perfect now, but we haven't ruled it out altogether. So many kids deserve a happy life and ours just keeps on getting better and better.

At the time of writing we are embarking on a dream of ours: to renovate a seventeenth-century country house. As a family, we have a lot to offer a small child – it may be the right thing to do. So who knows?

# CHAPTER 16

## As One Door Opens ...

When I went back to *The Bill* in late 2008 I had given them a few months' notice so that my character could be written out. It was a nice feeling and a lot of the original joy in the job came back as soon as I knew it was going to end and I was stepping off the treadmill. Somehow the episodes I would have filmed, the ones they wanted to tell me about while I was on my month off, had been rescheduled so I was now working on them. And it was tough: it was a cot death storyline. This was what they had half-hoped I would work on only days after my miscarriage.

Unbeknown to me, there were a lot of problems with the show at that time. Ultimately, I probably did them a big favour by going. Some time after I left they had to scale down the cast and crew. I'm thankful I wasn't around in the days when people were going to work on a daily basis and not knowing whether they'd still have a job when they went home. The series finally came off-air in the summer of 2010, about 18 months after I left, and it was a sad moment, but it was one of the longest-running shows on television and in its day it had been a really great programme. Despite the work schedule I loved *The Bill*, and it gave my career another dimension: I enjoyed playing Sam because she was a strong, rounded and flawed female. I had wonderful, happy times there, meeting some great people and laughing a lot. It would take too long to name-check all the amazing friends I made but they really were a team of some of the best actors in the business and the costume and make-up departments were some of the nicest people I've ever met.

There were one or two characters that definitely outstayed themselves at Sun Hill and I'm glad it never happened to me. The odd one had played a policeman so long they thought they really were members of the force; if their character got a promotion and a bigger office they behaved as if it was them who had been promoted. On one occasion Sam Nixon had to go to the office of a senior cop and it said in the script that she had to knock on the door.

When I did this, the actor concerned said to me, 'Why are you knocking on the door?'

'Because it says in the script that I knock on the door.'

'I have an open-door policy – my door's always open. Why don't you just walk in?'

*Hello*! We're actors, we do what it says in the script – we don't really work at Sun Hill.

One highlight of my time on the show was working with Les Dennis again. He came in to film a serious storyline about a man (Les) who kills his dad and puts the body in the freezer, but we struggled to keep a straight face. There were so many jokes: 'Dad's gone to Iceland', 'Fish fingers for supper', etc. It was like old times and I'm so thrilled for him that his life is finally very happy, with his new wife Claire, who is terrific; they have a lovely baby girl. His son Philip, whom I remember when he was a kid, is now an actor, too, and from everything I've heard he's a very gifted one.

It was only when I left *The Bill* that I truly realised what I'd missed by working so hard. Although I had always made Beau my top priority, it was sad to realise I'd missed so much of her day-to-day life. I don't resent the fact that Paul was more of a hands-on parent than me – I'm just very grateful he was there for her – but I do regret not being there, too, and not being one of the mums doing the school run every day.

When I left, my diary (which had been crammed with filming schedules) was empty and I loved that – I didn't want to do anything. But the very day when my departure was announced in the press I had a phone call from one of the producers on *Loose Women*. Already I'd appeared on the series a couple of times, promoting *The Bill*, and I loved the format. Nobody likes a good gossip more than me and it seemed perfect to have a group of women gassing away just like they do over coffee, over lunch, at the school gates or over the phone.

The last time I was on, one of the press team from ITV was there with me and in the taxi afterwards she told me the talent producer from the show had said about me, 'She'd make a great Loose Woman.' I think this was because I was talking to Gillian McKeith in the Green Room (long before she was on *I'm a Celebrity* …) about her food beliefs, about which she was evangelical. After a couple of minutes I realised everyone was listening to me probing her, so they were on the phone the minute they knew I was free. I tried out on one programme with Jane McDonald, Carol McGiffin, Sherrie Hewson and Jackie Brambles. I already knew Sherrie (we'd both done *The Russ Abbot Show*) and I'd been in a TV drama with her years before that when I was not long out of school. I remember she gave me a lift to Southampton for the recording of that play and I was bowled over. She was theatrical, used her hands a lot to illustrate what she was saying, wore a gipsy skirt and looked very attractive. I thought she was really cool and all actresses must be like that.

I also knew Lynda Bellingham, who wasn't on that first show with me. We'd worked together, but we also had mutual friends in Chris and Ingrid Tarrant and we'd enjoyed a great day out at the races, which ended back at Lynda's house, where she made wonderful pasta and we danced to Frank Sinatra round her kitchen. I also knew Denise Welch and again we had mutual friends in Mark Haddigan and his sister Lisa (Mark was very friendly with Denise's husband, Tim Healy). From time to time we ran into each other at Soho House, back in the days when I was in *Grease* and partying hard.

I only met Carol when I'd been a guest on the show. Coleen Nolan, one of the other regulars, was Shane's ex-wife and I remembered her being supportive of me when I was pregnant with Beau. Although she and Shane had an acrimonious break-up and I'm very loyal to him, I know no one outside a marriage can ever comment on what goes on inside it. When couples break up, often friends go with one half and not the other. I never consciously chose to be Shane's friend and not hers, but naturally we see a lot of him because we are god-parents to his baby daughter and he is Beau's godfather. When they were together they lived in a big house in Denham and we had many a good night there. Coleen and I don't often work together on *Loose Women* (we're in the same seat, we keep it warm for each other), but we meet up at work dos and still get on well. We've never talked about her relationship with Shane.

*Loose Women* was a completely new experience for me. I'd done presenting before but only as a manufactured version of myself; on the panel, I am the real me. It came at a time in my life when I finally know who I am and I'm no longer ashamed of any aspect of this. I've learnt the things you think make you different to everyone else and that you feel ashamed of are ultimately those that endear you to other people, and I've learnt the great value of truth. Now I always tell the truth even if it doesn't always put me in the best possible light.

I love the live aspect of the show and I quickly picked up that you have to be happy with what you bring to the table because you'll be talking about it to millions of people. When I joined I was self-editing because there were things I just didn't want to talk about to the whole world. Now I'm so comfortable in my seat that I can say more or less everything I feel. I won't talk about my loved ones in any revealing ways and I won't betray people's confidences or my own dignity (well, not too much!), but that still leaves the vast majority of subjects on the table.

I know it sounds really boring but we all get on well with each other. I see it as part of my job, whenever I'm in a company, to get on with the others, and it's especially important when you're going to open up about your life to a group of women. We start the day with a coffee session between 8.30 and 10 a.m., when we look through the papers and talk about the topics that will come on; we also have a good girlie chat – what we've done over the weekend, what's happening in our lives, everything from the dog being sick to really important developments in relationships. What's said is entrusted to that room; a lot of it is too personal to be used on the show and none of us ever betrays the mutual trust all Loose Women have.

Of course when you get a bunch of women together it can get hormonal at times. Lots of biological stuff is going on at times of the month and there are days when you get on better with one of the others than someone else and others when it reverses. We're like a family, we have our ups and downs, but ultimately we stick together.

After a couple of trial shows I was signed up and now I've done two years, appearing mostly twice a week, sometimes three times. The wonderful thing is that after the show I'm free and I can get back to my beloved home in time to pick up Beau from school. I want to act again, but I'm so happy with my life it would have to be something amazing to justify the time away from Beau and Paul.

After *The Bill* we made another major change to our lives: we moved out of London to live in our beloved Cotswolds. We'd always escaped there whenever we could, for long weekends and holidays. One of the best friends I have made is Emma Samms, who worked with me on *The Bill*, and she introduced us to the area of the Cotswolds where we are now living. After weekends at her fabulous home, we fell in love with the place. Once I was off the treadmill and we were down there, enjoying a walk, I said to Paul, 'Is there any reason why we shouldn't live here?' 'No, not now you've left *The Bill*,' he told me. 'I can run my business from an office anywhere.'

# Not That Kinda Girl

It was a good time for us to move because Beau was getting to the age when she would be going to secondary school and we wanted to find a really good school for her. We'd always dreamed of moving to the country and now there was no reason not to do this. So we started house hunting and were thrilled to find one we liked very quickly; we then looked around and found exactly the right school for Beau.

Sadly, the original house purchase fell through but we were determined to make the move and so we rented a wonderful place until we found the home of our dreams. This meant Beau could start school (which she loved) and she's in the right place to move on to the one we have chosen for her. Now we've got the house we want, too, so life on that front is perfect. All of us – and that includes Pepper, the Miniature Schnauzer – love it. Beau is the most wonderful, well-balanced child. As well as deciding early on that she was not going to be part of the madness of my dysfunctional family, I also decided that I was going to keep her away from all the body fascism that had affected me. She's got a perfectly normal relationship with food – she eats chocolate cake now and again, hallelujah! It's still 'poison' in my warped mind and I wrestle with my fear of eating too much, but I've kept it all away from Beau and not used her as a dumping ground for my own neuroses.

We're living on top of a hill with wonderful views in every direction. Of course, we've had a lot of work to do in getting it right but I'm not scared of a tin of paint and a brush. We love the fact that there's land around us, although we're not entirely sure what we're going to do with it. Now all we have to do is convert the coach house and do up the cottage in the grounds so that one day Nanny Chris and Nanny Val can come and live with us when they're both really old. We intend to stay in this house for the rest of our lives.

One person who will never live here with us and has never seen this house is my nan, Beau's Nanny Rose. In May 2010 she died at the grand old age of 95. She'd never smoked but she had more than her share of drinks over a long and busy lifetime. We noticed she wasn't herself the Christmas before she died, when she and Mum came to stay. She couldn't walk well without a stick, but that was because she should have had a hip replacement years before but didn't because she never liked doctors or hospitals.

In fact, she'd never in her life been in hospital until she had to go in with pneumonia after Christmas. Nan had given birth to all her babies at home. It was during one of her pregnancies, she told me, that her teeth had fallen out – is it any wonder I was scared of having a baby? She was also going deaf, her sight was really poor and she had a chest infection, too. She 'put up and shut up' – her lifelong philosophy – until she was so poorly that Mum called the GP. He said she needed to go into hospital for tests and that's when they found she had fluid on her lungs. She was in St Thomas's Hospital for three weeks, where she was treated with respect and dignity. I have nothing but praise for the Geriatric Ward there. Right to the end, she remained Nan: she had this young male physio who came to massage her chest and she flirted with him shamelessly, always trying to convince him she needed more physio.

After Nan went home, she seemed to give up: she wasn't eating and was too weak to even sit up properly, her paper-thin skin covered with bruises and cuts caused just by touching something, and her wounds had to be dressed all the time. I think she'd decided enough was enough. I was spending as much time as possible with her. 'Let me go,' she once said to me. This was a change. In hospital she kept saying, 'I've got to try my hardest.' So I said to her, 'Nan, you do what you want – you don't have to fight it.'

One day when she looked really bad Mum called in the GP again. 'Oh dear,' he said when he saw her – it was clear she was near the end. I was on the phone while the doctor was there and I asked if I should go that day or the next. 'Probably today,' he told me. And so we went, but she didn't die that day. Paul, Beau and I spent a few hours there but decided not to hang on: my nan was no longer there. That frail little body could never contain her big personality. I wanted Beau to see her before she died because she loved her Nanny Rose. She'll probably never meet another genuine old Cockney and she certainly won't be taught the words to wicked songs at school – Nan had Beau singing 'Tommy Tucker' from an early age. With the passing of Nan and her generation, so much of the old London has gone.

The following day, Mum and Auntie Shirley were with her. The two sisters were brought together at Nan's bedside, their old sibling rivalry gone; they were both Nan's daughters. They were completely there for her, but they couldn't have coped without each other. Shirley lived round the corner but she'd been sleeping at Mum's. That morning she popped home for a bath and a change of clothes. Mum was on her own at Nan's bedside, watching the rise and fall of her frail chest. She noticed her breathing had become irregular. Very peacefully, Nan's chest stopped moving and then she just slipped away.

\* \* \*

Paul had written down a list of the things Mum needed to do when the time came, like ringing the doctor and notifying everyone else who should know. She did all this before she rang me. I've always felt two of the really important events in any life are how you arrive on this planet and how you leave. I wanted to remember every second of my nan's departure. After all, Maxwell history was taking place.

So I asked Mum what she was doing when Nan died. She told me she was watching her and reading a book that she had got from a charity shop to try and cheer herself up.

'Just out of curiosity, Mum, what book were you reading?'

'*Being Jordan* by Katie Price,' she told me.

Maybe that's something I do have to edit out of the history books.

The task of organising Nan's funeral fell to me: Mum wasn't up to it. As you will know by now, I've slowly learnt how to cope with difficult times, to face up to my emotions, but I'd never been involved in a funeral before, let alone organised one, and this was a massive event for me. All my life I've hated driving past funeral parlours – I couldn't bear to look at them. Having been brought up by my grandparents, I always knew they were old and dreaded what would happen when they died. At first I had no idea what to do and I can honestly say arranging that funeral was the hardest single thing I've ever had to do. Somehow I had to keep it together and embrace the pain of losing Nan. I was determined to bring her back to life at the service so that everyone could celebrate her life – she meant the world to so many people. Nan spent her life singing, we could never really shut her up, and so we sang her favourite songs (no hymns) and ended the funeral with Vera Lynn's 'We'll Meet Again'. Nan would have loved it: she always thought she was a bit of a Vera (Grandad certainly had a thing for her and maybe this was why!).

At Nan's funeral I gave a tribute to her, and I'd like to repeat a little bit here so the memory of her lives on:

The phrase once met never forgotten must have been coined for my nan. From the moment I took my first breath she was there, along with my beloved Grandad Jim. She nurtured and loved me through my childhood. She's always been there, keeping my secrets and encouraging me to follow my dreams – she really thought I was the best thing since sliced bread.

Her childlike sense of fun and enthusiasm meant we had some right good laughs. She even managed to make me laugh after making me wait outside the betting shop in my Italia Conti boater and cape. I didn't mind – I was looking forward to Nan getting the chips. We were partners in crime: if only Grandad knew some of the things Nan and I got up to! Luckily, those secrets remain between me, Nan, the betting shop and the bingo hall.

When I am asked who inspired me, great actors or writers, I always say Nan. She was tough (she was still dancing on her one good leg at 4 a.m. on the Millennium). She was naughty, charismatic, everybody loved her; she had a wicked sense of humour and made up names for people – Grandad was always 'Fly Blower' and I was 'Granny Orlock'. Even when she was sitting quietly, there was a twinkle in her eye like she knew something we didn't. Only in her final hours did her twinkle fade. Her eyes closed and, holding our hands, she asked us to let her go.

Holding such a frail, small lady I realised that this body could no longer contain my nan's enormous personality. She was – and is – larger than life. Her personality needed more room to breathe. She was big enough to fill us all: her two sons, two daughters, seven grandchildren and 10 great grandchildren.

And this is where she will live now: we will recognise her in each other's character. She will live inside all our stories, in all our memories and in all our hearts.

Nan's death was a big deal in my life: she was such a larger-than-life character, always by Mum's side, and now she was gone. I'd been so scared that I wouldn't be able to get through the day and I was proud I'd managed to get through my tribute without breaking down. I had learnt how to cope with grief; I really could cry most days, and I do cry at least once a week whenever I think of her. The other day I was driving along in the car and a Stevie Wonder song came on the radio. I hadn't particularly associated it with my nan and her era, but Nan and Grandad loved 'I Just Called to Say I Love You' (which was what he sang) and I could see her face. Instead of getting scared by the fact that I was feeling my grief, I pulled over, turned the music up loud and had a bloody good cry. It felt marvellous, healthy. Later, I told Paul what it had happened to me and we had a hug. 'You see, it's not that bad! It's quite nice sometimes, to be sad,' he told me. Finally, I could understand how he must have felt about Lynne. Well, better late than never …

The first Christmas after Nan's death I sobbed as I put the decorations on the tree, aware she would not be there to celebrate with us. I still find it hard to believe I'll never again hear her sing the words: 'I'm not that kind of a girl …'

I'd always dreaded the effect of Nan's death on Mum. I knew it would be bad for me and for the rest of Nan's kids (Auntie Shirley, Uncle Jim and Uncle Alan), but I thought Mum would be hit hardest because she'd lived with Nan all her life and never left home. I was afraid she would fall apart because she would have no coping mechanism and so I'm really impressed with the way she's handled things. She's built a social life for herself, she's got friends and she gets out. I'm very proud of her.

So, Nan and Grandad, two great pillars of my life, have gone, but at least one ghost from my childhood has been laid to rest: I finally found my father.

# CHAPTER 17

# Father Unknown

Hints, whispered conversations overheard as a child, bits and pieces my mum let slip, standing outside the court while Nan went in to find out where my maintenance money was … All I knew about the father we never discussed was what I gleaned from these scraps.

I had learnt, with difficulty, to be comfortable with who I was and where I came from; I never felt any overwhelming desire to find my 'Father Unknown' – you don't miss what you've never had, there's no sense of loss as there is when someone you love leaves your life. I didn't even feel there was something missing, but I knew because of what he did, deserting my mum, I had grown up feeling I had to protect her from anything else hurting her like that.

As a person, a real human being, my father didn't exist to me. I never thought about *him*, the individual. I didn't even consider his genetic heritage. Whenever I was asked about my family's medical history, I just replied with all the ailments from Mum's side. Until Beau was born I didn't consider there was a whole other side to my genetic make-up, that there might be details there that I needed to know. It was having Beau that made me finally decide I had to trace my roots (when she was six and I was 41); this was something Paul and I had talked about in a casual way over the years and I knew he was behind me whatever I decided to do. But whenever I toyed with the idea of finding my father, I dismissed it because of Mum; I felt it would hurt her and she'd always tried her best to make sure I lacked for nothing.

Paul had always been very open about me not knowing who my dad was, and from time to time he would say, 'Why don't you find your dad? What's his name? What do you know about him?' He had already traced his own family tree, sitting up late at night in bed with his laptop. 'We should do yours,' he suggested, like a slight challenge. 'You could probably find your dad.' 'I will, one day I will,' I told him.

What you will have learnt about Paul by now is that he says what he means and he believes other people do, too. It was like when I told him I wanted kids; now I was telling him I would find my dad, so he believed me. And it was true enough: I knew at some point I was going to do it, but it was just a vague knowledge. It could be in 10 years' time or even further away – I certainly hadn't formulated any plans.

Not long after this it was Mum's birthday and we met for supper, just her and me, at Bertorelli's in Soho. I'm very good at daughterly gestures. I want to be a good daughter to her, to make her happy, but true to form, we started to niggle each other over our pasta. It's amazing how we can find things to argue about: any trivial disagreement can spark a full-on row. In the middle of this one, I blurted out, 'I can't even look for my dad because I'm worried it will upset you – I don't even have *that* right!'

'I'd love it,' she told me.

Mouth open, still in mid-rant, I stared at her. She'd completely stopped me in my tracks.

'What do you *mean*, you'd love it?'

'I'd love it if you found your dad.'

'I can't believe what I'm hearing! All my life, for years, I've believed that you would somehow feel like a failure if I so much as asked about my dad. I felt you would think I was looking for another parent after you've worked so hard to fill the gap. And now you're telling me you'd love it. *Really?*'

'Yes, I'd like to know if he's available,' said Mum.

My God! She'd carried a torch for him all these years. To be honest, I felt slightly resentful that what she was saying was, in effect, 'You can find your dad for me, not for your need.' I really wanted her to say straight away, 'Of course you need to know who your father is, of course you need to meet him – he's part of who you are.' She did eventually say those things, but on another day. Mum's the most kind-hearted woman you could ever meet, she wants to love and be loved, but she's had a lifetime of anxiety, depression and feeling inferior. When anything, good or bad, happens her first thought is, how am I going to cope? It always comes straight back to her and I understand and forgive her for this but it was good when she finally came round to seeing it from my perspective.

Right now, though, I was floored – she was happy, she wanted me to look for him. I hadn't planned to ambush her with the idea but it must have been on my mind. So the next time I spoke to her on the phone I asked her what she could tell me about him. She was quite forthcoming, telling me again that he looked like Paul Newman and when he sang in the pub his favourite song was 'Sixteen Tons' (an American song that was a huge hit in Britain and sung by Frankie Laine). I felt she was very much telling me her party line on him, things she felt it was safe to say. She enjoyed talking about him, telling me all about how she'd met him. So I pressed her for useful details and she told me the name of the print company where he had worked when she knew him. She told me his height, admitting he wasn't very tall – well, I think I'd worked that one out! And she gave me an address out of London, which had been the last one she knew, where the money for my maintenance came from.

She even told me that when I was a teenager at Italia Conti I was filming *A Place Like Home* in the town where he lived and she was convinced I would bump into him! The chances were incredibly low, but even if we had walked past one another neither of us would have had a clue what the other looked like.

My conversation with Mum was monumental in terms of communication between us. It was a complete first to be sitting there talking about my dad. It was a conversation I thought we'd never have and I can't overstress how important it was and the impact on me.

I didn't write down what she told me, I just remembered it. Afterwards, when I talked it all through with Paul, I was able to give him a couple of facts and figures: my dad's age, his last known address, the fact he had a son (Mum knew this because his wife was pregnant when she met her). Paul said, 'He can't have been all that bad – he paid maintenance for you and he's never gone to the newspapers and sold a story about you.' This had never occurred to me. I'd always been worried about journalists unearthing *him*, not the other way round, but now I was beginning to build up a picture. Paul went online but of course Murphy is a very common name and there were two or three who could be him, but one seemed more likely than the others. So what did I do? Nothing, big fat nothing, for four whole years.

I did think about it occasionally. I'd begun to realise how important the medical and biological history was for Beau, but I can see in retrospect that I was using this practical reason for finding him as a cover for my own emotional need. It gave me a motive and it also opened up lines of communication with Mum and Nan. If I said, 'I need to find him for Beau,' they understood and it took the onus from me. I wasn't saying, 'I need to find my father,' I was saying, 'I need to find out about my medical history because it could be very important for Beau.' I didn't realise it at the time but this practical motive was the tool I needed to start chipping away at the defences built round my own feelings. Then one day I was lying on Beau's bed, chatting away to her, when she asked about her grandfathers. Of course she knew all about Paul's dad dying but she was curious about her other grandfather. Mum had answered her honestly when she'd asked why she wasn't married so Beau knew he was out there, somewhere, and she knew I didn't know where he was.

'Why don't you find him? I'll help you! I'm good at finding things,' she told me.

'I will, darling, I *will*! I'll find him and get the answers to all the things you need to know.'

'No, you should find him for *you*, Mummy,' she said.

In her own way, Beau had understood I needed to do this for myself. Kids really do understand deep stuff and they can deal with it. Even if it involves pain, so long as they are given information in a truthful way they will be able to cope. I'm so impressed by her; if only I'd been credited with the same kind of intelligence as a child, I might have been told my own history in a proper way, not left to unravel some great (and slightly frightening) mystery. 'Wouldn't it be great for Mummy to find her dad?' Beau said to Paul.

Still I managed to bury my head in the sand. A few more months went by, until one evening Paul and I were watching the TV programme *Who Do You Think You Are?* in which the actress Kim Cattrall traced the heart-breaking story of her grandfather walking out on his family. She handled what must have been a distressing series of discoveries with great dignity. Paul and I looked at each other.

'Isn't she amazing?' I said.

'Yeah, she is. You know we've still got that address for your dad, don't you?'

We talked about it lightly, about how it probably wasn't the right address.

'You know, it's not far from where my mum lives,' said Paul. 'Why don't we just have a drive round there?'

He made it sound as if we were on a private investigator mission, as if we would be playing Secret Squirrel, like kids, and it would be fun. So I said: 'All right then, let's go – for a laugh.'

Paul went online again, checking the Electoral Register, and although the address had changed from the one we had four years ago there was another one in the same area that seemed to fit the bill. When we talked it through, I realised I felt strongly that I wanted to see him but not actually meet him. I thought I would sit in the car and watch from a distance just to see what he looked like. Did he look like me? Did Beau look like him?

But Paul didn't let me put it away again and pretend to forget it. The next day we were taking Beau over to stay with Nanny Chris. It was August, near the end of the long school holidays, and she was to sleep over. Paul suggested we combine the two things. He put the address in the Sat Nav and away we went. It still seemed like a big adventure, nothing to do with finding my father – it was just an address. I didn't seriously believe he would be there or even that it would be the right address.

'We can't just sit in the car and hope he comes out,' said Paul, as we got nearer.

'Why not?'

'He might not bloody well come out!'

'He will, eventually.'

'We can't sit there all night.'

'So what do you want to do?' I began to feel a bit scared – I didn't want to confront this man.

'I'll knock at the door,' Paul suggested.

'All right.'

Deep down, I guess I wanted him to do this and I was grateful he was taking control.

'Write down what you want me to say,' he told me.

So we agreed on a list of questions, starting with, 'Are you John Murphy?' and then asking if he'd worked at the printing company and whether he knew someone called Val Maxwell. If he answered 'yes' to either of these, we'd know we had our man. We were still laughing about it, pretending we were a couple of cops or private eyes. Meanwhile the Sat Nav was taking us through some very pretty scenery with large houses set well back from the road.

'What if he comes from money? Mum said he had a few quid, working in the print.' But I was joking when I said it – I really didn't care. The Sat Nav was saying we were two minutes away and the houses lining the road were lovely, really big now.

'Oh my God, Paul – it's going to be one of these!' I said.

'No, we've still got a little way and we're turning here.'

We drove into a huge council estate and I laughed at myself for thinking, even as a joke, that I'd find a rich branch of the family. We found the road easily enough but it was difficult tracing the number. It was about 5 p.m. but in summer so it was still light and it wasn't that we couldn't see; the numbers didn't seem to go in a logical way. We stopped the car and Paul asked a couple of people, dubious-looking characters but helpful. I slid down my seat in the street: my face was recognisable from *The Bill*.

'I can't get there with the car,' Paul told me. 'It's a block of flats down that alleyway.'

'You're not going down there. I won't be able to see you and there's no way I'm coming with you. Let's leave it, Paul. We should just leave it,' I said.

'No, we've come all this way,' he said. 'You stay here and I'll go and knock on the door. You don't have to see him and it won't do any harm – I'll just check if we've got the right address.'

'Take your phone with you,' I said, and I was worried as I watched him disappear up the alley. I was thinking one of the few things I knew about my father was that he had a grown-up son. Suppose the son was there and they didn't like coming face-to-face with his past? What if they beat the living daylights out of Paul? My imagination was running riot. This whole adventure had gone from me having a little nose from across the road to Paul being in danger – this wasn't what I'd signed up for. Paul, on the other hand, was not at all worried. He grew up in places like that, and at 6 foot tall and 14 stone he never, for a moment, felt there was any danger.

The block of flats (which I never saw) was a low-rise, six-storey block, probably built in the 1970s. There was a central staircase and a glass doorway that was open so Paul didn't need to use the entryphone. He went up to the second floor (my father's flat was to the left of the stairwell) and knocked on the door. While he was doing this, people were walking past the car and I had to put my head down and pretend to be looking at something so they didn't clock me properly and recognise me.

Twenty minutes went by, then half an hour. By now Paul must have found the right man, and there were two possible scenarios in my head: either it had all turned nasty and he was in a crumpled heap somewhere or he was talking to the man who was my 'Father Unknown'. I sent him a text.

'R U OK?'

Straight away the answer pinged back: 'Yeah, just having a chat with your dad.'

'Your dad' were not words I'd ever seen written down before, they weren't words that figured in my life (there was never any reason for anyone to reference 'your dad') but I knew something straight away: quite clearly, the man I love liked whoever he had found behind the front door. Paul would not refer to me as having a 'dad' if he did not like the outcome, and I felt strangely pleased.

I didn't text back because the next question would have to be: 'What's he like?' To text would be to acknowledge 45 years of curiosity. Anyway, what could he say in a text? But I sat there in a state of quiet excitement until Paul reappeared after about three-quarters of an hour. I saw him come down the alleyway and I was so relieved that he was on his own. All the while I'd been thinking, for Christ's sake don't bring him to the car! I don't want to meet him – I'm not up for that, it's not what I'm here for. I didn't want that big, life-changing moment to happen just yet, I wanted to be prepared, so it was great to see Paul with all his limbs and on his own.

'He's all right, actually,' were the first words he said as he climbed back into the car.

'Really?'

It was an uncomfortable feeling, keen as I was to find out everything about the man Paul had met. I felt like a kid asking for something. I was aware of the weight of what I wanted to know and how important it was to me. It was beginning to hit me in real terms that I had a dad, a flesh-and-blood father.

'What do you want to do?' said Paul. 'I didn't tell him you were in the car. Do you want to go back and meet him? Shall we sit here while I tell you all about it, or shall we get on the road and I'll tell you as we drive?' As ever, he was so sensitive to doing it the way with which I was most comfortable.

'Let's get going,' I said.

'OK, but before we go anywhere I've got something for you,' he told me.

He handed me a photo of my dad. Even as I think about it now, I can remember the weight of emotion I felt just seeing what he looked like.

'My God, oh my God, he looks like me!' I said.

It was a recent photo and the man in it was small, bald and with a very trimmed little beard, but he definitely did look like me.

As we drove away, Paul told me exactly what happened. After he knocked at the door it was answered by a man in a dressing gown. 'I didn't need to ask the questions,' he explained. 'It was you looking back at me – your little pointy chin and your little Irish eyes, a little leprechaun who looked like you. As soon as I asked if he was John Murphy, he said, "Yeah, who wants to know?" I told him my wife was trying to trace her father and he said, "You've got the wrong man," and started to close the door, but immediately he thought better of it and he said, "You'd better come in."'

So Paul went in and John Murphy offered him a cup of tea.

'I want to start by saying my wife does not want anything – she just needs answers to some questions,' he began.

'Well, I thought this day would come many years ago,' he said, 'but because it's been so long I thought the time had passed. I'll answer any questions. It's the least I can do.'

Paul said he was a fit man, who clearly took care of himself, and for a 70-year-old also good-looking, which pleased me. He had lived in Cyprus for six years and had returned to Britain about 18 months earlier so if we'd tried to find him when we first had the idea it would have been a lot more difficult. He was divorced but still in touch with his wife and three children. When he told my dad who I was and about my career, he had absolutely no idea; he didn't watch television, apart from sport. Then he added my dad was under the impression Mum had married and found me a new father because she had never fought him too hard over maintenance. He seemed very surprised and intrigued that Mum was still unattached and had brought me up as a single mum; he was just as surprised to learn my surname was still Maxwell – another reason why he would never have put two and two together, even if he had seen me on telly. Paul asked if he was willing to meet me, and he was. He gave him two telephone numbers, his landline and his mobile, so Paul gave him his mobile.

Paul told him that one thing I really would like was a photograph. On the coffee table between them was an envelope of pictures and John took one out and gave it to Paul. He explained that he had just been to Ireland to visit his aunt, and what he gave Paul was not just a picture of my dad, but also with him was his own father, my 92-year-old grandfather. Apparently his mother had only recently died in her late eighties. So far, so good with the gene pool, I thought. They are obviously a family who live a long time. I can't explain how happy I felt as I looked at the picture; it was a feeling of warmth inside me, of being complete. As I looked at his face for the first time in my life, I felt: I'm half of someone else, I'm not 100 per cent Mum – half of me belongs to this man. And Paul says he's all right, a nice man, and if Paul says it, that will do for me.

I knew how savvy Paul was and what a good judge of character; I also knew he would not let me be exposed to something that would hurt me. And I can't help thinking, if he'd found my father and it had been a disaster and the man was going to be bad for me or hurt me in some way, he would have just pretended it was the wrong address. I can't be sure because Paul is so straight, but protecting me will always come first.

Paul has been entrusted with the two most pivotal moments in my life: it was he who looked at the pregnancy test and knew before I did that I was expecting Beau, and he also met my father before I did. We have so much history as a couple.

With Beau at Nanny Chris's house, Paul and I sat up most of the night, talking it all through. He wanted to know if I was up for meeting my dad – and I was, but cautious, too. Even so, in the course of that one night he went from being 'John Murphy' to 'my father', words I had no experience of, but made me feel complete and whole. I put the picture of him on a high shelf in Paul's office – I didn't want Beau to find it until I was ready to talk it all through with her, too.

Paul took on the arrangements to meet, which we agreed would be in London when 'my father' was visiting his sister at The Oval (strange to think he had been going backwards and forwards to the area so close to my old home in Walworth, where Mum and Nan still lived all those years). With my schedule it became difficult to coordinate, and so we decided to go back to his home town and meet him in a hotel there at 7 o'clock in the evening, two weeks after Paul visited his flat.

Meanwhile I agonised about everything. 'Why has he chosen that hotel? Is he, like me, always trying to make a good impression? At least I'm not turning up needy, not asking for anything.' I wanted to look good; I wanted him to realise that he had an attractive daughter; I wanted him to think, she's quite pretty and she's done really well. So I chose a favourite dress, a red Orla Kiely one that I sometimes wear on *Loose Women*. It's my idea of a nice, daughterly dress – not too short, not revealing, not too sophisticated, but well made and quite expensive-looking. I wanted him to think, I may not have been around for her, but she's turned out lovely and it's a shame I didn't have a hand in it.

Only Paul and I knew what was happening. I didn't tell Mum or Beau. This had to be my time. I wasn't sure whether it would ever happen again – I might meet him just once, and so, at the risk of sounding selfish, I had to have this one for myself.

When the day arrived, I woke up to find I'd lost my voice. So many questions to ask and no voice to ask them with – it was pure stress. We arrived at the hotel before he did; it was one of those modern anonymous hotels in a big chain with a bar that looked like a mock pub. A couple of people recognised me and they were nudging each other and pointing me out to others. Two ladies came up. 'Hello Lisa, we love you on *The Bill* …' said one. '… and on *Loose Women*,' added her friend. Normally I love it when people come up and tell me they like what I'm doing. At this stage my face was in their homes twice a week with *The Bill* because, even though I had already left, the shows I'd filmed were still running and I was already a fixture on *Loose Women*. People are always nice when they come up to me but on this day I was thinking, all these people have no idea what's happening – they don't know 'that woman off the telly' is here to meet her dad for the first time ever! It felt surreal but I had a deep longing to see him. Even so, I was also scared, and when Paul said he was just popping to the loo I somehow found my voice and snapped, 'No, you bloody well aren't! You can't leave me here. Suppose he walks in while you're in the loo?'

'Just say hello.'

'Don't be stupid! I can't just say, "Hello Dad. Where have you been for the last 45 years?"'

I've never felt so vulnerable. I was holding onto Paul's hand like a child saying, 'Please don't leave me.' It was a strange feeling for me – I'm used to walking into parties and attending meetings on my own, but I couldn't just bump into my dad on my own. So Paul found us a quiet alcove and settled me there out of sight while he went to the loo. I couldn't see the bar or the hotel entrance and I was frantically thinking, please don't come in here. I don't want to meet you on my own. Apart from anything else, I had no voice, just a little squeak. He was going to think I'm some strange squeaking woman.

Just as I was thinking this, I heard a voice say: 'Hello, Paul. Oh, I'm glad you're wearing a jacket – I wasn't sure what to wear!' Clearly he was nervous, too. Paul was talking to him and it felt as though I was eavesdropping at my own reunion. I couldn't see him but I could hear them both chatting away. Surely he's going to come round and say hello, surely they're not going to stand in the bloody bar, I was thinking. At that moment they walked round, and without planning it I stood up. We said hello awkwardly and then we all sat down.

I'd come armed with a notebook and pen; I also had a list of questions, which made me feel like Jeremy Paxman. Paul had a tape recorder in his pocket so that we would always have a record of this meeting. But first of all he, my dad, offered to get us a drink and he brought me a glass of wine. I couldn't look into his eyes because it was like gazing into a mirror image of my own. One glance was enough, and from then on I kept my eyes on the floor, on the table, on Paul – anywhere other than look him full in the face. Every so often I'd shoot a look at him and afterwards Paul told me he was doing the same to me.

Paul, thank God, was able to talk, and he kept conversation going. We were all obviously uncomfortable because when I listen back to the tape the first 10 minutes or so are Paul and my father talking about the Ashes and Chelsea Football Club. They were just breaking the ice, and as the amount I know about either subject could be written on the back of a postage stamp it gave me a chance to weigh up this small, tanned man with a closely cropped white beard. Paul, bless him, isn't really that into sport either, but he knew how to keep the chat going. After a few minutes my reflexes kicked in and I went into audition mode. I told myself I was not going to allow myself to feel any of this, I was just going to take information from it. I'd spent a lifetime not allowing myself to feel anything for my father, and although I *wanted* to feel I was also worried that I could be rejected all over again.

Paul played a blinder, talking enough to let me get settled, and then I launched into my Q and A session. I didn't show any emotion, just went into interrogation mode. He seemed much better adjusted to the situation than I was. He was gentle and seemed very concerned with making me feel happy and comfortable. Also, he stressed he wanted to help me in any way that I needed.

He told me my family history, and if I'd entertained for the slightest second any thoughts of coming from money they were quickly dispelled. It turns out I'm from a long line of Irish poachers. Then he showed me a photo of a small man holding a gun almost bigger than he was; this was my great grandfather. It was clear from the pictures that I come from a long line of small, slim people. He told me something that pleased me: 'You're not a Murphy, you're a Ryan.'

'Why do you say that?' asked Paul.

'Because she's just like my mother's side of the family, the Ryans – she's the spitting image of my mother.'

I felt pleased because now I knew I had another strand of genetic history: the Ryans. The more diluted the pool, the better it sounded to me, and he had obviously adored his mother.

He told us he was proud of his Irish background and he and Paul joked about how common the name Murphy is in some parts of London. It turns out his father still lives at the address Mum knew, and for seven years as I drove to *The Bill* from Muswell Hill I must have gone past the end of his father's road, my grandfather's road. I may have passed him but we would not have known each other. From the photos it's clear both my dad and I favour his mum's side of the family so I wouldn't have noticed a resemblance.

We heard the medical background – not that there was anything significant, they seemed a very healthy bunch. He told us about moving to Greece and his subsequent divorce. He said his ex-wife knew about me (after all, she was the one who took my mum to see him when she was pregnant), but his two sons and his daughter did not know. He didn't offer to show me any pictures, and I'm glad – it may seem cold-hearted, but I didn't want to know anything about the children who had had him as their father all their lives. There's no benefit to me in finding out about them and I'm glad he did not want us to meet; I didn't want to play catch-up with three people with whom I have nothing in common except this man. Paul could see talk of his children made me uncomfortable so he interrupted and made it clear we did not want to know about them. Afterwards, he remembers me telling him that he was a bit harsh, which he thought was interesting as I was being protective towards my father.

Although Paul had given him a few details about my career, I told him the rest and he was quite taken aback. I really went into career mode, going through my whole CV as if he was a casting director – it was my way of covering the nerves. He heard all about my early success, my time in America, everything that had happened since. For a woman with a dodgy voice I certainly managed to talk some. He seemed intrigued about Mum never marrying and me growing up with Nan and Grandad, whom he remembered meeting. I talked around Mum being on her own, but I didn't feel it was right to tell him she had carried a torch for him all those years and she wasn't able to move on. I didn't know if he was the kind of man who could be trusted with such a massive compliment.

It was quite private in the alcove and we were all engrossed, exchanging information. My funny little voice held out, just about. When I listen to the tape I realise we were talking for a whole hour and 40 minutes – it didn't seem that long. In the middle of it we ordered chicken baguettes because Paul and I hadn't eaten since lunch, and my father insisted on paying. The whole evening was on him, which I think is what he wanted. He gave me a load of pictures, which he told me I could keep and have copied.

When it was time to say goodbye, we were both a bit awkward. I held out my hand to shake hands and he gave a little gesture as much as to say 'Come here', and we hugged each other. Had I allowed myself to succumb completely, I would probably have gone to pieces and sobbed like a baby. It surprised me that I really did feel like his kid; there was a definite connection, but I couldn't make sense of it. It's a connection so basic, raw and fundamental but I didn't know where to place it. What was I going to do with the information? Yes, I had the genetic stuff and I could tell Beau all about that when the time was right, but what about the rest of it?

Paul and I talked it through on the way home. Who should we tell? What do we do next? It's really hard to find your dad after 45 years, but it's even harder to decide what to do with him once you've found him. How much was he a part of my life? Did I want to include him? There isn't really a slot for him (my grandfather was a great father figure, and that will do for me); I don't need a father to take care of me because I'm a grown woman with a family of my own. I was also feeling some guilt about him, which is ridiculous really. I'd barged into his life; what was he supposed to do now? I knew he was pleased that I wasn't expecting him to be Pa Walton overnight, but he might be as confused as me about how we were supposed to proceed. He'd made it clear the ball was definitely in my court, though, which was good. I fully intended to keep it there, and so did Paul.

# CHAPTER 18

## *Finally Me*

There was another big hurdle ahead of me: telling Mum that I'd seen my father. I arranged to meet her in Marylebone High Street for coffee because I didn't want to tell her over the phone. She may have sensed something because she said, 'Have you done anything about the search for your dad?' 'Yeah I did, Mum – I found him,' I told her.

'Oh my Gawd!' she said, and her hands went involuntarily to her mouth; she then started crying. She was desperate to know what happened and kept urging me on. I told her he was a nice man, a charming man. 'I can so see what you saw in him,' I said. I think that was the kindest, most sensitive thing I could have said because I don't think anyone else had validated her choice to be with him before in her whole life. I was also very conscious of not saying he was the most amazing man ever and that my life felt suddenly complete – that would not have been fair to her. I had to give her what she needed as a player in this story but I also had to keep some feelings to myself, so I certainly didn't go down the road of saying I wished we could all have been one big happy family.

'Are you going to see him again?' she asked.

'I don't know, Mum. Now that I've found him, I don't feel I want a dad in my life. It felt OK to find him and I've done everything I needed to do in terms of finding out the medical history for Beau,' I told her.

I put it in terms of it being a practical mission rather than an emotional one, although her own reaction was totally emotional: she was so choked up she couldn't speak.

Soon afterwards, I spoke to my father (those strange words, 'father', 'dad') on the phone to talk about returning the pictures. It was a pleasant, non-committal chat. I left it to Paul to make the arrangements for us to meet up again but didn't tell Mum about it.

It was six weeks after our first meeting that we saw him again, towards the end of October 2009. We met for lunch at The Ivy Club in London. I'm a member and he'd told us he used to go to The Ivy with a friend he knew from Greece (another odd thought – we could have been having lunch in the same room). The Ivy Club is just round the corner from The Ivy and it's a fabulous place, with the feel of 1930s New York. It seemed like a good place to meet, a place that's quiet enough to talk – and of course, my voice had recovered. We invited our great friend Adam Garcia to come along towards the end of the meal. Adam had been estranged from his own father from an early age and had recently got back in contact with him. He had been very supportive of me all the way through and Paul thought it would be good for me to meet up with him after my dad had gone.

'Take from this what *you* want. You don't owe him anything,' Adam stressed to me beforehand.

The first thing we did was hand the photographs back; at least then the business was taken care of. Paul was brilliant again, talking easily and in a friendly way without giving him any ground. I was scared to open up too much in case he liked me and made some sort of gesture that showed he wanted to have an ongoing relationship. It was weird for me to hold back – I'm such a people-pleaser and I so like to be liked – but here I was, trying hard not to make myself too likeable. I wasn't going to give him any chance to suggest we might have a future. I didn't want to allow him the opportunity to let us down again – at least I think that's the reason why I held back. It's really hard to disentangle my true motives and feelings, but I knew I wanted to keep a distance.

We had a good lunch and a bit to drink; he's easy company, likes a drink, and he and Paul were chatting away. Occasionally I stood back, mentally, from the table and looked at us like an outsider. It was surreal. I was having lunch with my 'Father Unknown' and it was slowly becoming an enjoyable event for him and Paul – and in some ways for me, too. But I didn't want to become too comfortable; I was uncomfortable with how comfortable it was beginning to feel, if that makes any kind of sense.

At the previous meeting my father had said he had not told his children about me. I was happy with this. It was up to him whether he told them or not, but I didn't want a big family reunion.

He was really chuffed that I can sing and have been on stage in big musicals; that seemed to impress him more than the acting. Because he enjoys music, he seemed to think he had given me my musical gene. But you know what? He ain't claiming that one! That's got Nanny Rose written all over it.

When Adam arrived downstairs at the club, Paul looked over at me to see what I wanted to do. So I nodded to let him know Ad could come up and join us, even though my dad was still there.

'Does Adam know who I am?' he asked Paul.

'Yes, he does – Lisa does not have secrets,' he told him in a firm voice.

He wanted to make it clear to John Murphy that although he may have kept *me* a secret I was under no obligation to do the same. All the way through, although Paul liked him he made it clear there were ground rules. Adam and Paul sat either side of me, both very protective. It was a bit like The Management – they were my bodyguards. I felt like a president, knowing they would take a bullet for me. Apparently when I went to the loo my father said to Adam, 'I hear you have just met your father, too.' 'Yes, but I didn't really connect with him,' he told him. Adam is like Paul, very direct. He was there to look after me and he certainly didn't have any rose-tinted ideas about meeting fathers.

'What do you want from Lise?' Adam asked my father. He was at pains to make it clear it was going to be me calling the shots, but like Paul I think he could see my father was a good man. They were all drinking and getting a bit tipsy but I was completely sober. I had visions of my dad hanging out with us for the rest of the day, all pally, and everyone forgetting who this man was and what he had done to my life. He was charming and under any other circumstances I would have been delighted to spend a day with him, but not with the weight of my emotional baggage. I just felt, 'This is *my* life, these are *my* friends, you are not part of this. We've had lunch and that's enough.'

I didn't want to drift into a relationship with my dad over a few drinks. Also, I knew that I really did have a nice life, with really nice people in it, but I'd also spent 45 years sorting out a lot of shit to get to the place where I was and I didn't want to let someone else in for the best bits. Just by the nature of him being my dad, he can't plonk himself in my life. Luckily, my dad got up to go to the loo, and while he was away I told Paul, 'I want him to go now.' I think he already sensed this and was watching to make sure that I was OK.

As always, Paul was incredibly sensitive to my feelings and when my father returned he was on his feet. 'We're going to be going soon, John. Let me walk you outside and help you get a taxi,' he told him. There was no option to stay: Paul was in control. I stood up, and because he knew we were moving house I said, 'It's been really nice to have seen you before we move. We'll be in touch.' We had another awkward goodbye hug, but I enjoyed it. I felt he thought I was a lovely girl, he really liked me – that was a good feeling.

I haven't seen my father since, so my last view of him was waiting for the lift. Paul went with him and put him in a taxi while I stayed with Adam, who gave me lots of hugs and told me how honoured he felt at being allowed to meet my father. He reassured me that whatever I decided to do next would be right because I cannot be wrong, however you look at it – it's entirely up to me.

\* \* \*

I now had to tell Beau, and the chance came soon afterwards in a very easy, casual way. I didn't want to sit her down and make speeches about it, so one day when we were queuing at YO! Sushi in Brent Cross I simply said, 'Oh, I've got something to tell you.'

'Yes, Mummy?'

The look on her face said she knew what was coming.

'I found my dad.'

'I knew it, I knew it, I *knew* it!' she said, and she could hardly contain her excitement. 'What happened? What *happened*?'

'He was very nice, and Daddy liked him – he's the sort of man you could introduce to your friends.'

I saw her face quickly change from being really excited to worried I liked this man so much she might suddenly have a stranger as a grandfather. I'd always said to Beau, 'He's not my dad, he's my biological father – a dad is something different. Daddy is a dad; this man is not a dad to me.' So now she was hearing me refer to him as 'my dad'.

'He may be a dad to you but he's not a grandfather to me,' she told me, looking panic-stricken, as if she felt her whole world would somehow change.

'Nothing's going to change, Beau. Don't worry, it's still you, me, Daddy, Nanny Chris, Nanny Val and Nanny Rose. That's it. Nobody's joining our little family,' I told her.

I think I managed to reassure her. Over our food she told me she did not want to meet him. All along she had said I should find him for myself, not for anyone else. We tend to underestimate kids. She'd thought it through and she knew it mattered to me; now that I'd done it, she was happy for me but she did not want to be part of it. She was 10 years old and mature beyond her years in so many ways.

Mum told Nan, but she didn't say much.

'I'm glad you found your dad,' said Nan, the next time I saw her. 'That's all right then, all that, 'innit?'

'Yeah, I'm glad I did it, Nan,' I said.

'Good for you! It's all for Beau, isn't it?'

She and everyone else seemed to be a lot more comfortable with the idea that I'd searched for my father for Beau. Tough as she was, Nan was the one who brought me up all those years and it hurt her feelings that I still felt I had to find the missing link; if it was all for medical reasons, to protect Beau, then that was fine.

I haven't felt the need to keep in touch with John Murphy or to see him again. We don't send Christmas cards or anything. I got what I needed from those two meetings, and I respect the fact that he has done as he said he would, leaving it all to me to decide the pace and nature of our relationship. Deep down, there's a bit of me wondering why he doesn't want to keep in touch. Doesn't he miss me? I know this is irrational, and besides, I don't want him trying to be part of my life – I certainly don't want to feel responsible for how he feels or beholden to him in any way.

I don't know what will happen but I've a feeling there will be another meeting some day. Typically, when asked I have said, 'Yes, I'll see him again one day,' but I've done nothing about it. I'm glad I found him when I did. I have a friend who looked for his father and after lots of detective work managed to trace him, only to find it was too late and his father had died. I'm relieved that didn't happen to me because it would leave so many unresolved questions, but having met him, having seen how fit he is and having heard how long-lived his side of the family is, I don't feel the need to rush the next meeting. If my grandmother and grandfather on his side are anything to go by, we'll probably have plenty of time to fit in a couple more lunches.

I do wonder if he has seen me on television now. At our second meeting he told us he had looked for me on *The Bill*, but it was an episode I wasn't in so he'd hardly made a big effort to see me. I like that – I was really pleased to find he had no idea who I am and the only TV he watched was sport.

Even though all the way through I have tried to be realistic about what meeting my father would mean, at the back of my mind (and I expect it's the same for others in my situation) there was an idea that when I met this father person I would feel that in some way I had missed out, that my life would have been different and perhaps better with him. After two meetings, one thing of which I'm certain is my life would definitely not have been better had he been a fixture; the fact that he wasn't there for me caused a lot of pain, anxiety and hurt, but it's given me the life I have today. If I'd come from a perfectly 'normal' happily married couple ('married' is really the key word, because I don't think he and Mum would necessarily have been *happily* married) I don't think I would have done the things I've done, met the people I've met and finally found real happiness with Paul and Beau.

Mum might have been happier had they married, I don't know. But, equally, he might have caused her a lot of heartache, just as he did by not being around. She hasn't met him. I suspect she may want to do so to lay some ghosts, and maybe now Nan is not there to judge her she'd like to. Perhaps he feels the same way. Paul and I were talking about it once.

'Now they are both free, perhaps they could get together,' said Paul.

'Oh my Gawd, that's sick!' I shouted.

'Why is it sick? He's your dad.'

I can see in a strange way it makes sense, but it still doesn't feel right.

If John Murphy hasn't told his family, perhaps they will find out by reading this book. Then again, perhaps not; perhaps, like him, they don't really watch TV. And if he says nothing, why would they associate him with me? But I'm not worried about naming him or outing him as my dad. I've thought long and hard about this and I'm not anyone's dirty little secret any more. I'm not bitter or angry, but I felt it was my right to ask questions. John Murphy is part of my life story. I don't want to hurt anyone, I don't want to ruin anyone's life, but I've been without this information for 45 years and I'm at least entitled to the privilege of naming my father, a privilege I was denied for all those years when I was ashamed of my birth certificate with its 'Father Unknown' entry.

My mum asked very little from John Murphy – he himself said she didn't pursue him hard over maintenance. I have had nothing from him and I've never wanted anything either; just as he was never responsible for me, I'm not responsible for him. He may not have been prepared to own up about being my father for all those years, and now, whether he likes it or not, I am telling my story and he is part of it.

Finding my father has profoundly affected me for the better. In some strange way that I can't pinpoint, I feel healthier, more normal, better. Paul noticed it straight away. Every morning, in those first few months, I woke up feeling lighter, happier – it was as if I'd just learnt to breathe properly without thinking about it. And it's not thanks to John Murphy but simply to the fact that I now know with more clarity who I am and where I'm from.

In all this, Paul has been my saviour. He has not put a foot wrong in the whole process. It's such a sensitive area and I am such a complex character when it comes to anything to do with my 'illegitimacy' that he could so easily have offended me, rubbed me up the wrong way and hurt me by inadvertently saying the wrong thing, but he stepped delicately through the minefield of my emotions and did everything absolutely right. At every stage of the journey he would simply hug me and ask, 'Are you OK? You don't have to do anything, but if you want to do something, just tell me and I'll sort it out.'

In every important situation in my life, Paul has been there for me. He has allowed me to feel safe and, in turn, this has helped me to get in touch with my own feelings. He has given me Beau, not just by creating her but also by freeing me to believe I could be a good mother. And he has challenged what was painful and hurtful in my relationship with Mum, not to drive a wedge between us, but so that we could find a way to be happier in our relationship.

Paul's the best thing that ever happened to me and everyone who knows me can see it. Recently, Kate Thornton paid him a great tribute: she told me that she and a friend of hers (who both have little boys) said to each other when they met Paul,

'That's how we would like our sons to grow up.' Can there be a greater compliment?

For me, I now have the life I want, with the man I want, the daughter I wanted and even the house I wanted. I love my career, but my philosophy now is, what will be, will be. If it all ended tomorrow, it would not bother me. Today, I'm happy going for lunch with Paul and Beau, having half a shandy and a pie in a lovely country pub – I'm in a very happy place.

Yes, Paul and I will get married one day. I want to be married to him before I die, but without a big wedding, something very low-key. I love him in every sense of the word and feel like I'm his wife but I don't feel the need for a legally binding contract. It would be nice to have the same name as Beau, but we're so connected I don't think a change of name would make any difference. Every so often Paul says to me, 'I would marry you,' and I reply, 'I know.' Right now, that's all I need.

Before I started writing this book I went back to take a look at the Rockingham Estate, Elephant and Castle. It was almost exactly 30 years since the Maxwells moved out, but so much of my childhood is still there: the four-storey redbrick blocks of flats, the land between them where we played, the subway I walked through every day to the Elephant and Castle, the fence I had to climb to get to the Uxbridge Arms where Nan and Grandad spent so many happy hours.

The estate that seemed immense to me as a child now feels smaller, more intimate. I looked across from Stephenson House to Telford House, where my friend Caroline had lived. As children we waved across what seemed a wide gulf, and today the buildings seem so much closer. The flats are much the same: the iron balustrade, the yellow tiled walls, the sparkly concrete steps, the matching front doors, the little iron grille where I got my first glimpses of life below. Now the walls of the buildings bristle with satellite dishes and there are new modern windows.

I walked along Bath Terrace remembering how as a teenager I always gave this as my address because it sounded so much more upmarket than the Rockingham Estate. There's an Islamic Cultural Centre (it wasn't there when I was young), and Jail Park has been given a less forbidding name: Newington Gardens. The sandpit where I swapped my gold ring has gone, and now there are basketball courts. From some vantage points you can see the London Eye, a flag to tell the kids growing up there today there's another world out there across the river, the West End, something of which I had no concept when I was little.

Looking back at Stephenson House, I could feel the spirit of Nan and Grandad very strongly. As a child, everything I held cherished and dear was there, and the memories of those times are precious, indelible. Walking round the estate, I felt out of place: I'd come straight from the *Loose Women* set and I was dressed head to toe in cream cashmere. 'Why didn't you think to wear something more casual, you silly cow?' I said to myself. 'You're out of place here!' But then I remembered: little Lise was always overdressed when she lived here, so Nan and Grandad would still recognise me.

Some things never change.

# Acknowledgements

I'd especially like to thank my mother for her generosity in allowing me to finally tell the truth and for the wonderful relationship we now have.

I'd also like to thank my nan and grandad for their inspiration and Paul's mum, Chris Jessup, for her constant love and support.

Thank you to my lovely agent Peter Brooks and his assistant Gavin Denton-Jones, and thanks also to Caroline Sargeant, Laura James and Danielle Foreman for their help with the memories.

# *Picture Credits*

## Section 1:
Page 3, bottom left: © Ron Howard
Page 3, bottom right: © Ron Howard
Page 4, top: © Frazer Ashford/Arenpal.com
Page 5, top right: © BBC
Page 6, middle row, right: © Mirrorpix
Page 8, top left: © Mike Lawn

## Section 2:
Page 2, bottom right: © Doug McKenzie
Page 4, top: © talkbackThames
Page 4, bottom left: © Radio Times
Page 8, top left: © Richard Young/Rex Features
Page 8, top right: © Oliver/GoffPhotos.com
Page 8, bottom left: © Ken McKay/Rex Features
Page 8, bottom right: © Sven Arnstein